6. Enter your class ID code to join a class.

IF YOU HAVE A CLASS CODE FROM YOUR TEACHER

a. Enter your class code and click [Next]

b. Once you have joined a class, you will be able to use the Discussion Board and Email tools.

c. To enter this code later, choose **Join a Class**.

IF YOU DO NOT HAVE A CLASS CODE

a. If you do not have a class ID code, click [Skip]

b. You do not need a class ID code to use *iQ Online*.

c. To enter this code later, choose **Join a Class**.

7. Review registration information and click Log In. Then choose your book. Click **Activities** to begin using *iQ Online*.

IMPORTANT

- After you register, the next time you want to use *iQ Online*, go to www.iQOnlinePractice.com and log in with your email address and password.
- The online content can be used for 12 months from the date you register.
- For help, please contact customer service: eltsupport@oup.com.

WHAT IS iQ ONLINE ?

All new activities provide essential skills **practice** and support.
Vocabulary and Grammar **games** immerse you in the language and provide even more practice.
Authentic, engaging **videos** generate new ideas and opinions on the Unit Question.

Go to the Media Center to download or stream all **student book audio**.

Use the **Discussion Board** to discuss the Unit Question and more.

Email encourages communication with your teacher and classmates.

Automatic grading gives immediate feedback and tracks progress.
Progress Reports show what you have mastered and where you still need more practice.

OXFORD
UNIVERSITY PRESS

198 Madison Avenue
New York, NY 10016 USA

Great Clarendon Street, Oxford, OX2 6DP, United Kingdom

Oxford University Press is a department of the University of Oxford.
It furthers the University's objective of excellence in research, scholarship,
and education by publishing worldwide. Oxford is a registered trade
mark of Oxford University Press in the UK and in certain other countries

Adult Content Director: Stephanie Karras
Publisher: Sharon Sargent
Managing Editor: Mariel DeKranis
Development Editor: Eric Zuarino
Head of Digital, Design, and Production: Bridget O'Lavin
Executive Art and Design Manager: Maj-Britt Hagsted
Design Project Manager: Debbie Lofaso
Content Production Manager: Julie Armstrong
Image Manager: Trisha Masterson
Image Editor: Liaht Ziskind
Production Coordinator: Brad Tucker

ISBN: 978 0 19 481952 7 Student Book 5 with iQ Online pack
ISBN: 978 0 19 481953 4 Student Book 5 as pack component
ISBN: 978 0 19 481802 5 iQ Online student website

Printed in China
This book is printed on paper from certified and well-managed sources.

ACKNOWLEDGEMENTS

*The authors and publisher are grateful to those who have given permission to
reproduce the following extracts and adaptations of copyright material:*

p. 5 from "My Stroke of Insight: A Brain Scientist's Personal Journey,"
from *Focus 580AM* with David Inge, WILL Radio, University of Illinois, July 21,
2008, http://will.illinois.edu. Used by permission.; p. 27 from *The Woman
Warrior: Memoirs of a Childhood Among Ghosts* by Maxine Hong Kingston.
Copyright © 1975, 1976 by Maxine Hong Kingston. Used by permission
of Alfred A. Knopf, an imprint of the Knopf Doubleday Publishing Group,
a division of Random House LLC and Abner Stein. All rights reserved.;
p. 33 "Voluntourism" from the *Amateur Traveler*, Episode 125, February 16,
2008, http://Amateur.com by Chris Christensen. Used by permission of
Chris Christensen.; p. 40 "Having Fun with Science, Science Festival,
2006," University of Cambridge, http://mediaplayer.group.cam.ac.uk. Used
by permission of University of Cambridge/Cambridge Science Festival.;
p. 40 from *The Sedgwick Reserve* produced by UC Agriculture and Natural
Resources, UCTV, May 3, 2004, http://www.uctv.tv. Copyright © 2004
Regents of the University of California. Used by permission.; p. 62 from *Wild
Survivors: Camouflage & Mimicry,* July 9, 1997.; p. "The Campaign to Humanize
the Coffee Trade," from American Public Media's "American RadioWorks."
Copyright © ℗ 2001 American Public Media. Used with permission. All
rights reserved.; p. 91 "The Campaign to Humanize the Coffee Trade," from
American Public Media's "American RadioWorks." Copyright © ℗ 2001
American Public Media. Used with permission. All rights reserved.; p. 97 from
"UN Global Compact," http://www.unep.org. Used by permission of United
Nations Global Compact.; p. 97 from "The 2014 State of the Union between
Business and Society" by Georg Kell, Executive Director UN Global Compact
from the Oslo 2014 Business for Peace Summit, http://businessforpeace.no.
Used by permission.; p. 109 from "Organizational Description" of Save the
Children. Used by permission of Save the Children.; p. 119 Environmental
Psychology, a lecture by Dr. Traci Craig, http://www.class.uidaho.edu. Used
by permission of Dr. Traci Craig, Associate Professor of Social Psychology,
University of Idaho.; p. 127 © 2008 NPR®. News report by NPR's Neal Conan
was originally broadcast on NPR's *Talk of the Nation*® on May 26, 2008, and is
used with the permission of NPR. Any unauthorized duplication is strictly
prohibited.; p. 145 from "Bee Sting Therapy," May 29, 2007, http://wunc.org.
Reprinted by permission.; p. 145 from "Doc in a Box?" originally published in
World Vision Report. Used by permission of World Vision, www.worldvision.org.;
p. 154 from "Boulder Bike-to-School Program goes International" Interview
with Tim Carlin, *Colorado Matters,* http://www.kcfr.org. Audio produced by
Colorado Public Radio for Colorado Matters. Printed transcript transcribed
by Oxford University Press. Used by permission of Public Broadcasting of
Colorado, Inc. dba Colorado Public Radio.; p. 175 from "The Reindeer People"
by Lorne Matalon, http://homelands.org. Used by permission of Lorne
Matalon.; p. 182 "High-Tech Nomads," from American Public Media's "The
Savvy Traveler." Copyright © ℗ 2001 American Public Media. Used with
permission. All rights reserved.; p. 205 from "Energy: What's the Least
Worst Option" from *BBC News: Science & Environment,* posted November 25,
2013, http://www.bbc.com/news/science-environment-25051351.
BBC © 2014. Used by permission.; p. 211 "Tapping the Energy of the Tides"
by Amy Quinton, from New Hampshire Public Radio News, July 13, 2007,
http://www.nhpr.org. Used by permission of New Hampshire Public Radio.

Illustrations by: p. 32 Stacy Merlin; p. 82 Marc Kolle; p. 110 Stacy Merlin;
p. 116 Greg Paprocki; p. 119 Greg Paprocki; p. 144 Stacy Merlin; p. 166 Marc
Kolle; p. 172 Stacy Merlin; p. 197 Stacy Merlin; p. 226 Marc Kolle.

*We would also like to thank the following for permission to reproduce the following
photographs:* Cover: David Pu'u/Corbis; Video Vocabulary (used throughout
the book): Oleksiy Mark/Shutterstock; p. 3 Dieter Spears/Getty Images;
p. 5 Jemal Countess/WireImage/Getty Images; p. 7 Science Photo Library/
Alamy; p. 10 CW Images/Alamy (Rock), Jon Hicks/Corbis UK Ltd. (Crowd);
p. 13 The Library of Congress: 3b26080u; p. 24 Peter Muller/Corbis UK Ltd.;
p. 27 Christopher Felver/Corbis UK Ltd.; p. 31 Frans Lanting/Corbis;
p. 32 Blend Images - Inti St Clair/Getty Images (Office), Vicki Beaver/Alamy
(Museum); p. 33 Blend Images/Ariel Skelley/Getty Images; p. 40 Witold
Skrypczak/Alamy; p. 41 MShieldsPhotos/Alamy; p. 54 Imfoto/Shutterstock;
p. 58 Peter Adams/Getty Images; p. 59 Rex Features via AP Images, Mega
Pixel/Shutterstock; p. 60 dov makabaw/Alamy (Covent garden), Frans
Lanting Studio/Alamy (Camouflaged insect); p. 62 Lisa Moore/Alamy
(Caterpillar), Norbert Wu/Science Faction/Co/Corbis UK Ltd. (Flounder fish),
zsirosistvan/Shutterstock (Moth), Romeo Mikulic/Shutterstock (Mantis),
Getty Images (Ptarmigan), Martin Harvey/Alamy (Snake); p. 67 Halil
Terzioglu/Shutterstock; p. 78 YAY Media AS/Alamy; p. 87 Blaine Harrington/
AGE fotostock; p. 88 FocusChina/Alamy (Traffic), FloridaStock/Shutterstock
(Polar bear), AGE fotostock Spain, S.L./Alamy (Puffin); p. 91 John Jairo
Bonilla/Epa/Corbis UK Ltd.; p. 95 Ianni Dimitrov/Alamy; p. 96 Aurora Photos/
Alamy; p. 97 Image Source/Corbis UK Ltd.; p. 114 BremecR/Getty Images;
p. 115 Scott B Smith Photography/Getty Images, Le Club Symphonie/Ian
Nolan/Getty Images; p. 127 Getty Images; p. 138 Johnny Greig/Getty Images;
p. 143 Cadalpe/cultura/Corbis; p. 145 William Caram/Alamy (Shipping
containers), ChameleonsEye/Shutterstock (Beekeeper); p. 151 Razumovskaya
Marina Nikolaevna/Shutterstock; p. 154 Emily Minton Redfield
Photography; p. 170 Colin Anderson/Getty Images; p. 171 MichaelSvoboda/
Getty Images, Michael S. Nolan/AGE fotostock; p. 172 Huchen Lu/Getty
Images; p. 175 Getty Images; p. 179 Hamid Sardar/Corbis UK Ltd.;
p. 182 Frank Herholdt/Alamy; p. 200 Jochen Tack/Alamy; p. 201 Leo Francini/
Alamy, chartcameraman/Shutterstock, viki2win/Shutterstock, Abel Leao/
Getty Images; p. 202 Photodisc/Oxford University Press (Oil rig), 2013
Bloomberg/Getty Images (Fracking), RG Images/Oxford University Press
(Wind turbines), elxeneize/Shutterstock (Solar panels), Michael Utech/
Getty Images (Nuclear power station), Ashley Cooper pics/Alamy (Coal
mine); p. 205 A.P.S. (UK)/Alamy; p. 211 Press Association Images;
p. 224 PhotosIndia.com LLC/Alamy; Back Cover: mozcann/iStockphoto.

SHAPING learning TOGETHER

We would like to acknowledge the teachers from all over the world who participated in the development process and review of the Q series.

Special thanks to our *Q: Skills for Success* Second Edition Topic Advisory Board

Shaker Ali Al-Mohammad, Buraimi University College, Oman; **Dr. Asmaa A. Ebrahim**, University of Sharjah, U.A.E.; **Rachel Batchilder**, College of the North Atlantic, Qatar; **Anil Bayir**, Izmir University, Turkey; **Flora Mcvay Bozkurt**, Maltepe University, Turkey; **Paul Bradley**, University of the Thai Chamber of Commerce Bangkok, Thailand; **Joan Birrell-Bertrand**, University of Manitoba, MB, Canada; **Karen E. Caldwell**, Zayed University, U.A.E.; **Nicole Hammond Carrasquel**, University of Central Florida, FL, U.S.; **Kevin Countryman**, Seneca College of Applied Arts & Technology, ON, Canada; **Julie Crocker**, Arcadia University, NS, Canada; **Marc L. Cummings**, Jefferson Community and Technical College, KY, U.S.; **Rachel DeSanto**, Hillsborough Community College Dale Mabry Campus, FL, U.S.; **Nilüfer Ertürkmen**, Ege University, Turkey; **Sue Fine**, Ras Al Khaimah Women's College (HCT), U.A.E.; **Amina Al Hashami**, Nizwa College of Applied Sciences, Oman; **Stephan Johnson**, Nagoya Shoka Daigaku, Japan; **Sean Kim**, Avalon, South Korea; **Gregory King**, Chubu Daigaku, Japan; **Seran Küçük**, Maltepe University, Turkey; **Jonee De Leon**, VUS, Vietnam; **Carol Lowther**, Palomar College, CA, U.S.; **Erin Harris-MacLead**, St. Mary's University, NS, Canada; **Angela Nagy**, Maltepe University, Turkey; **Huynh Thi Ai Nguyen**, Vietnam; **Daniel L. Paller**, Kinjo Gakuin University, Japan; **Jangyo Parsons**, Kookmin University, South Korea; **Laila Al Qadhi**, Kuwait University, Kuwait; **Josh Rosenberger**, English Language Institute University of Montana, MT, U.S.; **Nancy Schoenfeld**, Kuwait University, Kuwait; **Jenay Seymour**, Hongik University, South Korea; **Moon-young Son**, South Korea; **Matthew Taylor**, Kinjo Gakuin Daigaku, Japan; **Burcu Tezcan-Unal**, Zayed University, U.A.E.; **Troy Tucker**, Edison State College-Lee Campus, FL, U.S.; **Kris Vicca**, Feng Chia University, Taichung; **Jisook Woo**, Incheon University, South Korea; **Dunya Yenidunya**, Ege University, Turkey

UNITED STATES Marcarena Aguilar, North Harris College, TX; **Rebecca Andrade**, California State University North Ridge, CA; **Lesley Andrews**, Boston University, MA; **Deborah Anholt**, Lewis and Clark College, OR; **Robert Anzelde**, Oakton Community College, IL; **Arlys Arnold**, University of Minnesota, MN; **Marcia Arthur**, Renton Technical College, WA; **Renee Ashmeade**, Passaic County Community College, NJ; **Anne Bachmann**, Clackamas Community College, OR; **Lida Baker**, UCLA, CA; **Ron Balsamo**, Santa Rosa Junior College, CA; **Lori Barkley**, Portland State University, OR; **Eileen Barlow**, SUNY Albany, NY; **Sue Bartch**, Cuyahoga Community College, OH; **Lora Bates**, Oakton High School, VA; **Barbara Batra**, Nassau County Community College, NY; **Nancy Baum**, University of Texas at Arlington, TX; **Rebecca Beck**, Irvine Valley College, CA; **Linda Berendsen**, Oakton Community College, IL; **Jennifer Binckes Lee**, Howard Community College, MD; **Grace Bishop**, Houston Community College, TX; **Jean W. Bodman**, Union County College, NJ; **Virginia Bouchard**, George Mason University, VA; **Kimberley Briesch Sumner**, University of Southern California, CA; **Kevin Brown**, University of California, Irvine, CA; **Laura Brown**, Glendale Community College, CA; **Britta Burton**, Mission College, CA; **Allison L. Callahan**, Harold Washington College, IL; **Gabriela Cambiasso**, Harold Washington College, IL; **Jackie Campbell**, Capistrano Unified School District, CA; **Adele C. Camus**, George Mason University, VA; **Laura Chason**, Savannah College, GA; **Kerry Linder Catana**, Language Studies International, NY; **An Cheng**, Oklahoma State University, OK; **Carole Collins**, North Hampton Community College, PA; **Betty R. Compton**, Intercultural Communications College, HI; **Pamela Couch**, Boston University, MA; **Fernanda Crowe**, Intrax International Institute, CA; **Vicki Curtis**, Santa Cruz, CA; **Margo Czinski**, Washtenaw Community College, MI; **David Dahnke**, Lone Star College, TX; **Gillian M. Dale**, CA; **L. Dalgish**, Concordia College, MN; **Christopher Davis**, John Jay College, NY; **Sherry Davis**, Irvine University, CA; **Natalia de Cuba**, Nassau County Community College, NY; **Sonia Delgadillo**, Sierra College, CA; **Esmeralda Diriye**, Cypress College & Cal Poly, CA; **Marta O. Dmytrenko-Ahrabian**, Wayne State University, MI; **Javier Dominguez**, Central High School, SC; **Jo Ellen Downey-Greer**, Lansing Community College, MI; **Jennifer Duclos**, Boston University, MA; **Yvonne Duncan**, City College of San Francisco, CA; **Paul Dydman**, USC Language Academy, CA; **Anna Eddy**, University of Michigan-Flint, MI; **Zohan El-Gamal**, Glendale Community College, CA; **Jennie Farnell**, University of Connecticut, CT; **Susan Fedors**, Howard Community College, MD; **Valerie Fiechter**, Mission College, CA; **Ashley Fifer**, Nassau County Community College, NY; **Matthew Florence**, Intrax International Institute, CA; **Kathleen Flynn**, Glendale College, CA; **Elizabeth Fonsea**, Nassau County Community College, NY; **Eve Fonseca**, St. Louis Community College, MO; **Elizabeth Foss**, Washtenaw Community College, MI; **Duff C. Galda**, Pima Community College, AZ; **Christiane Galvani**, Houston Community College, TX; **Gretchen Gerber**, Howard Community College, MD; **Ray Gonzalez**, Montgomery College, MD; **Janet Goodwin**, University of California, Los Angeles, CA; **Alyona Gorokhova**, Grossmont College, CA; **John Graney**, Santa Fe College, FL; **Kathleen Green**, Central High School, AZ; **Nancy Hamadou**, Pima Community College-West Campus, AZ; **Webb Hamilton**, De Anza College, San Jose City College, CA; **Janet Harclerode**, Santa Monica Community College, CA; **Sandra Hartmann**, Language and Culture Center, TX; **Kathy Haven**, Mission College, CA; **Roberta Hendrick**, Cuyahoga Community College, OH; **Ginny Heringer**, Pasadena City College, CA; **Adam Henricksen**, University of Maryland, MD; **Carolyn Ho**, Lone Star College-CyFair, TX; **Peter Hoffman**, LaGuardia Community College, NY; **Linda Holden**, College of Lake County, IL; **Jana Holt**, Lake Washington Technical College, WA; **Antonio Iccarino**, Boston University, MA; **Gail Ibele**, University of Wisconsin, WI; **Nina Ito**, American Language Institute, CSU Long Beach, CA; **Linda Jensen**, UCLA, CA; **Lisa Jurkowitz**, Pima Community College, CA; **Mandy Kama**, Georgetown University, Washington, DC; **Stephanie Kasuboski**, Cuyahoga Community College, OH; **Chigusa Katoku**, Mission College, CA; **Sandra Kawamura**, Sacramento City College, CA; **Gail Kellersberger**, University of Houston-Downtown, TX; **Jane Kelly**, Durham Technical Community College, NC; **Maryanne Kildare**, Nassau County Community College, NY; **Julie Park Kim**, George Mason University, VA; **Kindra Kinyon**, Los Angeles Trade-Technical College, CA; **Matt Kline**, El Camino College, CA; **Lisa Kovacs-Morgan**, University of California, San Diego, CA; **Claudia Kupiec**, DePaul University, IL; **Renee La Rue**, Lone Star College-Montgomery, TX; **Janet Langon**, Glendale College, CA; **Lawrence Lawson**, Palomar College, CA; **Rachele Lawton**, The Community College of Baltimore County, MD; **Alice Lee**, Richland College, TX; **Esther S. Lee**, CSUF & Mt. SAC, CA; **Cherie Lenz-Hackett**, University of Washington, WA; **Joy Leventhal**, Cuyahoga Community College, OH; **Alice Lin**, UCI Extension, CA; **Monica Lopez**, Cerritos College, CA; **Dustin Lovell**, FLS International Marymount College, CA; **Carol Lowther**, Palomar College, CA; **Candace Lynch-Thompson**, North Orange County Community College District, CA; **Thi Thi Ma**, City College of San Francisco, CA; **Steve Mac Isaac**, USC Long Academy, CA; **Denise Maduli-Williams**, City College of San Francisco, CA; **Eileen Mahoney**, Camelback High School, AZ; **Naomi Mardock**, MCC-Omaha, NE; **Brigitte Maronde**, Harold Washington College, IL; **Marilyn Marquis**, Laposita College CA; **Doris Martin**, Glendale Community College; Pasadena City College, CA; **Keith Maurice**, University of Texas at Arlington, TX; **Nancy Mayer**, University of Missouri-St. Louis, MO; **Aziah McNamara**, Kansas State University, KS; **Billie McQuillan**, Education Heights, MN; **Karen Merritt**, Glendale Union High School District, AZ; **Holly Milkowart**, Johnson County Community College, KS; **Eric Moyer**, Intrax International Institute, CA; **Gino Muzzatti**, Santa Rosa Junior College, CA; **Sandra Navarro**, Glendale Community College, CA; **Than Nyeinkhin**, ELAC, PCC, CA; **William Nedrow**, Triton College, IL; **Eric Nelson**, University of Minnesota, MN; **Than Nyeinkhin**, ELAC, PCC, CA; **Fernanda Ortiz**, Center for English as a Second Language at the University of Arizona, AZ; **Rhony Ory**, Ygnacio Valley High School, CA; **Paul Parent**, Montgomery College, MD; **Dr. Sumeeta Patnaik**, Marshall University, WV; **Oscar Pedroso**, Miami Dade College, FL; **Robin Persiani**, Sierra College, CA; **Patricia Prenz-Belkin**, Hostos Community College, NY; **Suzanne Powell**, University of Louisville, KY; **Jim Ranalli**, Iowa State University, IA; **Toni R. Randall**, Santa Monica College, CA; **Vidya Rangachari**, Mission College, CA; **Elizabeth Rasmussen**, Northern Virginia Community College, VA; **Lara Ravitch**, Truman College, IL;

iii

Deborah Repasz, San Jacinto College, TX; **Marisa Recinos**, English Language Center, Brigham Young University, UT; **Andrey Reznikov**, Black Hills State University, SD; **Alison Rice**, Hunter College, NY; **Jennifer Robles**, Ventura Unified School District, CA; **Priscilla Rocha**, Clark County School District, NV; **Dzidra Rodins**, DePaul University, IL; **Maria Rodriguez**, Central High School, AZ; **Josh Rosenberger**, English Language Institute University of Montana, MT; **Alice Rosso**, Bucks County Community College, PA; **Rita Rozzi**, Xavier University, OH; **Maria Ruiz**, Victor Valley College, CA; **Kimberly Russell**, Clark College, WA; **Stacy Sabraw**, Michigan State University, MI; **Irene Sakk**, Northwestern University, IL; **Deborah Sandstrom**, University of Illinois at Chicago, IL; **Jenni Santamaria**, ABC Adult, CA; **Shaeley Santiago**, Ames High School, IA; **Peg Sarosy**, San Francisco State University, CA; **Alice Savage**, North Harris College, TX; **Donna Schaeffer**, University of Washington, WA; **Karen Marsh Schaeffer**, University of Utah, UT; **Carol Schinger**, Northern Virginia Community College, VA; **Robert Scott**, Kansas State University, KS; **Suell Scott**, Sheridan Technical Center, FL; **Shira Seaman**, Global English Academy, NY; **Richard Seltzer**, Glendale Community College, CA; **Harlan Sexton**, CUNY Queensborough Community College, NY; **Kathy Sherak**, San Francisco State University, CA; **German Silva**, Miami Dade College, FL; **Ray Smith**, Maryland English Institute, University of Maryland, MD; **Shira Smith**, NICE Program University of Hawaii, HI; **Tara Smith**, Felician College, NJ; **Monica Snow**, California State University, Fullerton, CA; **Elaine Soffer**, Nassau County Community College, NY; **Andrea Spector**, Santa Monica Community College, CA; **Jacqueline Sport**, LBWCC Luverne Center, AL; **Karen Stanely**, Central Piedmont Community College, NC; **Susan Stern**, Irvine Valley College, CA; **Ayse Stromsdorfer**, Soldan I.S.H.S., MO; **Yilin Sun**, South Seattle Community College, WA; **Thomas Swietlik**, Intrax International Institute, IL; **Nicholas Taggert**, University of Dayton, OH; **Judith Tanka**, UCLA Extension–American Language Center, CA; **Amy Taylor**, The University of Alabama Tuscaloosa, AL; **Andrea Taylor**, San Francisco State, CA; **Priscilla Taylor**, University of Southern California, CA; **Ilene Teixeira**, Fairfax County Public Schools, VA; **Shirl H. Terrell**, Collin College, TX; **Marya Teutsch-Dwyer**, St. Cloud State University, MN; **Stephen Thergesen**, ELS Language Centers, CO; **Christine Tierney**, Houston Community College, TX; **Arlene Turini**, North Moore High School, NC; **Cara Tuzzolino**, Nassau County Community College, NY; **Suzanne Van Der Valk**, Iowa State University, IA; **Nathan D. Vasarhely**, Ygnacio Valley High School, CA; **Naomi S. Verratti**, Howard Community College, MD; **Hollyahna Vettori**, Santa Rosa Junior College, CA; **Julie Vorholt**, Lewis & Clark College, OR; **Danielle Wagner**, FLS International Marymount College, CA; **Lynn Walker**, Coastline College, CA; **Laura Walsh**, City College of San Francisco, CA; **Andrew J. Watson**, The English Bakery; **Donald Weasenforth**, Collin College, TX; **Juliane Widner**, Sheepshead Bay High School, NY; **Lynne Wilkins**, Mills College, CA; **Pamela Williams**, Ventura College, CA; **Jeff Wilson**, Irvine Valley College, CA; **James Wilson**, Consomnes River College, CA; **Katie Windahl**, Cuyahoga Community College, OH; **Dolores "Lorrie" Winter**, California State University at Fullerton, CA; **Jody Yamamoto**, Kapi'olani Community College, HI; **Ellen L. Yaniv**, Boston University, MA; **Norman Yoshida**, Lewis & Clark College, OR; **Joanna Zadra**, American River College, CA; **Florence Zysman**, Santiago Canyon College, CA;

CANADA Patricia Birch, Brandon University, MB; **Jolanta Caputa**, College of New Caledonia, BC; **Katherine Coburn**, UBC's ELI, BC; **Erin Harris-Macleod**, St. Mary's University, NS; **Tami Moffatt**, English Language Institute, BC; **Jim Papple**, Brock University, ON; **Robin Peace**, Confederation College, BC;

ASIA Rabiatu Abubakar, Eton Language Centre, Malaysia; **Wiwik Andreani**, Bina Nusantara University, Indonesia; **Frank Bailey**, Baiko Gakuin University, Japan; **Mike Baker**, Kosei Junior High School, Japan; **Leonard Barrow**, Kanto Junior College, Japan; **Herman Bartelen**, Japan; **Siren Betty**, Fooyin University, Kaohsiung; **Thomas E. Bieri**, Nagoya College, Japan; **Natalie Brezden**, Global English House, Japan; **MK Brooks**, Mukogawa Women's University, Japan; **Truong Ngoc Buu**, The Youth Language School, Vietnam; **Charles Cabell**, Toyo University, Japan; **Fred Carruth**, Matsumoto University, Japan; **Frances Causer**, Seijo University, Japan; **Jeffrey Chalk**, SNU, South Korea; **Deborah Chang**, Wenzao Ursuline College of Languages, Kaohsiung; **David Chatham**, Ritsumeikan University, Japan; **Andrew Chih Hong Chen**, National Sun Yat-sen University, Kaohsiung; **Christina Chen**, Yu-Tsai Bilingual Elementary School, Taipei; **Hui-chen Chen**, Shi-Lin High School of Commerce, Taipei; **Seungmoon Choe**, K2M Language Institute, South Korea; **Jason Jeffree Cole**, Coto College, Japan; **Le Minh Cong**, Vungtau Tourism Vocational College, Vietnam; **Todd Cooper**, Toyama National College of Technology, Japan; **Marie Cosgrove**, Daito Bunka

University, Japan; **Randall Cotten**, Gifu City Women's College, Japan; **Tony Cripps**, Ritsumeikan University, Japan; **Andy Cubalit**, CHS, Thailand; **Daniel Cussen**, Takushoku University, Japan; **Le Dan**, Ho Chi Minh City Electric Power College, Vietnam; **Simon Daykin**, Banghwa-dong Community Centre, South Korea; **Aimee Denham**, ILA, Vietnam; **Bryan Dickson**, David's English Center, Taipei; **Nathan Ducker**, Japan University, Japan; **Ian Duncan**, Simul International Corporate Training, Japan; **Nguyen Thi Kieu Dung**, Thang Long University, Vietnam; **Truong Quang Dung**, Tien Giang University, Vietnam; **Nguyen Thi Thuy Duong**, Vietnamese American Vocational Training College, Vietnam; **Wong Tuck Ee**, Raja Tun Azlan Science Secondary School, Malaysia; **Emilia Effendy**, International Islamic University Malaysia, Malaysia; **Bettizza Escueta**, KMUTT, Thailand; **Robert Eva**, Kaisei Girls High School, Japan; **Jim George**, Luna International Language School, Japan; **Jurgen Germeys**, Silk Road Language Center, South Korea; **Wong Ai Gnoh**, SMJK Chung Hwa Confucian, Malaysia; **Sarah Go**, Seoul Women's University, South Korea; **Peter Goosselink**, Hokkai High School, Japan; **Robert Gorden**, SNU, South Korea; **Wendy M. Gough**, St. Mary College/Nunoike Gaigo Senmon Gakko, Japan; **Tim Grose**, Sapporo Gakuin University, Japan; **Pham Thu Ha**, Le Van Tam Primary School, Vietnam; **Ann-Marie Hadzima**, Taipei; **Troy Hammond**, Tokyo Gakugei University International Secondary School, Japan; **Robiatul 'Adawiah Binti Hamzah**, SMK Putrajaya Precinct 8(1), Malaysia; **Tran Thi Thuy Hang**, Ho Chi Minh City Banking University, Vietnam; **To Thi Hong Hanh**, CEFALT, Vietnam; **George Hays**, Tokyo Kokusai Daigaku, Japan; **Janis Hearn**, Hongik University, South Korea; **Chantel Hemmi**, Jochi Daigaku, Japan; **David Hindman**, Sejong University, South Korea; **Nahn Cam Hoa**, Ho Chi Minh City University of Technology, Vietnam; **Jana Holt**, Korea University, South Korea; **Jason Hollowell**, Nihon University, Japan; **F. N. (Zoe) Hsu**, National Tainan University, Yong Kang; **Kuei-ping Hsu**, National Tsing Hua University, Hsinchu City; **Wenhua Hsu**, I-Shou University, Kaohsiung; **Luu Nguyen Quoc Hung**, Cantho University, Vietnam; **Cecile Hwang**, Changwon National University, South Korea; **Ainol Haryati Ibrahim**, Universiti Malaysia Pahang, Malaysia; **Robert Jeens**, Yonsei University, South Korea; **Linda M. Joyce**, Kyushu Sangyo University, Japan; **Dr. Nisai Kaewsanchai**, English Square Kanchanaburi, Thailand; **Aniza Kamarulzaman**, Sabah Science Secondary School, Malaysia; **Ikuko Kashiwabara**, Osaka Electro-Communication University, Japan; **Gurmit Kaur**, INTI College, Malaysia; **Nick Keane**, Japan; **Ward Ketcheson**, Aomori University, Japan; **Nicholas Kemp**, Kyushu International University, Japan; **Montchatry Ketmuni**, Rajamangala University of Technology, Thailand; **Dinh Viet Khanh**, Vietnam; **Seonok Kim**, Kangsu Jongro Language School, South Korea; **Suyeon Kim**, Anyang University, South Korea; **Kelly P. Kimura**, Soka University, Japan; **Masakazu Kimura**, Katoh Gakuen Gyoshu High School, Japan; **Gregory King**, Chubu Daigaku, Japan; **Stan Kirk**, Konan University, Japan; **Donald Knight**, Nan Hua/Fu Li Junior High Schools, Hsinchu; **Kari J. Kostiainen**, Nagoya City University, Japan; **Pattri Kuanpulpol**, Silpakorn University, Thailand; **Ha Thi Lan**, Thai Binh Teacher Training College, Vietnam; **Eric Edwin Larson**, Miyazaki Prefectural Nursing University, Japan; **David Laurence**, Chubu Daigaku, Japan; **Richard S. Lavin**, Prefectural University of Kumamoto, Japan; **Shirley Leane**, Chugoku Junior College, Japan; **I-Hsiu Lee**, Yunlin; **Nari Lee**, Park Jung PLS, South Korea; **Tae Lee**, Yonsei University, South Korea; **Lys Yongsoon Lee**, Reading Town Geumcheon, South Korea; **Mallory Leece**, Sun Moon University, South Korea; **Dang Hong Lien**, Tan Lam Upper Secondary School, Vietnam; **Huang Li-Han**, Rebecca Education Institute, Taipei; **Sovannarith Lim**, Royal University of Phnom Penh, Cambodia; **Ginger Lin**, National Kaohsiung Hospitality College, Kaohsiung; **Noel Lineker**, New Zealand/Japan; **Tran Dang Khanh Linh**, Nha Trang Teachers' Training College, Vietnam; **Daphne Liu**, Buliton English School, Taipei; **S. F. Josephine Liu**, Tien-Mu Elementary School, Taipei ; **Caroline Luo**, Tunghai University, Taichung; **Jeng-Jia Luo**, Tunghai University, Taichung; **Laura MacGregor**, Gakushuin University, Japan; **Amir Madani**, Visuttharangsi School, Thailand; **Elena Maeda**, Sacred Heart Professional Training College, Japan; **Vu Thi Thanh Mai**, Hoang Gia Education Center, Vietnam; **Kimura Masakazu**, Kato Gakuen Gyoshu High School, Japan; **Susumu Matsuhashi**, Net Link English School, Japan; **James McCrostie**, Daito Bunka University, Japan; **Joel McKee**, Inha University, South Korea; **Colin McKenzie**, Wachirawit Primary School, Thailand; **Terumi Miyazoe**, Tokyo Denki Daigaku, Japan; **William K. Moore**, Hiroshima Kokusai Gakuin University, Japan; **Kevin Mueller**, Tokyo Kokusai Daigaku, Japan; **Hudson Murrell**, Baiko Gakuin University, Japan; **Frances Namba**, Senri International School of Kwansei Gakuin, Japan; **Keiichi Narita**, Niigata University, Japan; **Kim Chung Nguyen**, Ho Chi Minh University of

Industry, Vietnam; **Do Thi Thanh Nhan**, Hanoi University, Vietnam; **Dale Kazuo Nishi**, Aoyama English Conversation School, Japan; **Huynh Thi Ai Nguyen**, Vietnam; **Dongshin Oh**, YBM PLS, South Korea; **Keiko Okada**, Dokkyo Daigaku, Japan; **Louise Ohashi**, Shukutoku University, Japan; **Yongjun Park**, Sangji University, South Korea; **Donald Patnaude**, Ajarn Donald's English Language Services, Thailand; **Virginia Peng**, Ritsumeikan University, Japan; **Suangkanok Piboonthamnont**, Rajamangala University of Technology, Thailand; **Simon Pitcher**, Business English Teaching Services, Japan; **John C. Probert**, New Education Worldwide, Thailand; **Do Thi Hoa Quyen**, Ton Duc Thang University, Vietnam; **John P. Racine**, Dokkyo University, Japan; **Kevin Ramsden**, Kyoto University of Foreign Studies, Japan; **Luis Rappaport**, Cung Thieu Nha Ha Noi, Vietnam; **Lisa Reshad**, Konan Daigaku Hyogo, Japan; **Peter Riley**, Taisho University, Japan; **Thomas N. Robb**, Kyoto Sangyo University, Japan; **Rory Rosszell**, Meiji Daigaku, Japan; **Maria Feti Rosyani**, Universitas Kristen Indonesia, Indonesia; **Greg Rouault**, Konan University, Japan; **Chris Ruddenklau**, Kindai University, Japan; **Hans-Gustav Schwartz**, Thailand; **Mary-Jane Scott**, Soongsil University, South Korea; **Dara Sheahan**, Seoul National University, South Korea; **James Sherlock**, A.P.W. Angthong, Thailand; **Prof. Shieh**, Minghsin University of Science & Technology, Xinfeng; **Yuko Shimizu**, Ritsumeikan University, Japan; **Suzila Mohd Shukor**, Universiti Sains Malaysia, Malaysia; **Stephen E. Smith**, Mahidol University, Thailand; **Moon-young Son**, South Korea; **Seunghee Son**, Anyang University, South Korea; **Mi-young Song**, Kyungwon University, South Korea; **Lisa Sood**, VUS, BIS, Vietnam; **Jason Stewart**, Taejon International Language School, South Korea; **Brian A. Stokes**, Korea University, South Korea; **Mulder Su**, Shih-Chien University, Kaohsiung; **Yoomi Suh**, English Plus, South Korea; **Yun-Fang Sun**, Wenzao Ursuline College of Languages, Kaohsiung; **Richard Swingle**, Kansai Gaidai University, Japan; **Sanford Taborn**, Kinjo Gakuin Daigaku, Japan; **Mamoru Takahashi**, Akita Prefectural University, Japan; **Tran Hoang Tan**, School of International Training, Vietnam; **Takako Tanaka**, Doshisha University, Japan; **Jeffrey Taschner**, American University Alumni Language Center, Thailand; **Matthew Taylor**, Kinjo Gakuin Daigaku, Japan; **Michael Taylor**, International Pioneers School, Thailand; **Kampanart Thammaphati**, Wattana Wittaya Academy, Thailand; **Tran Duong The**, Sao Mai Language Center, Vietnam; **Tran Dinh Tho**, Duc Tri Secondary School, Vietnam; **Huynh Thi Anh Thu**, Nhatrang College of Culture Arts and Tourism, Vietnam; **Peter Timmins**, Peter's English School, Japan; **Fumie Togano**, Hosei Daini High School, Japan; **F. Sigmund Topor**, Keio University Language School, Japan; **Tu Trieu**, Rise VN, Vietnam; **Yen-Cheng Tseng**, Chang-Jung Christian University, Tainan; **Pei-Hsuan Tu**, National Cheng Kung University, Tainan City; **Hajime Uematsu**, Hirosaki University, Japan; **Rachel Um**, Mok-dong Oedae English School, South Korea; **David Underhill**, EEExpress, Japan; **Ben Underwood**, Kugenuma High School, Japan; **Siriluck Usaha**, Sripatum University, Thailand; **Tyas Budi Utami**, Indonesia; **Nguyen Thi Van**, Far East International School, Vietnam; **Stephan Van Eycken**, Kosei Gakuen Girls High School, Japan; **Zisa Velasquez**, Taihu International School/Semarang International School, China/Indonesia; **Jeffery Walter**, Sangji University, South Korea; **Bill White**, Kinki University, Japan; **Yohanes De Deo Widyastoko**, Xaverius Senior High School, Indonesia; **Dylan Williams**, SNU, South Korea; **Jisuk Woo**, Ichean University, South Korea; **Greg Chung-Hsien Wu**, Providence University, Taichung; **Xun Xiaoming**, BLCU, China; **Hui-Lien Yeh**, Chai Nan University of Pharmacy and Science, Tainan; **Sittiporn Yodnil**, Huachiew Chalermprakiet University, Thailand; **Shamshul Helmy Zambahari**, Universiti Teknologi Malaysia, Malaysia; **Ming-Yuli**, Chang Jung Christian University, Tainan; **Aimin Fadhlee bin Mahmud Zuhodi**, Kuala Terengganu Science School, Malaysia;

TURKEY **Shirley F. Akis**, American Culture Association/Fomara; **Gül Akkoç**, Boğaziçi University; **Seval Akmeşe**, Haliç University; **Ayşenur Akyol**, Ege University; **Ayşe Umut Aribaş**, Beykent University; **Gökhan Asan**, Kapadokya Vocational College; **Hakan Asan**, Kapadokya Vocational College; **Julia Asan**, Kapadokya Vocational College; **Azarvan Atac**, Piri Reis University; **Nur Babat**, Kapadokya Vocational College; **Feyza Balakbabalar**, Kadir Has University; **Gözde Balikçi**, Beykent University; **Deniz Balım**, Haliç University; **Asli Başdoğan**, Kadir Has University; **Ayla Bayram**, Kapadokya Vocational College; **Pinar Bilgiç**, Kadir Has University; **Kenan Bozkurt**, Kapadokya Vocational College; **Yonca Bozkurt**, Ege University; **Frank Carr**, Piri Reis; **Mengü Noyan Çengel**, Ege University; **Elif Doğan**, Ege University; **Natalia Donmez**, 29 Mayis Üniversite; **Nalan Emirsoy**, Kadir Has University; **Ayşe Engin**, Kadir Has University; **Ayhan Gedikbaş**, Ege University; **Gülşah Gençer**, Beykent University; **Seyit Ömer Gök**, Gediz University; **Tuğba Gök**, Gediz University; **İlkay Gökçe**, Ege University; **Zeynep Birinci Guler**, Maltepe University; **Neslihan Güler**, Kadir Has University; **Sircan Gümüş**, Kadir Has University; **Nesrin Gündoğu**, T.C. Piri Reis University; **Tanju Gurpinar**, Piri Reis University; **Selin Gurturk**, Piri Reis University; **Neslihan Gurutku**, Piri Reis University; **Roger Hewitt**, Maltepe University; **Nilüfer İbrahimoğlu**, Beykent University; **Nevin Kaftelen**, Kadir Has University; **Sultan Kalin**, Kapadokya Vocational College; **Sema Kaplan Karabina**, Anadolu University; **Eray Kara**, Giresun University; **Beylü Karayazgan**, Ege University; **Darren Kelso**, Piri Reis University; **Trudy Kittle**, Kapadokya Vocational College; **Şaziye Konaç**, Kadir Has University; **Güneş Korkmaz**, Kapadokya Vocational College; **Robert Ledbury**, Izmir University of Economics; **Ashley Lucas**, Maltepe University; **Bülent Nedium Uça**, Dogus University; **Murat Nurlu**, Ege University; **Mollie Owens**, Kadir Has University; **Oya Özağaç**, Boğaziçi University; **Funda Özcan**, Ege University; **İlkay Özdemir**, Ege University; **Ülkü Öztürk**, Gediz University; **Cassondra Puls**, Anadolu University; **Yelda Sarikaya**, Cappadocia Vocational College; **Müge Şekercioğlu**, Ege University; **Melis Senol**, Canakkale Onsekiz Mart University, The School of Foreign Languages; **Patricia Sümer**, Kadir Has University; **Rex Surface**, Beykent University; **Mustafa Torun**, Kapadokya Vocational College; **Tansel Üstünloğlu**, Ege University; **Fatih Yücel**, Beykent University; **Şule Yüksel**, Ege University;

THE MIDDLE EAST **Amina Saif Mohammed Al Hashamia**, Nizwa College of Applied Sciences, Oman; **Jennifer Baran**, Kuwait University, Kuwait; **Phillip Chappells**, GEMS Modern Academy, U.A.E.; **Sharon Ruth Devaneson**, Ibri College of Technology, Oman; **Hanaa El-Deeb**, Canadian International College, Egypt; **Yvonne Eaton**, Community College of Qatar, Qatar; **Brian Gay**, Sultan Qaboos University, Oman; **Gail Al Hafidh**, Sharjah Women's College (HCT), U.A.E.; **Jonathan Hastings**, American Language Center, Jordan; **Laurie Susan Hilu**, English Language Centre, University of Bahrain, Bahrain; **Abraham Irannezhad**, Mehre Aval, Iran; **Kevin Kempe**, CNA-Q, Qatar; **Jill Newby James**, University of Nizwa; **Mary Kay Klein**, American University of Sharjah, U.A.E.; **Sian Khoury**, Fujairah Women's College (HCT), U.A.E.; **Hussein Dehghan Manshadi**, Farhang Pajooh & Jaam-e-Jam Language School, Iran; **Jessica March**, American University of Sharjah, U.A.E.; **Neil McBeath**, Sultan Qaboos University, Oman; **Sandy McDonagh**, Abu Dhabi Men's College (HCT), U.A.E.; **Rob Miles**, Sharjah Women's College (HCT), U.A.E.; **Michael Kevin Neumann**, Al Ain Men's College (HCT), U.A.E.;

LATIN AMERICA **Aldana Aguirre**, Argentina; **Claudia Almeida**, Coordenação de Idiomas, Brazil; **Cláudia Arias**, Brazil; **Maria de los Angeles Barba**, FES Acatlan UNAM, Mexico; **Lilia Barrios**, Universidad Autónoma de Tamaulipas, Mexico; **Adán Beristain**, UAEM, Mexico; **Ricardo Böck**, Manoel Ribas, Brazil; **Edson Braga**, CNA, Brazil; **Marli Buttelli**, Mater et Magistra, Brazil; **Alessandra Campos**, Inova Centro de Linguas, Brazil; **Priscila Catta Preta Ribeiro**, Brazil; **Gustavo Cestari**, Access International School, Brazil; **Walter D'Alessandro**, Virginia Language Center, Brazil; **Lilian De Gennaro**, Argentina; **Mônica De Stefani**, Quality Centro de Idiomas, Brazil; **Julio Alejandro Flores**, BUAP, Mexico; **Mirian Freire**, CNA Vila Guilherme, Brazil; **Francisco Garcia**, Colegio Lestonnac de San Angel, Mexico; **Miriam Giovanardi**, Brazil; **Darlene Gonzalez Miy**, ITESM CCV, Mexico; **Maria Laura Grimaldi**, Argentina; **Luz Dary Guzmán**, IMPAHU, Colombia; **Carmen Koppe**, Brazil; **Monica Krutzler**, Brazil; **Marcus Murilo Lacerda**, Seven Idiomas, Brazil; **Nancy Lake**, CEL-LEP, Brazil; **Cris Lazzerini**, Brazil; **Sandra Luna**, Argentina; **Ricardo Luvisan**, Brazil; **Jorge Murilo Menezes**, ACBEU, Brazil; **Monica Navarro**, Instituto Cultural A. C., Mexico; **Joacyr Oliveira**, Faculdades Metropolitanas Unidas and Summit School for Teachers, Brazil; **Ayrton Cesar Oliveira de Araujo**, E&A English Classes, Brazil; **Ana Laura Oriente**, Seven Idiomas, Brazil; **Adelia Peña Clavel**, CELE UNAM, Mexico; **Beatriz Pereira**, Summit School, Brazil; **Miguel Perez**, Instituto Cultural, Mexico; **Cristiane Perone**, Associação Cultura Inglesa, Brazil; **Pamela Claudia Pogré**, Colegio Integral Caballito / Universidad de Flores, Argentina; **Dalva Prates**, Brazil; **Marianne Rampaso**, Iowa Idiomas, Brazil; **Daniela Rutolo**, Instituto Superior Cultural Británico, Argentina; **Maione Sampaio**, Maione Carrijo Consultoria em Inglês Ltda, Brazil; **Elaine Santesso**, TS Escola de Idiomas, Brazil; **Camila Francisco Santos**, UNS Idiomas, Brazil; **Lucia Silva**, Cooplem Idiomas, Brazil; **Maria Adela Sorzio**, Instituto Superior Santa Cecilia, Argentina; **Elcio Souza**, Unibero, Brazil; **Willie Thomas**, Rainbow Idiomas, Brazil; **Sandra Villegas**, Instituto Humberto de Paolis, Argentina; **John Whelan**, La Universidad Nacional Autonoma de Mexico, Mexico

UNIT 1

UNIT QUESTION

How does language affect who we are?

A Discuss these questions with your classmates.

1. What difficulties might an English speaker visiting your home country have while trying to communicate?

2. Do people who know two languages have different thoughts in each language or just different words for them?

3. Look at the photo. What are the people using to communicate? What are other non-standard forms of communication?

B Listen to *The Q Classroom* online. Then answer these questions.

1. Marcus and Felix believe that since language is tied to culture, it makes up part of our identity. What point can you add to the discussion to show you agree or disagree?

2. Sophy talks about ways to show respect in English, such as not using a lot of contractions. Can you think of any other ways you speak differently when talking to adults in English?

C Go to the Online Discussion Board to discuss the Unit Question with your classmates.

D Work with a partner. Read the following situations and discuss them. Then choose one and role-play it for the class.

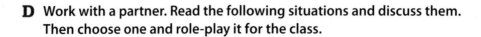

Have you ever experienced one of these difficulties in communicating?

1. Two friends see each other across a large, crowded, noisy restaurant. They try to communicate different issues, such as the time (one person is late), where to sit, and whether or not to leave.

2. A tourist who doesn't speak the language is lost in a big city. He or she tries to get directions from a local resident to get to a specific location (such as a hospital, a train station, a restaurant, or a museum).

3. A patient in a doctor's office tries to explain to the doctor how he or she woke up with a terrible headache and weak muscles and now is unable to speak.

E With your partner, use this mind map to brainstorm causes and effects of communication difficulties such as those in Activity D or another situation. Then discuss the questions below using your mind map.

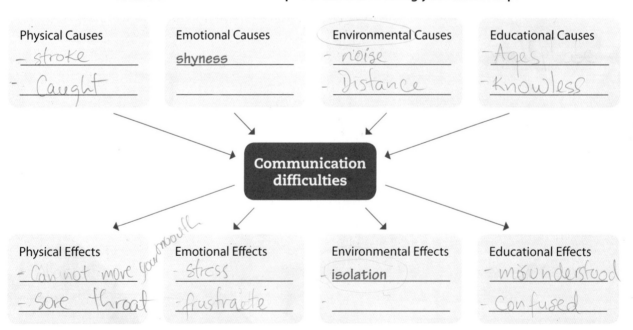

Physical Causes
- stroke
- Caught

Emotional Causes
shyness

Environmental Causes
- noise
- Distance

Educational Causes
- Ages
- Knowless

Communication difficulties

Physical Effects
- Can not move your mouth
- Sore throat

Emotional Effects
- Stress
- frustracte

Environmental Effects
- isolation

Educational Effects
- misunderstood
- Confused

1. What do you think are the most common causes of communication difficulties?

2. What are the most harmful effects?

LISTENING 1 | My Stroke of Insight: A Brain Scientist's Personal Journey

UNIT OBJECTIVE ▶▶▶

You are going to listen to an interview with Dr. Jill Bolte Taylor, a neuroanatomist who had a stroke and later wrote a book titled *My Stroke of Insight: A Brain Scientist's Story*. She describes the effects of her stroke in her book and in this interview with David Inge of the radio station WILL from the University of Illinois. As you listen to the interview, gather information and ideas about how language affects who we are.

PREVIEW THE LISTENING

Dr. Jill Bolte Taylor

A. **PREVIEW** How do you think Dr. Taylor's ability to think and communicate was affected when she had a stroke? Check (✓) your prediction.

☑ She could think using language, but could not speak.

☐ She could not think or speak using language.

B. **VOCABULARY** Read aloud these words from Listening 1. Check (✓) the ones you know. Use a dictionary to define any new or unknown words. Then discuss with a partner how the words will relate to the unit.

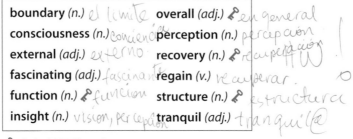

boundary *(n.)* el límite   overall *(adj.)* 🔑 en general
consciousness *(n.)* conciencia   perception *(n.)* percepción
external *(adj.)* externo   recovery *(n.)* 🔑 recuperación
fascinating *(adj.)* fascinante   regain *(v.)* recuperar
function *(n.)* 🔑 función   structure *(n.)* 🔑 estructura
insight *(n.)* visión, percepción   tranquil *(adj.)* tranquil@

🔑 Oxford 3000™ words

iQ ONLINE **C.** Go online to listen and practice your pronunciation.

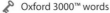

WORK WITH THE LISTENING

🔊 **A.** **LISTEN AND TAKE NOTES** Read the key phrases in the chart that introduce important ideas. Listen to the interview and take notes on what the speaker says about them.

Introduction

Key Phrases	Notes
1. The right hemisphere and the big picture	major poits the big picture
2. The left hemisphere and language	details - using language communication

Call-in Show

Key Phrases	Notes
3. Memories and a sense of identity	- loose future and past
4. Stroke victims and English speakers in a foreign country	

Tip for Success

Remember that main ideas are always complete sentences, whereas topics are just key words or phrases.

B. Use your notes to write the main ideas about each key phrase that Taylor explains to her listeners. Compare your sentences with a partner.

Introduction

1. The right hemisphere and the big picture

   The right hemisphere is charactinzed to register de general information from the enviroment, without focos on details.

2. The left hemisphere and language

However, the left hemisphere is looking for details and use the communication.

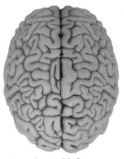

The right and left hemispheres of the human brain

Call-in Show

3. Memories and a sense of identity

_____

_____

4. Stroke victims and English speakers in a foreign country

_____

_____

C. Listen again. Circle the answer that best completes each statement.

Introduction

1. When Jill Bolte Taylor had her stroke in 1996, she was working at (Harvard / Indiana) University.

2. Dr. Taylor describes her feeling during her stroke as one of (peace and tranquility / panic and fear).

3. The right hemisphere of the brain is concerned with (overall perception / details).

4. The right and left hemispheres (have to / don't have to) work together for people to have a normal perspective.

5. During Dr. Taylor's stroke, she lost use of the (right / left) hemisphere of her brain.

Call-in Show

6. The behavioral psychologists mentioned by the caller believed that language could be lost only if a person (remained conscious / lost consciousness).

7. Dr. Taylor lost her perception of (past and present / past and future).

8. When Dr. Taylor lost the basic human ability to use language, she (no longer saw herself / still saw herself) as a human being.

D. Circle the best answer for each question.

1. What main purpose did Dr. Taylor have for agreeing to a radio interview?
    a. to help sell more copies of her book
    b. to teach listeners about neuroanatomy
    c. to explain the effects of a stroke
    d. to raise money for brain research

2. Which phrase explains what Dr. Taylor was referring to when she said "that person went offline."
    a. her loss of the ability to use a computer
    b. her loss of consciousness
    c. her loss of the ability to use language
    d. her loss of data connected to memories

3. Which quotation supports the concept that Jill Bolte Taylor did *not* picture herself as less than perfect.
    a. "... I was now an infant in a woman's body."
    b. "... there's a whole part of us that is non-language ..."
    c. "... I lost all of the consciousness of the language center."
    d. "... the rest of my left hemisphere was, was swimming in a pool of blood."

E. Read the statements. Write whether you would use the left hemisphere or right hemisphere of your brain. Explain your answer.

1. You call your friends by their names. _____

   _____

2. You go outside and think it's cold. _____

   _____

3. A picture reminds you of when you were younger. _____

   _____

4. You remember your home address. _____

   _____

5. You enjoy the movie you're watching. _____

   _____

F. **VOCABULARY** Here are some words from Listening 1. Read the paragraphs. Then fill in the blanks with the correct words from the list.

boundary (n.)	function (n.)	recovery (n.)
consciousness (n.)	insight (n.)	regain (v.)
external (adj.)	overall (adj.)	structure (n.)
fascinating (adj.)	perception (n.)	tranquil (adj.)

Vocabulary Skill Review

Using new words after you learn them will help ensure that they become part of your active vocabulary.

The brain is one of the most _fascinating_ organs in
                                        1
the human body, partly because it is such a mystery. It is studied

by doctors called neurologists and neuroanatomists, who hope to

gain a(n) _insight_ into the way the brain works. The
            2

structure of the brain is important: it is divided into two equal
     3

sections called hemispheres. One part, the cerebral cortex, coordinates what

we think and feel with what we see and our _perception_ of the
                                              4

outside world. Each part of the brain has a specific _function_ ,
                                                         5

and if injured, it may become unable to perform this role.

A stroke occurs when blood flow to part of the brain is cut off due

to a hemorrhage (heavy bleeding); this can result in an inability to

speak or move. Stroke victims sometimes lose _consciousness_ and
                                                  6

later have no memory of what has happened. They may not be aware of

external events or things around them. The line between what
   7

is real and unreal may become unclear, and the inability to understand

this _boundary_ may cause confusion. However, some patients
       8

experience the opposite feeling of _tranquil_ euphoria, a sense
                                       9

of calm when they are disconnected from the real world. For all stroke

victims, _recovery_ depends on the seriousness of the stroke, but
           10

with a lot of physical and speech therapy, patients can _regain_
                                                            11

their ability to walk and communicate. Although the _overall_
                                                        12

survival rate for stroke victims is not bad, on the whole, 40 percent have

some resulting disability.

SAY WHAT YOU THINK

Discuss the questions in a group.

1. Do you think you focus more on "the big picture" and general ideas or details? Would you say that you are more "right-brained" or "left-brained," according to the ideas in the Listening?

2. Which effect of a stroke would upset you more, the loss of the ability to speak or the loss of your past memories? Why?

3. Look at one of the pictures below and describe your overall perception. This will engage the right hemisphere of your brain, the side that looks at the big picture. Then, describe the details of the other picture. This will engage the left hemisphere of your brain, the side that looks at details.

   Which description was easier for you? What would Dr. Taylor say?

Picture A

Picture B

| Listening Skill | Making inferences |

Speakers do not always state their ideas or opinions directly. They may give facts or examples and expect the listener to draw a logical conclusion, or *make an inference*. It is important, however, to make sure you don't make inferences that were not suggested by the information.

If you are not sure what someone is implying, here are some phrases to check your understanding.

> So, do you mean that . . . ?
> So, are you saying that . . . ?
> So, would you say that . . . ?

A. Listen to the excerpts from Listening 1. Circle the best inference for each one.

1. a. People have no idea how the brain works.
   b. People don't understand the exact functions of the different parts of the brain.

2. a. A normal, healthy person uses both hemispheres of the brain.
   b. Different people prefer to use different hemispheres of the brain.

3. a. Dr. Taylor found an advantage in the consequences/effects of her stroke.
   b. Dr. Taylor was very upset about losing some of her brain's abilities.

4. a. Dr. Taylor feels that foreign tourists function somewhat as if they were brain-damaged.
   b. Dr. Taylor feels that foreign tourists make up for the lack of language skills by increasing other communicative abilities.

B. Choose two of the situations below or use your own ideas. Write some sentences that imply the ideas, but do not state them directly.

Your concerns about learning English
Your communication difficulties with grandparents
Your thoughts on teenage slang and text abbreviations
Your feelings about your language classes
Your fears about a miscommunication with a best friend

Your sentence: _____

Your sentence: _____

C. Work with a partner. Take turns reading the sentences about your situation. Can your partner infer what you are trying to say?

D. Go online for more practice making inferences.

In classes such as literature and history, reports or lectures often follow chronological, or time, order. The title of Listening 2, "The Story of My Life," suggests that you will listen to part of an autobiography.

When preparing to take notes, it is always a good idea to write down key words you expect to hear, leaving room to add information. For information you expect to be given in chronological order, think about the words you might hear the speaker use to indicate time order, such as:

at first	then	later
before	in the beginning	during that time
first, second, last	after that	soon
while	in 1954	on Monday

These words and phrases are important and you should write them down as you hear them, even if you have to go back and fill in some information.

A good note-taking tool for a lecture that will present information chronologically is a vertical or horizontal timeline. As you are listening, write dates or time phrases on one side of the timeline. On the other side, write corresponding key events and details. Remember you can always finish the timeline later.

A. Listen to a lecture on early childhood language development. Which set of words would you use in a timeline about this lecture? Check (✓) the best answer.

☐ first year of language instruction, second year, third year, fourth year

☐ 0–12 months, 18 months, 24 months, 30 months

☐ childhood, teenage years, adulthood

☐ age 1, age 2, age 3, age 4

B. Add the time words you chose in Activity A to the timeline below. Then listen again and complete the timeline with the corresponding events and details. Compare your answers with a partner.

children learn words from parents

 **C.** Go online for more practice organizing notes in chronological order using a timeline.

LISTENING 2 | The Story of My Life

UNIT OBJECTIVE You are going to listen to an excerpt from an audiobook of Hellen Keller's autobiography, *The Story of My Life*. Helen Keller (1880–1968) lost her sight and her hearing from an illness when she was 19 months old. She learned to communicate through hard work with her teacher, Annie Sullivan. As you listen to the excerpt, gather information and ideas about how language affects who we are.

PREVIEW THE LISTENING

Anne Sullivan and
Helen Keller

A. **PREVIEW** In what ways do you predict that a child who lost her sight and hearing at such a young age would try to communicate? Write your ideas and then share them with the class.

- Body language
- Braille method
- Sign language

B. **VOCABULARY** Read aloud these words from Listening 2. Check (✓) the ones you know. Use a dictionary to define any new or unknown words. Then discuss with a partner how the words will relate to the unit.

adequate *(adj.)* 🔑 *adecuado*	invariably *(adv.)* *invariablemente*
fragment *(n.)* *fragmento*	outburst *(n.)* *explosión* Homework!
gesticulate *(v.)* *gesticular*	persist *(v.)* *persistir*
imitate *(v.)* *imitar*	reveal *(v.)* 🔑 *revelar*
incident *(n.)* 🔑 *incidente*	sentiment *(n.)* *sentimiento*
intense *(adj.)* 🔑 *intenso*	tangible *(adj.)* *palpable*

→ ✱ Use google classroom or hand write turn in tuesday 9/10.

🔑 Oxford 3000™ words

 **C.** Go online to listen and practice your pronunciation.

WORK WITH THE LISTENING

A. **LISTEN AND TAKE NOTES** Listen to Helen Keller's story. As you listen, add main events from the story to the timeline. Then compare your timeline with a partner.

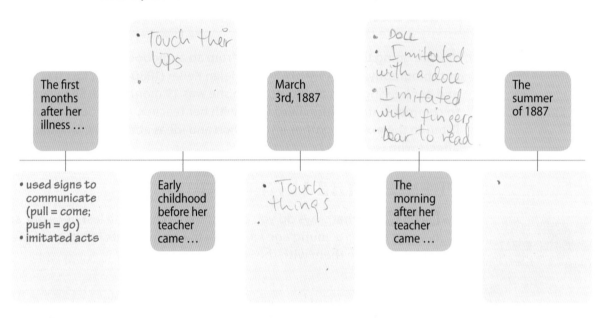

- Touch their lips

The first months after her illness …

- DOLL
- Imitated with a doll
- Imitated with fingers
- bear to read

March 3rd, 1887

The summer of 1887

- used signs to communicate (pull = come; push = go)
- imitated acts

Early childhood before her teacher came …

- Touch things

The morning after her teacher came …

Critical Thinking **Tip**

In Activity B you are asked to number the descriptions in chronological order. **Identifying** the logical order of events is an important critical thinking skill.

B. Read these descriptions of Helen Keller's emotions during periods of her childhood. Use your notes to number the described events in chronological order from 1 (the earliest) to 7 (the last). Check your answers with a partner.

_5_ Helen could make finger signs to spell many words but became impatient because she didn't understand how the actions connected with the words.

_1_ Helen used her hands, touched every object, and felt protected by her mother who understood her crude signs to communicate.

_4_ Helen's desire to communicate grew so strong that she was often angry and had passionate outbursts.

_7_ Helen began to grow confident as she explored with her hands and learned the names and uses for objects.

_3_ Helen was able to figure out what was going on around her and could imitate actions, but she felt different from others.

_2_ Helen touched people's lips and imitated their movements, but became frustrated when it did not produce any result.

_6_ Helen felt free and hopeful once the mystery of language was revealed to her, and she was eager to learn.

C. Read the lists of examples and descriptions from the audiobook excerpt. Then listen again. Match the examples with the descriptions.

a. a doll
b. pushing someone to tell her to go
c. her teacher
d. the strength of the sun
e. water
f. her mother
g. breaking the doll
h. Helen's saying "She brought me my hat, and I knew I was going out"

_b_ 1. an example of Helen's simple "crude signs" to communicate

f _e_ 2. the person to whom Helen owed "all that was bright and good in my long night"

h _g_ 3. an example of Helen's ability to figure out what was going on around her

c _f_ 4. the person "who had come to reveal all things to me, and, more than all things else, to love me"

_d_ 5. the way Helen knew that the "sweet southern spring" season had begun

_a_ 6. the gift that "the little blind children at the Perkins Institution had sent"

_e_ 7. the "living word" that "awakened [her] soul" and made Helen finally realize what language was

g _h_ 8. the action that Helen said made her feel satisfied and showed she knew "neither sorrow nor regret"

D. Circle the best answers to these questions.

1. How would you describe Anne Sullivan's teaching method?
    a. She persisted in teaching Helen one word at a time until she learned it correctly.
    b. She taught Helen in a traditional classroom/style, but used her fingers to spell words.
    c. She used Helen's sense of smell to connect a word with an object.
    d. She gave in to Helen's anger by allowing her to play outside when she got frustrated.

2. What is one point Helen Keller would probably NOT agree with?
   a. Children who are deaf and blind can learn to communicate effectively.
   b. Children who are deaf and blind are forever locked in a world of silence.
   c. Children who are deaf and blind should be encouraged to face their challenges.
   d. Children who are deaf and blind need special teachers to acquire language skills.

3. What can you infer from Keller's words, ". . . the more I handled things and learned their names and uses, the more joyous and confident grew my sense of kinship with the rest of the world"?
   a. Learning how to use things made Keller happier.
   b. Without words, Keller felt separate from the world.
   c. Confidence is not possible without language.
   d. Her family was happy that Keller understood the names for things.

E. Read the statements. Write *T* (true) or *F* (false). Then correct the false statements.

____ 1. Helen Keller did not communicate with anyone until she met her teacher, Anne Sullivan.

_____

____ 2. Helen Keller knew she was different before she met Anne Sullivan.

_____

____ 3. Anne Sullivan taught Helen Keller that everything has a name.

_____

____ 4. Helen Keller never became frustrated after meeting Anne Sullivan.

_____

____ 5. Helen Keller called the day she met Anne Sullivan the most important day of her life.

_____

F. VOCABULARY Here are some words from Listening 2. Read the sentences. Circle the answer that best matches the meaning of each bold word.

1. Children learn to speak by **imitating** words and trying to sound like adults.
   a. duplicating   b. ignoring

2. When we were trying to use our hands to communicate without language, we found that the way we **gesticulated** did not always get the message across.

   a. made signs   b. complained loudly

3. There were many **incidents** when it was clear that she could understand me, even though she never said anything directly.

   a. accidents   b. events

4. The experience was so **intense** that it caused the woman to cry.

   a. powerful   b. unexpected

5. If you don't feel your language skills are **adequate** for that job, then you should not apply!

   a. sufficient   b. not good enough

6. Those who are bilingual **invariably** get jobs more easily and are grateful to their parents for making them learn a second language.

   a. occasionally   b. consistently

7. These passionate **outbursts** helped the little boy get his way because no one could ignore the noise he made.

   a. quick explosion of feeling   b. loud sad songs

8. Without **tangible** evidence to support their theory, the researchers didn't feel confident publishing their study.

   a. popular; widely accepted   b. clearly visible or concrete

9. The answer to the mystery was not **revealed** until the last few pages of the book.

   a. explained; shown   b. hidden; unknown

10. If that annoying sound **persists**, I will have to complain to the neighbors. I can't sleep!

    a. fades away   b. keeps up

11. Because the stroke victim had lost some of her vision, she could only make out **fragments** of the picture and had to connect the pieces in her mind.

    a. little pieces   b. soft colors

12. There was no strong **sentiment** visible in the man's face, no feeling of anger or sorrow.

    a. line   b. emotion

G. Go online for more practice with the vocabulary.

H. Go online to listen to *Losing a Native Language* and check your comprehension.

Q? SAY WHAT YOU THINK

A. Discuss the questions in a group.

1. In the 21st century, do you think it is better for a child like Helen Keller to have a private tutor at home or learn in a school setting?

2. Helen Keller felt lost and empty without language. She was angry and even violent at times when she couldn't communicate. What are some emotions that are hard to put into words, and how do different people express them?

3. What message do you think Helen Keller wants readers to get from her descriptions of her childhood before and after she met her teacher?

B. Before you watch the video, discuss the questions in a group.

1. How might people have treated Helen Keller and Jill Bolte Taylor when they were unable to use language easily?

2. In what ways have people spoken to you differently when they realize English is not your native language?

C. Go online to watch the video about communicating with elders. Then check your comprehension.

> **demeaning** *(adj.)* insulting or disrespectful
>
> **dementia** *(n.)* serious mental disorder caused by brain disease or injury that affects the ability to think, remember, and behave
>
> **incompetence** *(n.)* lack of skill or ability to do your job or a task as it should be done

D. Think about the unit video, Listening 1, and Listening 2 as you discuss these questions.

1. If Helen Keller and Jill Bolte Taylor could meet, what do you think they would talk about?

2. What mental attitudes did Helen Keller and Jill Bolte Taylor have in common? In what ways were their attitudes different?

3. What similar feelings might the elderly, Helen Keller, and Jill Bolte Taylor have in common about the way others treat them?

Knowledge of prefixes helps you expand your vocabulary. Here are prefixes that are added to adjectives to give an opposite or negative meaning.

il- **il**legal
im- **im**possible
in- **in**capable
ir- **ir**regular
un- **un**thinkable

With *il-*, *im-*, and *ir-*, there are patterns, but also exceptions.

Use *il-* for words that begin with *l*.	**il**legal, **il**logical (but **un**lawful)
Use *im-* for words that begin with *p*, *m*, and *b*.	**im**possible, **im**measurable (but **un**popular)
Use *ir-* for words that begin with *r*.	**ir**relevant, **ir**regular (but **un**reliable)

The prefix *dis-* is the form that is most often used to form the negative of verbs, though *un-* is also used.

disobedecer
disgusto deshacer

disagree   **dis**obey   **dis**qualify   **dis**like   **un**do   **un**tie desatar

Both *dis-* and *un-* are also used for participial adjectives.

dissatisfied   **dis**appointing   **un**decided   **un**ending

A. Write the correct negative prefix on the line in front of the adjectives.

1. Dr. Taylor said that she was able to enjoy the experience of being

   ____connected from the left hemisphere of her brain.

2. Dr. Taylor told the caller she wasn't ____conscious even though she

   had had a stroke.

3. The caller was surprised that the neuroanatomist could get help in

   spite of her ____regular style of communicating.

4. A stroke victim who wasn't a doctor like Taylor was could have been

   ____aware of what was happening.

5. Helen Keller's parents might have thought that a teacher without direct experience with blindness would have been more ____sensitive toward Helen's condition.

6. Helen Keller was ____patient with her teacher's attempts to teach her the difference between *mug* and *water*.

B. Write sentences to describe Helen Keller and Jill Bolte Taylor and their experiences. Use one of these adjectives in a negative form in each sentence. Compare sentences with a partner.

adequate	conscious	perfect	tangible
capable	connected	possible	usual
comfortable	measurable	satisfied	visible

Helen Keller's earliest attempts to communicate were inadequate.

1. _____

2. _____

3. _____

4. _____

 C. Go online for more practice with negative prefixes.

Grammar | Passive voice

En lugar

1. The **passive voice** is used to put the emphasis on the object of the verb instead of the subject.

For example, imagine we want to talk about why Jill Bolte Taylor lost her language ability—because of the effects of a stroke on her brain. The most important part of the sentence is *her brain* and not *a stroke*. Therefore, instead of the active sentence *A stroke damaged Taylor's brain* we would say:

☐ Taylor's brain **was damaged** by a stroke.

2. The passive voice is used when the subject of the sentence isn't known.

☐ This audiobook **was recorded** in 2007.

If we don't know (and don't care) who recorded the audiobook, it sounds awkward to say *Somebody recorded this audiobook in 2007*. The important element of the sentence is *this audiobook*, so it sounds better at the beginning of the sentence.

3. The passive voice is only used with **transitive verbs** (verbs that take an object).

✓ Helen Keller **was taught** a new way to speak.

✗ Dr. Taylor's stroke was happened in the morning.

4. In passive sentences, the verb tense is indicated in the verb *be*. Modal verbs can also be made passive.

Past perfect passive	Past passive	Present perfect passive
had been found	was lost	has been studied
Present passive	**Future passive**	**Modal passive**
is taken	will be given	may be revealed could be gained

se puede usar con futuro presente.

The active voice is more common than the passive voice. Overusing the passive voice can make your speaking sound flat, impersonal, or too formal. This is why some word-processing grammar checks underline passive sentences. However, there are times when the passive voice is more appropriate and should be used.

 **Tip for Success**

Remember that not all sentences with a form of *be* + a participle are passive!
This article was written by Helen Keller is passive.
I was tired after a long, difficult day is not passive. It is the simple past of the verb *be* + an adjective.

A. Read these sentences from Helen Keller's story. Write *P* if the underlined verb is passive and *A* if it is active.

___P___ **1.** I felt my teacher sweep the fragments to one side of the hearth, and I had a sense of satisfaction that the cause of my discomfort <u>was removed</u>.

___A___ **2.** She brought me my hat, and I knew I <u>was going out</u> into the warm sunshine.

___P___ **3.** This thought, if a wordless sensation <u>may be called</u> a thought, made me hop and skip with pleasure.

___A___ **4.** Someone <u>was drawing</u> water, and my teacher placed my hand under the spout.

___A___ **5.** As the cool stream gushed over one hand she <u>spelled</u> into the other the word *water*, first slowly, then rapidly.

___P___ **6.** I stood still; my whole attention <u>was fixed</u> upon the motions of her fingers.

___P___ **7.** Suddenly I felt a misty consciousness as of something forgotten—a thrill of returning thought; and somehow the mystery of language <u>was revealed</u> to me.

___P___ **8.** I knew then that "w-a-t-e-r" meant the wonderful cool something that <u>was flowing</u> over my hand.

B. Work with a partner. Discuss whether the passive or the active version of the sentence sounds more natural. (Sometimes one is clearly better; sometimes both can sound all right, although the emphasis is different.)

1. a. I forgot my textbook.
   b. My textbook was forgotten by me.

2. a. Some scientists made many significant advances in the field of neuroscience in the last century.
   b. Many significant advances in the field of neuroscience were made in the last century.

3. a. Louis Braille invented a system of writing for the blind known as Braille.
   b. Braille, a system of writing for the blind, was invented by Louis Braille.

4. a. Someone added Braille signs to places such as elevators and restrooms.
   b. Braille signs have been added to places such as elevators and restrooms.

5. a. Today, some blind children may attend regular public schools.
   b. Today, regular public schools may be attended by some blind children.

C. Go online for more practice with the passive voice.

D. Go online for the grammar expansion.

Pronunciation | Emphatic word stress

Speakers engage their audiences by emphasizing key words in three main ways.

1. Saying key words more loudly
2. Making the vowels in the key syllables longer
3. Using a higher pitch for stressed words

Key words in sentences are usually content words (nouns, verbs, adjectives, and adverbs).

We also stress words that provide new information or information that contrasts with or corrects previous information. New or particularly important information often comes at the end of a clause or sentence.

Listen and practice the examples.

> She's a SCIENTIST. (noun)
> She was COMPLETELY CONSCIOUS. (adverb + adjective)
> He was RESPONSIBLE. (adjective)
> She ISOLATED herself. (verb)

Any word (pronouns, auxiliaries, prepositions) can be stressed, however, when the speaker wants to emphasize a particular point. Notice which words indicate corrective or contrasting information.

Listen and practice the examples.

> A: She's a SCIENTIST?   B: No, she's a DENTIST.
> A: Are you AFRAID of oral reports?   B: YES! I NEVER take SPEAKING classes.
> A: Can Gary speak MANDARIN?   B. HE can't, but LISA can.

When you emphasize key words, a strong rhythm develops and key words stand out clearly to listeners. Knowing how stress and intonation work will help you with both speaking fluency and listening comprehension.

A. Jill Bolte Taylor is a strong and dynamic speaker. Listen to her describe the morning of her stroke. Circle the key words you hear emphasized; then compare transcripts with a partner and discuss the ways Dr. Taylor uses stress to help engage her listeners.

Then I would have this wave of clarity that would bring me and reattach me

back to normal reality, and I could pursue my plan, and my—the only plan that

I had in my head was to call work and that somebody at work would get me help. Um, but it—it took, uh, over 45 minutes for me to figure out what number to dial and how to dial and by the time, um, I got the information I could not see uh the, the phone number on my business card. I couldn't pick the numbers out from the background pixels, cause all I could see were pixels. Uh, and it's a you know, it's a, big drama. By the time my colleague, I'm very fortunate he was at his desk. I spoke. I said "Woo Woo Woo Woo Er" I had no, no language and when he spoke to me he sounded "Woo Woo Wer." He sounded like a golden retriever. So, uh, but he did recognize that it was I and that I needed help and then eventually he did get me help.

B. In a group, take turns adding some expressive details to these sentence starters, stressing key words so your listeners understand what information is important or contrastive.

1. We use our right brains to . . . , and our left brains to . . .

2. Many ESL learners have difficulty . . . , but I . . .

3. When I had to stand up in front of the class to give a speech, . . .

4. I'll never forget the day when (name of a person) asked me . . .

5. When I went to visit my relatives in . . . , I couldn't . . .

6. Taylor's experience made me think about . . .

7. My worst experience trying to speak English was when . . .

 C. Go online for more practice with emphatic word stress.

One way to make your speaking more interesting is to use *similes* and *metaphors*. These devices create images that help listeners experience the intensity of something you are describing.

A **simile** is a way of describing something by comparing it to another thing. Similes include the word *like* or *as*.

> Learning English is **like** climbing a mountain.
> The baby's skin was as soft **as** silk.

[handwritten: → seda]

[handwritten note: Simile/metaphor Compare two things]

Some similes become so common in a language that they become idioms. *[handwritten: ≠]*

> as pretty as a picture   as gentle as a lamb
> as sharp as a tack   roar like a lion

[handwritten note: Simile (like/as) metaphor does not]

A **metaphor** describes something as if it were something else. Here, *words* are being compared to *swords that cut through the silence*.

> His **words** were swords that cut through the silence.

Metaphors can be quite indirect. Here, *his heart* is being described as if it were something that could actually *break*, such as glass.

> His **heart** was broken.

A. Match the parts of the phrases to form common similes in English.

1. You are as light as _c_
2. That horse can run like _h_
3. When I lost my diamond ring, I cried like _a_
4. You are as busy as _b_
5. His words cut me like _e_
6. Please be as quiet as _f_
7. The children were as good as _g_
8. My sister can swim like _d_

    a. a baby
    b. a bee
    c. a feather
    d. a fish
    e. a knife
    f. a mouse
    g. gold
    h. the wind

B. Discuss the similes in Activity A in a group and compare them to similes commonly used in your native/home countries.

[handwritten: "Requirement": at least 1 simile or metaphor in speech!]

C. Work with a partner. Explain what the underlined metaphors from Listening 1 and Listening 2 mean. What are the literal meanings of the words?

1. These are all the memories associated with who I had been, and when that person went <u>offline</u>, which is the best way for me to explain it, I lost all of her likes and dislikes.

2. You wake up one day and you're in <u>the heart</u> of China.

3. That <u>living</u> word awakened my soul.

4. There were barriers still, it is true, but barriers that could in time be <u>swept</u> away.

5. . . . words that were to make the world <u>blossom</u> for me.

D. Work with a partner. Describe one of the items or situations below in a short paragraph. Use your imagination and be expressive! Use similes and metaphors. Then read your description to the class.

My room is a disaster area. It looks like a tornado blew through, scattering my papers like leaves in an autumn wind. If you can wade through the piles of clothes near my bed, . . .

1. Your room or home

2. Your friend or someone you know

3. Learning a new language

4. Speaking in front of the class

5. Being a tourist in a foreign country

 E. Go online for more practice using figurative language.

 **UNIT OBJECTIVE** ▶▶▶▶ In this assignment, you are going to narrate a personal experience involving language loss or a difficulty communicating. As you prepare your narrative, think about the Unit Question, "How does language affect who we are?" Use information from Listening 1, Listening 2, the unit video, and your work in this unit to support your narration. Refer to the Self-Assessment checklist on page 28.

CONSIDER THE IDEAS

Maxine Hong Kingston, a Chinese-American writer, was born in the United States, but her parents spoke only Chinese at home. In her autobiographical novel, *The Woman Warrior*, she describes her discomfort speaking English after years of silence in American school and narrates a painful experience in Chinese school. Read this excerpt. Then discuss the questions with a group.

Maxine Hong Kingston

When I went to kindergarten and had to speak English for the first time, I became silent. A dumbness—a shame—still cracks my voice in two, even when I want to say "hello" casually, or ask an easy question in front of the check-out counter, or ask directions of a bus driver. I stand frozen, or I hold up the line with the complete, grammatical sentence that comes squeaking out at impossible length. "What did you say?" says the cab driver, or "Speak up," so I have to perform again, only weaker the second time. A telephone call makes my throat bleed and takes up that day's courage. . . .

Not all of the children who were silent at American school found voice at Chinese school. One new teacher said each of us had to get up and recite in front of the class, who was to listen. My sister and I had memorized the lesson perfectly. We said it to each other at home, one chanting, one listening. The teacher called on my sister to recite first. It was the first time a teacher had called on the second-born to go first. My sister was scared. She glanced at me and looked away; I looked down at my desk. I hoped that she could do it because if she could, then I wouldn't have to. She opened her mouth and a voice came out that wasn't a whisper, but it wasn't a proper voice either. I hoped that she would not cry, fear breaking up her voice like twigs underfoot. She sounded as if she were . . . weeping and strangling. She did not pause or stop to end the embarrassment. She kept going until she said the last word, and then she sat down. When it was my turn, the same voice came out, a crippled animal running on broken legs. You could hear splinters in my voice, bones rubbing jagged against one another. I was loud, though. I was glad I didn't whisper.

1. How did Hong Kingston's communication difficulties affect her identity?

2. In what ways can you relate to Hong Kingston's story about language and silence?

3. Discuss the similes and metaphors Hong Kingston uses. Which ones affected you the most?

PREPARE AND SPEAK

A. **GATHER IDEAS** Work in a group. Follow these steps to gather ideas.

1. Brainstorm examples of stories about language-related difficulties that you can use as models or inspiration for your own narrative. What makes these stories compelling? Are they serious or humorous?

2. Briefly describe your ideas to your group. Ask your group where they think your story should begin and end.

B. **ORGANIZE IDEAS** Follow these steps to prepare your narrative.

1. Use a timeline like the one on page 12 to organize the main events and/or emotional states in your story. Choose your starting and ending points. Make sure the emotions and events between are in chronological order.

2. Work with a partner. Practice narrating your stories to each other.

C. **SPEAK** Narrate your experience in groups or for the whole class. As you listen to your classmates, write down similes and metaphors that you especially liked. At the end of the activity, share these with the whole class. Refer to the Self-Assessment checklist below before you begin.

 Go online for your alternate Unit Assignment.

CHECK AND REFLECT

A. **CHECK** Think about the Unit Assignment as you complete the Self-Assessment checklist.

Yes	No	SELF-ASSESSMENT
☐	☐	I was able to speak fluently about the topic.
☐	☐	My partner, group, and class understood me.
☐	☐	I used the correct negative prefixes for adjectives.
☐	☐	I used the active voice and the passive voice appropriately.
☐	☐	I used similes and metaphors to make my language more interesting.
☐	☐	I emphasized words in the correct places to express my meaning.

 B. **REFLECT** Go to the Online Discussion Board to discuss these questions.

1. What is something new you learned in this unit?

2. Look back at the Unit Question—How does language affect who we are? Is your answer different now than when you started this unit? If yes, how is it different? Why?

TRACK YOUR SUCCESS

Circle the words you have learned in this unit.

Nouns
boundary
consciousness
fragment
function 🔑 AWL
incident 🔑 AWL
insight AWL
outburst
perception AWL
recovery 🔑 AWL
sentiment
structure 🔑 AWL

Verbs
gesticulate
imitate
persist AWL
regain
reveal 🔑 AWL

Adjectives
adequate 🔑 AWL
external AWL
fascinating
intense 🔑 AWL

overall 🔑 AWL
tangible
tranquil

Adverb
invariably AWL

🔑 Oxford 3000™ words
AWL Academic Word List

Check (✓) the skills you learned. If you need more work on a skill, refer to the page(s) in parentheses.

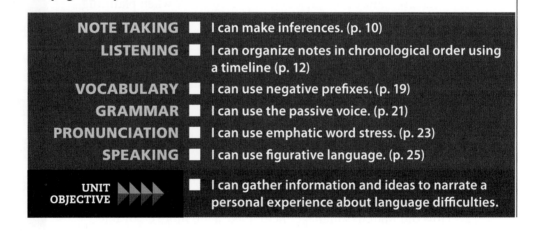

NOTE TAKING	☐ I can make inferences. (p. 10)
LISTENING	☐ I can organize notes in chronological order using a timeline (p. 12)
VOCABULARY	☐ I can use negative prefixes. (p. 19)
GRAMMAR	☐ I can use the passive voice. (p. 21)
PRONUNCIATION	☐ I can use emphatic word stress. (p. 23)
SPEAKING	☐ I can use figurative language. (p. 25)
UNIT OBJECTIVE ▶▶▶▶	☐ I can gather information and ideas to narrate a personal experience about language difficulties.

UNIT 2

Education

LISTENING	▶	listening for examples
NOTE TAKING	▶	organizing notes in a Venn diagram
VOCABULARY	▶	compound words
GRAMMAR	▶	comparative structures
PRONUNCIATION	▶	intonation with choices
SPEAKING	▶	discussing preferences and alternatives

UNIT QUESTION

Where can work, education, and fun overlap?

A Discuss these questions with your classmates.

1. What are some of the factors that you consider when planning a vacation?

2. Can you describe a time when you felt work or school was fun?

3. Look at the photo. What aspects of this man's job would you consider work or educational? What aspects are fun?

B Listen to *The Q Classroom* online. Then answer these questions.

1. In what ways does Sophy think that fun and work overlap at school? Do you agree with her?

2. How did Marcus's manager help make a job more enjoyable? Have you had any similar experiences?

 C Go to the Online Discussion Board to discuss the Unit Question with your classmates.

UNIT OBJECTIVE ▶▶▶▶ Listen to an interview from *The Amateur Traveler* and two university reports. Gather information and ideas to plan an alternative school trip and present it in a persuasive way.

D Write the goals in the appropriate part of the Venn diagram. If you think a goal can describe education and work, write it in the center area where the circles overlap.

appreciate cultures	have fun	meet new people
discover new ideas	help society	pass tests
earn money	interact with others	play sports
get good grades	keep to a schedule	solve problems
get promoted	learn a language	think critically

Critical Thinking **Tip**

In Activity D you will complete a Venn diagram. **Diagramming** the relationships between ideas is one way of analyzing information. You will learn more tips about organizing notes in a Venn diagram on page 39.

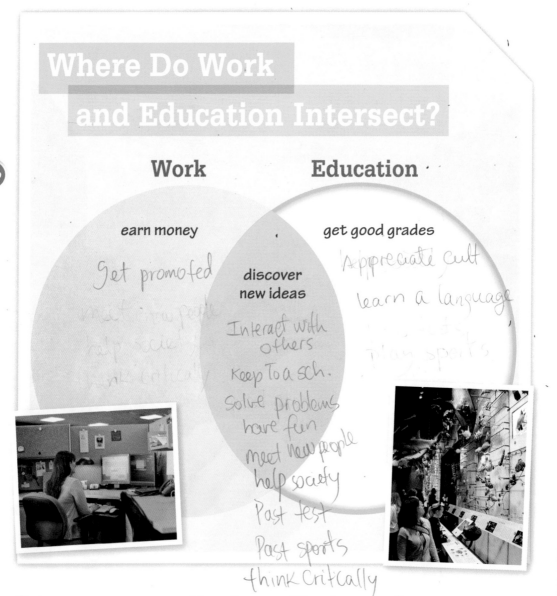

Where Do Work and Education Intersect?

Work   **Education**

earn money   get good grades

Get promoted

discover new ideas

Appreciate cult
learn a language

meet new people
help society
think critically

Interact with others
Keep To a sch.
Solve problems
have fun
meet new people
help society
Past test
Past sports
think Critically

Play sports

E In a group, compare your Venn diagrams. What does your diagram say about your attitudes toward education and work? Do you think work can be educational? Do you think education can be work?

LISTENING 1 | Voluntourism

You are going to listen to an interview titled "Voluntourism" from the Amateur Traveler Web site. Linda Stuart talks with show host Chris Christensen about the nonprofit organization Global Citizens Network (GCN). As you listen to the interview, gather information and ideas about where work, education, and fun can overlap.

PREVIEW THE LISTENING

A. **PREVIEW** If a *volunteer* is someone who does work without pay, and *tourism* is the business of travel, what do you think *voluntourism* is? Write your own definition.

It's a person who travel for works in a
non profit ~~organization~~ organization.

B. **VOCABULARY** Read aloud these words from Listening 1. Check (✓) the ones you know. Use a dictionary to define any new or unknown words. Then discuss with a partner how the words will relate to the unit.

demographics (n.) demografía   indigenous (adj.) indigena

diverse (adj.) diversa   preservation (n.) preservacion

ecological (adj.) ecologica   prompt (v.) 🔑 sugerir, estimular.

enticing (adj.) tentadora.   raise awareness (phr.) crear conciencia

expedition (n.)   range (n.) 🔑 distancia

immerse oneself in (phr.) sumergirse en   validate (v.) validar

🔑 Oxford 3000™ words

 C. Go online to listen and practice your pronunciation.

WORK WITH THE LISTENING

A. **LISTEN AND TAKE NOTES** Look at the Web page for Global Citizens Network. Then listen to the interview and use the Web page to take notes. Compare your answers with a partner.

Global Citizens Network

Serving the volunteer tourist for _16_ years.
1

Essential information:

Average age range _30_ to _55_   Average group size _4_ to _12_
2   3   6   7

Trip length _1_ to _2_ weeks   Fees range from $ _9,000_ to $ _24000_.
4   5   8   9

Some of our projects include:

working on _Construction_ of a health center
10

teaching _English_ ,
11

helping indigenous groups preserve their _Culture_ .
12

Volunteers get to:

practice _new language_ , try new _food_ , learn weaving and other new skills.
13   14

We have programs around the world in urban and _rural_ areas in
15

Mexico, Ecuador, _Tailan_ , _Guatemala_ ,
16   17

B. Read the list of characteristics of tourists. Use your notes to help you determine if each phrase describes traditional tourists (*TT*), volunteer tourists (*VT*), or both (*TT + VT*). Compare your answers with a partner.

_TT + VT_ 1. Pay the cost of travel arrangements

_TT_ 2. Might take a long weekend trip

_TT_ 3. Can choose to go to any country around the world

_VT + TT_ 4. Practice a second language

_VT_ 5. Hope to get away from work for a while

_TT_ 6. Can travel with children

_____ VT _____ 7. Expect to have activities planned by the people they visit

_____ TT _____ 8. Have the option for a weekend or a long-term vacation

_____ VT + TT _____ 9. Usually travel in small, unrelated groups

_____ Vt + TT _____ 10. Support the economy of the countries they visit

_____ Vt + TT _____ 11. May need to get immunizations

_____ VT _____ 12. Might visit clinics or orphanages

C. **Listen again and answer the questions. Compare answers with a partner.**

1. According to Stuart, what is the overall purpose of Global Citizens Network?

2. Some people might believe that volunteer vacations are just for wealthy people, young men, or bilingual people. What would Stuart say in response?

3. What effects do volunteer vacations have on both the travelers and the countries they visit?

D. **Write a short review of the Global Citizens Network program for a local newspaper. You can present a positive, negative, or neutral view of the program, but make sure to back up your ideas with specific details. Then read your commentary aloud to a partner.**

E. **VOCABULARY** **Here are some words and phrases from Listening 1. Read the sentences. Then write each bold word or phrase next to the correct definition. Write each verb in its base form.**

1. The senior citizens from Canada went on a cross-cultural **expedition** to explore Peru.

2. The nonprofit organization wanted to work with the **indigenous**, or native, people of Guatemala who are descendents of the Mayans.

3. The ads for cheap airfare, great weather, and quiet beaches were **enticing**.

4. Even though this position demands a wide **range** of high-level skills, the company tries to create an anti-stress environment.

5. We will have to **validate** our visas before we are allowed in that country.

6. By learning more about the importance of keeping our culture, we work toward the **preservation** of our traditions.

Tip for Success

Remember that in abbreviations such as GCN and UN, each letter is pronounced separately, with stress on the final letter. In acronyms, letters are pronounced together as a word, such as TOEFL and UNICEF.

Vocabulary
Skill Review

In Unit 1, you learned about negative prefixes, such as *un-* and *dis-*. *Non-* is a prefix that means *not*, and *anti-* means *against*. Find words in Activity E with negative prefixes.

7. Many parents believe their children will be at a disadvantage if they are not exposed to **diverse** groups from many different countries.

8. The **demographics** from the study show that 10 percent of the people there cannot read, but the data are unreliable.

9. When I travel, I like to **immerse myself in** the new culture by eating at small restaurants and talking to the people there.

10. The **ecological** project involved planting more trees to protect the hillsides.

11. It's important to educate people about global issues. Seeing how others live helps **raise awareness** of the need to protect some cultures.

12. The desire to learn a new language **prompted** me to go abroad to study for the first time.

a. _____ (n.) the act of maintaining something in its original state or in good condition

b. _____ (v.) to state officially that something is useful and of an acceptable standard

c. _____ (phr.) to become completely involved in (something)

d. _____ (adj.) very different from each other

e. _____ (n.) an organized journey with a particular purpose

f. _____ (v.) to make (somebody) decide to do (something)

g. _____ (n.) data relating to populations and groups of people

h. _____ (adj.) very attractive and interesting

i. _____ (n.) a variety of things or experiences of a particular type

j. _____ (adj.) belonging to a particular place, rather than coming to it from someplace else

k. _____ (phr.) to increase knowledge of or interest in (something)

l. _____ (adj.) connected to the relation of living things to each other and to their environment

 F. Go online for more practice with the vocabulary.

Q ? SAY WHAT YOU THINK

A. Discuss the questions in a group.

1. Linda Stuart says that one of the benefits of voluntourism is that it's an "eye-opening experience" and it helps people see that it's "not us versus them, but it's us all together." What does she mean by that? Do you agree?

2. In what ways has this interview been successful or unsuccessful in motivating you to take a volunteer vacation?

3. Think of a place in the world that could benefit from the contributions of volunteer tourists. What kind of work could people do there? How could it be fun?

B. Before you watch the video, discuss the questions in a group.

1. How popular do you think voluntourism has become in recent years? Had you ever heard of this travel opportunity before?

2. Which country would you like to visit as a volunteer tourist but not as a traditional tourist, and vice versa? Why?

iQ ONLINE

C. Go online to watch the video about Global Volunteers. Then check your comprehension.

> **boat people** *(n.)* people who escape their country in small boats to find safety in another country
>
> **enriching** *(adj.)* improving the quality of something *enriquesedor ora*
>
> **irrigation** *(n.)* a system of pipes used to supply water to an area of land *Riego*
>
> **mass exodus** *(n.)* situation in which many people leave a place at the same time *exodo masivo*
>
> **transformational** *(adj.)* causing a complete change in someone *transformacional*

In an interview, a lecture, or a report, a speaker often provides examples so the listener can understand key ideas better. Active listeners can use different strategies to notice examples.

- Listen for phrases that introduce examples: *for example*, *take for instance*, *for instance*, *as an example*, *let me give you an example*, *including*, and *such as*.
- Notice rising intonation that signals items in a list. A speaker who is listing examples will use rising intonation for each item in a list except for the last one. The rising intonation works like a comma to let the listener know the speaker is not finished.

Listen to this example. Notice how the speaker identifies the main point and then lists examples. Pay attention to the speaker's rising intonation.

> There is a wide range of opportunities. Others include individual placement; some are in rural areas versus urban areas; others may be more of a tutoring or English teaching placements . . .

One way to take notes involving examples or other details is to write the main point on the left and examples on the right.

Main point	Examples
Range of volunteer opportunities	individual placement
	rural vs. urban
	tutoring or English teaching

A. Listen to the excerpts. Use the chart to take notes. Make sure you have two examples of each main point.

Main point	Examples
1. Small-scale development projects	
2. Motivating reasons	
3. Countries GCN works in	

B. Take turns asking and answering these questions with a partner about the Global Volunteers and Amateur Traveler interviews. Then ask some questions of your own.

1. What are some reasons people would be interested in voluntourism?

2. What types of people take these trips?

3. What kinds of projects do voluntourists work on?

4. What countries do GCN and Global Volunteers operate in?

 C. Go online for more practice listening for examples.

Note-taking Skill | Organizing notes in a Venn diagram

Finding the relationships between items is a critical thinking skill that is often necessary when taking and organizing notes. A Venn diagram is a special type of graphic organizer that can provide a visual representation of these relationships. Lists are useful when information about distinct categories is provided during a lecture, but in many academic fields, the objective of a discussion or lecture may be to find similarities and differences between items or to classify them according to specific criteria. A Venn diagram consists of at least two overlapping circles. Inside the overlapping areas is where similarities between the items are listed.

Look back at the Venn diagram on page 32. You were asked to think about the goals of work and education. Figuring out which goals fit in each area in the circles helped you answer the unit question: Where can work, education, and fun overlap?

A. Look at Activity B on pages 34–35. Use a Venn diagram to show traits of traditional tourists and volunteer tourists.

Traditional Tourists   Volunteer Tourists

B. Listen to a short discussion on studying abroad or working at an internship during college. Take notes using a Venn diagram. Compare your notes with a partner.

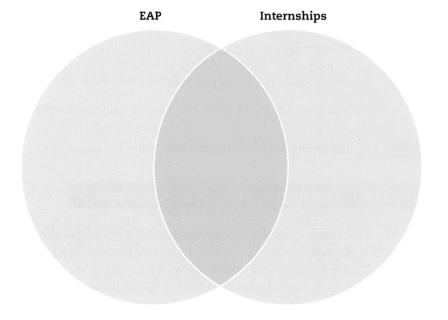

EAP   Internships

 C. Go online for more practice with organizing notes in Venn diagrams.

LISTENING 2 | Science Fairs and Nature Reserves

 You are going to listen to two university reports, "The Cambridge Science Festival," about a science fair in England, and "The Sedgwick Reserve," about protected lands in California. They present different experiences that have been developed to engage students in science. As you listen to the reports, gather information and ideas about where work, education, and fun can overlap.

PREVIEW THE LISTENING

The Sedgwick Reserve

A. PREVIEW Write five information questions (questions using *wh-* words) about things you would like to know about these programs.

B. **VOCABULARY** Read aloud these words from Listening 2. Check (✓) the ones you know. Use a dictionary to define any new or unknown words. Then discuss with a partner how the words will relate to the unit.

atmosphere *(n.)* 🔑	familiarize *(v.)*	pioneer *(v.)*
collaboration *(n.)*	impact *(n.)* 🔑	resource *(n.)* 🔑
coordinator *(n.)*	interactive *(adj.)*	restore *(v.)* 🔑
exhibit *(n.)* 🔑	outreach *(n.)* alcance	site *(n.)* 🔑

🔑 Oxford 3000™ words

 C. Go online to listen and practice your pronunciation.

WORK WITH THE LISTENING

A. **LISTEN AND TAKE NOTES** Listen to the university reports. Use the T-charts to take notes about the goals and outcomes of each science event as you listen.

Science Festival

a science fair

Goals	Outcomes

Sedgwick Reserve

Goals	Outcomes

B. Use your notes from the T-charts in Activity A to answer these questions.

1. The science festival at Cambridge and the nature programs at the Sedgwick Reserve have two specific goals for students beyond just making science fun. What are they?

2. What are three or four of the ways the speakers mentioned that help their programs accomplish these goals?

3. What does *public outreach* mean, and why is it an important goal of both Cambridge University and the Sedgwick Reserve?

C. Use your notes to place these details about the science programs in the correct circles in the Venn diagram on page 43. (You can use the letters to save space.) If a detail describes both programs, write the letter in the overlapping area. Then listen again and correct any information.

a. ecosystems and biology	g. open to the public
b. in school buildings	h. week-long event
c. students from all grades	i. over 45,000 visitors
d. geology and engineering	j. praised by teachers
e. inspires interest in science	k. year-long experience
f. interactive/hands-on activities	l. on-going research projects

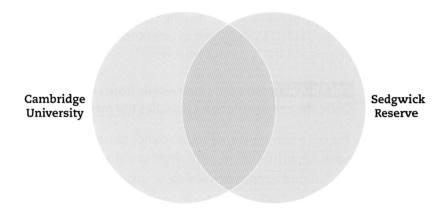

Cambridge
University

Sedgwick
Reserve

D. Read the statements. Write *T* (true) or *F* (false). Then correct each false statement.

_____ 1. Volunteers help run both the Sedgwick Natural Reserve and the Cambridge Science Festival.

_____ 2. Before the actual festival at Cambridge, a truck tours the city to introduce science at local schools.

_____ 3. The Cambridge Science Festival takes place only on Saturday.

_____ 4. For the Cambridge organizers, the goal of getting more people to understand the importance of science in our lives is even more important than encouraging young people to study science.

_____ 5. Sedgwick Nature Reserve is an open-use area in Santa Barbara for the public to enjoy.

_____ 6. The Kids in Nature program focuses on children from low-performing schools.

_____ 7. One goal of the Kids in Nature program is to encourage boys to become scientists.

_____ 8. Professor Thorsch at UCSB is concerned that most schools are "teaching by telling" rather than "teaching by doing."

E. Read the sentences. Circle the answer that best completes each statement.

1. The Cambridge Science Festival is the (most important / largest / most expensive) public event each year at the university.

2. The major goal of the Cambridge Science Festival is to break down the barriers between (children and the university / parents and their children's teachers / scientists and the community).

3. The Sedgwick Nature Reserve is (one of 30 nature reserves / the only nature reserve / the biggest nature reserve) in the University of California system.

4. (Restoring woodlands / Playing computer games / Writing reports about plants) is NOT mentioned as one of the activities of the Kids in Nature program at the Sedgwick reserve.

F. **VOCABULARY** Here are some words from Listening 2. Read the sentences. Circle the answer that best matches the meaning of each bold word.

1. The **outreach** programs bring science to rural areas so children there have equal opportunities to learn about chemistry and physics.
   a. designed to provide a service to underprivileged people in a community
   b. designed to be not only educational but also entertaining and motivating

2. The **atmosphere** in the classroom was so energized that students didn't mind working very hard.
   a. a mood or feeling in a particular location
   b. the mixture of gases that surrounds the Earth

3. If it is a hands-on, **interactive** show, students are motivated to participate in the demonstrations.
   a. involving several speakers at the same time
   b. involving the input or actions of audience members

4. When we visit a science **exhibit** related to elasticity, we expect to find a demonstration on how an object can stretch and bend.
   a. a written report
   b. a show or display

5. We need to choose a new **site** for that research project because the current building is too far away from our labs.
   a. a place or location
   b. a plan or idea

6. Because of the old building's historical value, the city decided to **restore** it and bring it back to life.
   a. repair; return to its original condition
   b. tear down and replace with something better

7. Schools that are famous for research such as Oxford University and the University of California **pioneer** ideas and often discover ways to cure diseases and solve problems.
   a. travel to new areas
   b. be the first to do or try something

8. The **coordinator** of the program was responsible for bringing workers together while developing that project.
   a. a person who manages
   b. a person who investigates or inspects

9. With all of the **resources** available in the library, students can find enough information for their reports.
   a. raw materials such as wood or metal
   b. materials that can be used to help achieve a goal

10. The **collaboration** between environmental organizations and governments is extremely important for the success of ecological programs.
    a. the act of working together
    b. the act of working independently or separately

11. When the result of an experiment has an **impact** on science, it influences scientific ideas and may change our perspectives.
    a. a collision or accident with somebody or something
    b. a powerful effect of one thing on something else

12. Since we are new to the campus, we need to **familiarize** ourselves with the labs before we do any experiments.
    a. get acquainted with conditions
    b. begin a close relationship with somebody

G. Go online for more practice with the vocabulary.

H. Go online to listen to *Turning a Hobby into Work* and check your comprehension.

SAY WHAT YOU THINK

A. Discuss the questions in a group.

1. Which of the two science programs would you most enjoy participating in? Why?

2. What should teachers be more concerned about: whether students are interested and excited about what they need to learn or whether they are learning as much information as possible about the subject?

B. Think about the unit video, Listening 1, and Listening 2 as you discuss the questions.

1. In what ways are Global Citizens Network and Global Volunteers similar to and in what ways are they both different from the science and nature programs at Cambridge University and the Sedgwick Reserve?

2. Which speakers were most persuasive in making you want to participate in the programs they were talking about? How did they persuade you?

3. How might going abroad to study or testing video games for a software company be considered areas where work, education, and fun overlap? Can you think of other examples?

Vocabulary Skill | Compound words

Compounds are made up of two or more words, usually a combination of nouns, adjectives, and verbs. The most common compounds are nouns (*nature reserve*), but there are also compound adjectives (*short-term*) and verbs (*underline*).

Over time, compounds tend to become written as single words (*classroom*). Sometimes the words are hyphenated (*short-term*), and sometimes the words remain separate (*high school*) although they are considered one-word units.

Compound words are listed as separate entries in the dictionary. Since there are no strict rules for how compounds are written, it is important to check a dictionary to see if a compound is written as one word, as two words, or with a hyphen.

> **class·room** 🔑 /'klæsrum; -rʊm/ *noun*
> a room where a class of children or students is taught: *classroom activities* ◆ *the use of computers in the classroom*

> ˈ**high school** 🔑 *noun* [C, U]
> a school for young people between the ages of 14 and 18
> ↻ collocations at EDUCATION ↻ see also JUNIOR HIGH SCHOOL, SENIOR HIGH SCHOOL

> ˌ**short-ˈterm** *adj.* **1** [usually before noun] lasting a short time; designed only for a short period of time in the future: *a short-term loan* ◆ *to find work on a short-term contract* ◆ *short-term plans* ◆ *a short-term solution to the problem* ◆ *His short-term memory* (= the ability to remember things that happened a short time ago) *is failing.* ↻ compare LONG-TERM **2** [only before noun] (of a place) where you only stay for a short time: *a short-term parking garage* ◆ *short-term patients* (= who only stay in a hospital for a short time)

Compounds are content words, so they are stressed in a sentence. Within the compound itself, there is usually a strong stress on the first word and a lighter stress on the second (*WOODlands*, *HOMEwork*). If the first word has more than one syllable, the stress is the same as it is in the word by itself (*DAta*, *DAtabase*).

All dictionary entries are from the *Oxford Advanced American Dictionary for learners of English* © Oxford University Press 2011.

A. Write the words in the right column on the correct lines.

1. computer _____   boomer

2. baby _____   reach

3. eye _____ cultural

4. out _____ ground

5. net _____ view

6. grass _____ opening

7. senior _____ game

8. cross _____ lands

9. over _____ citizen

10. testing _____ working

B. Work with a partner. Take turns reading the compound words in Activity A aloud. Listen for your partner's stress on the first word. Check a dictionary to find out if the compounds are written as one word (with or without a hyphen) or two.

C. Complete these sentences with compounds from Activity A.

1. Realizing how much fun science can be is a(n)

   _____ experience for many teenagers.

2. Students walked through the _____ while they

   were at the Sedgwick Reserve.

3. GCN specializes in _____ programs for those

   who want to help indigenous groups while traveling.

4. A small community is often the _____ for new

   ideas that later spread to larger cities if they are successful.

5. The _____ center on campus provides a place for

   students from diverse communities to meet.

6. An American born right after World War II, between 1946 and 1964,

   is called a(n) _____.

iQ ONLINE **D.** Go online for more practice with compound words.

UNIT OBJECTIVE ▶▶▶▶ At the end of this unit, you are going to give a persuasive presentation about an alternative school trip. For your presentation, you will need to discuss preferences and alternatives.

Grammar | Comparative structures

When discussing similarities and differences, comparative structures can be used with various word forms.

Word form	Comparison	Negative comparison	Intensified comparison	Comparison of equality
Adjective	clearer than more enticing than	less aware	much clearer than much less aware than	as enticing as
Adverb	faster than more slowly than	less slowly than	much faster than much more/less slowly than	as fast as as slowly as
Noun	more exhibits than more time than	fewer exhibits than less time than	many more/fewer exhibits than much less time than	as many exhibits as as much time as
Verb	travels more than	travels less than	travels much more/less than	travels as much as

Remember: When making comparisons, you must compare parallel elements.

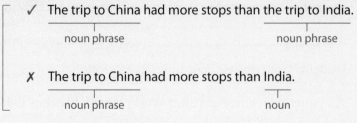

✓ The trip to China had more stops than the trip to India.
    noun phrase   noun phrase

✗ The trip to China had more stops than India.
    noun phrase   noun

Tip for Success

Even native speakers sometimes get confused when using pronouns with comparisons. Is it correct to say *Jane is taller than me* or *Jane is taller than I*? To find the answer, complete the sentence in your head: *Jane is taller than I am.* Therefore, the correct comparison is *Jane is taller than I.*

Repetition of elements in a comparison can be avoided in two ways:

1. Using a synonym of the element compared

   The Cambridge science demonstrations covered more fields than **the Stanford exhibits.**

2. Using pronouns (*this, that, these, those, the one, the ones, mine, yours, his, hers, ours, theirs, other,* and *others*)

   The meals we ate in Lebanon were better than **those in England.**

A. Circle the correct words to complete these comparative sentences. Avoid repetition in the comparative.

1. My father has traveled less than (I / me).

2. I don't like these travel options as much as (them / those).

3. The Cambridge program is shorter than the (Sedgwick one / Sedgwick program).

4. Jose's science project is more interactive than (Tim / Tim's).

5. The flight to Dubai was twice as long as (the flight to Frankfurt / the one to Frankfurt).

6. Volunteer vacations usually cost less money than (regular trips / regular vacations).

7. Your method for solving that problem takes more time than (me / my way).

8. An expedition to China is more enticing than (England / a term in England).

Tip for Success

When making a comparison, make sure to stress the comparative words and phrases. *PHY-sics is MORE IN-ter-est-ing than CHEM-is-try.*

B. Work with a partner. Take turns reading the sentences below and then restating the comparison using a comparative structure from the Grammar box.

1. The trip to Peru costs $5,000. The trip to Bolivia costs $5,000.

   A: The trip to Peru costs $5,000 and the trip to Bolivia costs $5,000.
   B: The trip to Peru costs as much as the trip to Bolivia.

2. A science fair sounds good. A nature expedition sounds exciting.

3. The bus trip is ten hours long. The train ride is five hours long.

4. The grasslands stretch for 50 miles. The woodlands cover 25 miles.

5. GCN needs 50 volunteers. Earthwatch needs 50 volunteers.

6. The wagon moves slowly, at five miles per hour. The tractor moves slowly, at ten miles per hour.

 C. Go online for more practice with comparative structures.

D. Go online for the grammar expansion.

Pronunciation	Intonation with choices

Choice Statements

When a list of choices is given in a series, rising intonation starts on the stressed syllable of each choice, pitch drops on *or*, and the sentence ends with a rise-fall intonation that signals the end of the choices. Listen to this example.

☐ With GCN, we can take an expedition to Mexico, Peru, or Argentina.

If the last item ends in a stressed syllable, glide up and down on that word. Listen to this example.

☐ They need to find out if that institute is in China or Japan.

Choice Questions

Questions that offer the listener two or more possible choices (or answers) have rising intonation starting with the stressed syllable in the first choice, a drop in pitch on *or*, and a rise and then a low fall (or a glide up and down) on the last choice. Listen to these examples.

Did they visit Saudi Arabia, Lebanon, or Egypt?

Is it a science fair or a science camp?

If the choice question is an information question, the *wh-* clause ends with rise-fall intonation. The pitch rises on each choice, falls on *or*, and ends with a rise-fall or a glide-fall on the last choice. Listen to these examples.

What did they build in Mexico, schools or houses?

Where are the exhibits, in the school, at the beach, or in the park?

A. Work with a partner. Mark the intonation in these sentences and take turns reading them. Then listen and check your answers. Correct any sentences whose stress you didn't mark correctly.

Tip for Success

Remember, the answer to a choice question is not *Yes* or *No*; the answer should be one of the choices.

1. Who paid for the travel expenses, the students or the school?

2. Would you choose to initiate a new project or work on an old one?

3. I'm not sure if I prefer Cambridge, Oxford, Harvard, or Stanford.

4. Which adjective is best: *compelling*, *liberating*, or *enticing*?

5. You have your choice of staying in a tent, a home, or a hotel.

6. Can everyone go on a volunteer vacation, including children, teens, and adults?

B. Complete the questions. Give two choices for three of the questions and more than two choices for the other questions. Then ask and answer the questions with a partner. Pay attention to your intonation patterns.

1. Where would you like to travel, _____

_____?

2. What kind of ethnic food would you like to try, _____

_____?

3. How long does it take to plan a vacation, _____

_____?

4. Which activities are both fun and educational, _camping, or Expedition trips_

_____?

5. What kind of outdoor places do you like to explore, _____

_____?

6. Who is the best coordinator for a trip to _____, _____

_____?

C. Go online for more practice with intonation with choices.

In a meeting or a planning session, discussion often involves expressing preferences and offering alternatives. Additionally, you might need to investigate people's past preferences to help make choices about future actions.

Here are some common expressions for talking about preferences and alternatives.

To talk about past preferences	To talk about current preferences
prefer + noun or noun phrase Students **preferred** the expedition to China.	*preference* + *is* + infinitive **My preference is to attend** a science fair.
choose + infinitive Students **chose to visit** indigenous people.	*would rather (not)* + verb I**'d rather do** something that helps society.
first/second choice + *be* My **first choice was** to visit a nature reserve.	*If it were up to me, . . .* **If it were up to me,** we'd do an ecological study.
had hoped + infinitive I **had hoped to spend** the summer volunteering in Tanzania.	*I like . . . more than . . .* **I like** studying in my dorm **more than** in the lab.
	I'd like + infinitive **I'd like to explore** the idea of working abroad.

A. With a partner, take turns asking and answering these questions about the Listening texts. Use expressions for preferences and choices in your answers. Pay attention to your intonation in any choice questions.

1. Does Linda Stuart prefer the volunteering or the tourist side of voluntourism?

   A: Does Linda Stuart prefer the volunteering or the tourist side of voluntourism?
   B: Stuart would rather be a volunteer than a tourist.

2. Does Stuart's organization choose to take large or small groups of travelers?

3. If it were up to the speaker from Cambridge, would the science fair there have many more participants?

4. What does the professor at UC Santa Barbara hope to show the young students, especially girls?

5. Do you think the students in the Kids in Nature program would rather learn about plants in the classroom or at the nature reserve?

6. Do you think the children who go to the science fair will choose to become scientists and study at Cambridge?

7. Could you tell if the director's preference would be to have more visitors to the reserve?

B. Work in groups of three. Create a short role-play to present to the class. Student A is a travel agent. Students B and C want to take a trip. Student A asks B and C about their travel preferences—destination, length of trip, activities, etc. Use as many different structures as you can.

A: *Would you prefer a relaxing vacation or a learning expedition?*
B: *My preference is to take a relaxing vacation.*
C: *Hmm. I'd like to explore the possibility of an expedition to a country in Africa!*

 **C.** Go online for more practice with discussing preferences and alternatives.

Unit Assignment · Plan and present a school trip

UNIT OBJECTIVE ▶▶▶▶ In this assignment, you are going to work with a group to plan a fun and meaningful vacation that you will try to convince your classmates to join. As you prepare your presentation, think about the Unit Question, "Where can work, education, and fun overlap?" Use information from Listening 1, Listening 2, the unit video, and your work in this unit to support your presentation. Refer to the Self-Assessment checklist on page 56.

CONSIDER THE IDEAS

A. Read these two end-of-program evaluations from two people who went on a school trip to study mountain and forest environments.

1.

The trip started out great. I really liked the scenery. Unfortunately, I hurt my back the second day when we spent the whole day setting up tents and digging trenches. I would have preferred more help from the teachers with that work. Then I got a bad sunburn from looking for research specimens in the sun all day, and that evening I got more mosquito bites than I have ever gotten in my life before. Next time, I would prefer to camp somewhere without mosquitoes.

I thought the project was interesting, certainly more interesting than regular classroom study, but we weren't able to collect as many specimens as we needed for our research, so we couldn't finish our project. That was pretty disappointing. Oh, and the food was worse than the school cafeteria's.

2.

This school trip was better than any other school trip I have ever taken. We worked hard (maybe harder than I have ever worked before!), saw some amazing sights, and learned a lot. I prefer this kind of hands-on learning to just reading textbooks. I think I learn better when I actually do something myself.

The only thing I didn't like about the trip was some of the other students. I think they just didn't want to be there. I'd rather do this kind of expedition with people who are as motivated as I am. Maybe you should charge more money for the trip, and then only people who really want to be there will come.

B. Compare the two experiences of hands-on school trips described here. What did the two participants like and not like?

C. Which do you think plays a bigger role in how much someone enjoys a trip such as this one: the person's attitude or what he or she actually experiences on the trip?

PREPARE AND SPEAK

A. **GATHER IDEAS** An organization has requested your help in planning a five-day alternative vacation for students over spring break. They want the vacation to be meaningful and educational, but also fun. The organization has received funding for a large group, so money does not have to be considered.

1. In a group, brainstorm trip ideas by asking each other questions. Find out preferences and make comparisons. Make notes of your ideas.

   Would you rather work on a science project or do volunteer work?
   Which type of trip do you think would be more fun?

2. Look at your list of ideas and choose one trip to present to the class.

B. ORGANIZE IDEAS **Follow these steps to prepare your presentation.**

1. As a group, complete the chart below with details about your trip.

Alternative spring break	
Plan	
Location	
Purpose of program	
Opportunities for fun, learning, work	
Benefits	
Travel details	

2. Choose one person in the group to present each different part of the trip plan. One person should add a summary comment about why the class should vote for your trip.

C. SPEAK **Practice your parts of the presentation individually and then together as a group. Then present your alternative spring break plan as a group to the class. Refer to the Self-Assessment checklist on page 56 before you begin.**

D. After you listen to all of the class presentations, vote on which trip to take. You can vote for your own trip, but you don't have to. Your teacher may call on volunteers to explain why they chose the trip they did.

I thought the trip to Antarctica was more exotic than any of the others.

 Go online for your alternate Unit Assignment.

CHECK AND REFLECT

A. **CHECK** Think about the Unit Assignment as you complete the Self-Assessment checklist.

Yes	No	SELF-ASSESSMENT
☐	☐	I was able to speak fluently about the topic.
☐	☐	My partner, group, and class understood me.
☐	☐	I used comparative structures correctly.
☐	☐	I used vocabulary from the unit to express my ideas.
☐	☐	I used correct intonation to ask question and list choices.
☐	☐	I discussed preferences and alternatives.

 B. **REFLECT** Go to the Online Discussion Board to discuss these questions.

1. What is something new you learned in this unit?

2. Look back at the Unit Question—Where can work, education, and fun overlap? Is your answer different now than when you started this unit? If yes, how is it different? Why?

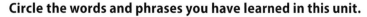

TRACK YOUR SUCCESS

Circle the words and phrases you have learned in this unit.

Nouns
atmosphere 🔑
baby boomer
collaboration
coordinator AWL
database
demographics
exhibit 🔑 AWL
expedition
grasslands
impact 🔑 AWL
nature reserve
networking 🔑 AWL
outreach

overview
preservation
range 🔑 AWL
resource 🔑 AWL
site 🔑 AWL
testing ground
woodlands

Verbs
familiarize
pioneer
prompt 🔑
restore 🔑 AWL
underline
validate AWL

Adjectives
cross-cultural
diverse AWL
ecological
enticing
eye-opening
indigenous
interactive AWL
short-term

Phrases
immerse oneself in
raise awareness

🔑 Oxford 3000™ words
AWL Academic Word List

Check (✓) the skills you learned. If you need more work on a skill, refer to the page(s) in parentheses.

LISTENING	☐ I can listen for examples. (p. 38)
NOTE TAKING	☐ I can organize notes in a Venn diagram. (p. 39)
VOCABULARY	☐ I can use compound words. (p. 46)
GRAMMAR	☐ I can use comparative structures. (p. 48)
PRONUNCIATION	☐ I can use intonation with choices. (p. 50)
SPEAKING	☐ I can discuss preferences and alternatives. (p. 52)
UNIT OBJECTIVE ▶▶▶	☐ I can gather information and ideas to plan an alternative school trip and present it in a persuasive way.

UNIT QUESTION

How can the eyes deceive the mind?

A Discuss these questions with your classmates.

1. Have your eyes ever "played tricks" on you, causing you to see something that wasn't there or not see something that was? Explain what you saw.

2. Do you like to go to movies that have sophisticated visual effects? Do you just enjoy the illusions, or do you want to figure out how the visual effects were created?

3. Look at the photos. How does each serve to deceive the mind?

B Listen to *The Q Classroom* online. Then answer these questions.

1. What examples do the students give of the eyes deceiving the mind?

2. What is a mirage, and what examples of mirages do Yuna and the teacher give?

 C Go online to watch the video about the wheel illusion. Then check your comprehension.

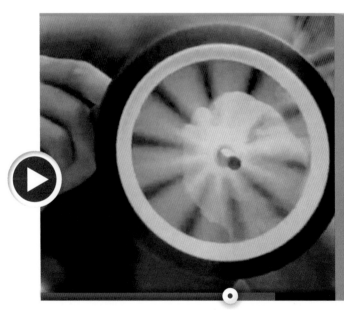

backwards *(adv.)* in the opposite direction from the usual one

detect *(v.)* discover or notice something, especially something that is not easy to see, hear, etc.

flicker *(v.)* move with small, quick movements

shutter speed *(n.)* the length of time that a camera's shutter (the part that allows light through the lens) remains open

spoke *(n.)* a thin piece of metal that connects the center of a wheel to its outer edge

 D Go to the Online Discussion Board to discuss the Unit Question with your classmates.

E Look at these examples of visual deception. Discuss their purpose with a partner.

F Read these examples of visual deception that people use. Check (✓) the ones that you have tried yourself. Can you think of other examples?

- ☐ a large hat
- ☐ dark glasses
- ☐ tinted windows
- ☐ hair coloring
- ☐ elevated shoes
- ☐ makeup
- ☐ teeth whitening products
- ☐ a wig
- ☐ different clothing styles

G Discuss these questions in a group.

1. In what ways are the examples of animal deception similar to those that people use? In what ways are they different?

2. Look at the examples of human visual deception in Activity F. What are some reasons that people use them?

3. Give an example of one type of deception in Activity F that you have used yourself. Why did you use it? Do you think that other people were truly deceived? Why or why not?

4. What fields other than biology might study types of deception?

Good listeners use their prior knowledge of a topic to make predictions about what a speaker might say about it. As you listen, your mind is working to compare what you know with what the speaker says. When a speaker shares thoughts or ideas that match your current understanding, you confirm your knowledge about a topic. When a speaker says something that differs from what you know or previously thought, you begin to ask yourself questions and explore new ideas. This is part of active, rather than passive, listening.

Before listening to a lecture, it's a good idea to think about everything you know about a topic. Some good strategies include the following:

- reading any materials an instructor has assigned before the lecture so you are already familiar with the information
- looking over class notes that lead up to the lecture
- talking with classmates about the topic so you share details you already know
- thinking about the title of the lecture or presentation
- writing some key words related to the topic in a graphic organizer for note taking
- writing a few questions you have about the topic, and leaving room for notes if your teacher answers them

A. Write some of the ways the pictures and activities on pages 58–60 helped you activate your prior knowledge about visual deception and optical illusions.

B. You are going to listen to a short description of Sherlock Holmes, a fictional British detective who uses visual deception to investigate crimes. Before you listen, think about the deceptive techniques used by detectives. Make a list of key words and questions related to the topic. Compare your ideas with a partner.

C. Listen to the description of Sherlock Holmes. Use the chart to take notes.

What disguises does he use?	What purpose do they have?	Who does he deceive?

D. Go online for more practice with using prior knowledge to prepare and organize notes.

LISTENING 1 | Wild Survivors

You are going to listen to an excerpt from a National Geographic television documentary, *Wild Survivors*, that explores some ways in which animals use a certain type of visual deception in order to survive. As you listen to the documentary, gather information and ideas about how the eyes can deceive the mind.

PREVIEW THE LISTENING

A. PREVIEW Work with a partner. What types of environment or background are these animals and insects trying to match and why?

caterpillar

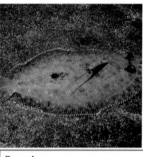
flounder

moth

praying mantis

ptarmigan

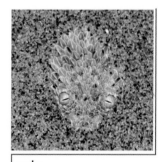
snake

B. VOCABULARY Read aloud these words from Listening 1. Check (✓) the ones you know. Use a dictionary to define any new or unknown words. Then discuss with a partner how the words will relate to the unit.

Homework

adapt *(v.)* 🔑	**mature** *(v.)*	**prey** *(n.)*
camouflage *(n.)*	**mimic** *(v.)*	**resemble** *(v.)*
elaborate *(adj.)*	**obvious** *(adj.)* 🔑	**survival** *(n.)*
infinite *(adj.)*	**predator** *(n.)*	**virtually** *(adv.)* 🔑

🔑 Oxford 3000™ words

C. Go online to listen and practice your pronunciation.

WORK WITH THE LISTENING

A. **LISTEN AND TAKE NOTES** Before you listen, use your prior knowledge about animals and camouflage to add notes to the chart. Then listen to the documentary and complete the chart. Edit your notes, if necessary.

Animal	Type of camouflage	How it works
1. Ptarmigan		
2. Caterpillars		
3. Praying mantis		
4. Desert snake		
5. Flounder		

B. Use your notes to summarize these types of deception with one example of each. Compare your answers with a partner.

1. physical change:

     praying mantis   caterpillar

2. chemical change:

     Caterpillar, flounder

3. adaptation:

Snake

⏺ **C. Listen again. Circle the word or phrase that best completes each statement.**

1. The ptarmigan lives in Europe and (North America / Asia / Africa).

2. In the winter, the ptarmigan grows long white feathers on its (head / feet / back).

3. Camouflage is the (last / best / only) protection for the ptarmigan in the Pacific Northwest.

4. The moth lays eggs (between two / on the underside of / on top of) oak tree leaves.

5. The caterpillars mimic the (movement / scent / color) of the oak tree flowers.

6. The caterpillars use camouflage to avoid being eaten by (snakes / rats / birds).

7. The body of a praying mantis can look just like (a predator / a flower / another insect).

8. The (lizard / frog / spider) is prey for the desert snake.

9. When it hides on the ocean floor, only the (fin / tail / eyes) of the flounder can be seen.

10. *Survival of the fittest* is a synonym for (adaptation to the environment / natural selection / useful traits).

D. Write questions about the documentary, based on your notes and the phrases provided. Take turns asking and answering questions in a group.

1. ptarmigan's summer appearance

   What color is a ptarmigan in summer?

2. adaptation

3. mimicry

4. moths and caterpillars

Are moths and caterpillars examples for phisycal chahge)

5. survival of the fittest

_____

Vocabulary
Skill Review
_____

In Unit 2, you learned
about compound
words that have a
unique definition
in the dictionary.
Find two compound
words in the
paragraphs in the
vocabulary activity,
one in which the two
words are joined and
one in which they
remain separate.

E. **VOCABULARY** Here are some words from Listening 1. Read the
paragraphs. Then write each bold word next to the correct definition.

Animals and plants are in a constant battle for **survival** as they compete for
limited resources. In the process of natural selection, the species that can **adapt**
to the challenges of their environment will survive. Those that are not capable of
adapting move out or die out. Different animals use different ways of coping in
their environment. For example, animals that are **predators** learn how to hunt
in ways that allow them to surprise their **prey**. The prey, in turn, sometimes use
camouflage, such as changing colors, to protect themselves.

1. _____ *(n.)* animals that kill and eat other animals

2. _____ *(n.)* the way in which an animal's color or shape
matches its surroundings and makes it difficult
to be seen

3. _____ *(n.)* the state of continuing to exist

4. _____ *(n.)* animals that are hunted, killed, and eaten
by other animals

5. _____ *(v.)* to change in order to be more suitable for
a new situation

In addition to using color for camouflage, some animals naturally
resemble the shape of a rock or a leaf, so they can hide very well in their
environment. Some birds can **mimic** other birds and so in springtime they
defend their nests from predators by copying the call of a stronger or more
dangerous bird. Disguises like these allow many animals to **mature**, safe from
predators until they are old enough to defend themselves.

6. _____ *(v.)* to copy the behavior of someone or something

7. _____ *(v.)* to be or look like something or someone else

8. _____ *(v.)* to become fully grown or developed

There's an almost **infinite** variety of living things on the planet, so
scientists are constantly discovering new examples of animals using these
tricks to survive. Some are **obvious**, and some are harder to see. However,
what is clear is that **virtually** every species has developed a clever and
elaborate system to protect itself and ensure its survival.

9. _____ (adj.) complicated; done or planned carefully

10. _____ (adv.) almost or nearly

11. _____ (adj.) easily seen or understood; clear

12. _____ (adj.) without end or limits

 F. Go online for more practice with the vocabulary.

 SAY WHAT YOU THINK

Discuss the questions in a group.

1. Listening 1 mainly describes how animals use camouflage to hide from predators. In what ways do you think predators can use camouflage to their advantage?

2. In what ways can people camouflage themselves to blend in with their environment (for example, a group of other people)? What are some advantages to looking like other people? What are some disadvantages?

3. For what reasons might a person want to stand out in his or her environment, or look different from other people?

| Listening Skill | Recognizing appositives that explain |

An **appositive** is a phrase that gives additional information in a sentence. Grammatically, an appositive is extra; you could remove it and still have a complete sentence. Functionally, an appositive often serves to provide a definition or explanation of the word or idea just before. Scientific or specialized terms are commonly defined by appositives with *or*.

In writing, appositives are set off by commas. In speaking, appositives are marked by intonation. Listen to these sentences and note the intonation of the appositives.

> The chameleon, *a type of lizard*, changes its skin color to match its background.
>
> The animal most famous for its ability to camouflage itself is the chameleon, *a type of lizard*.
>
> Chameleons are oviparous, *or egg-laying*, animals.

A. Listen to these excerpts from *Wild Survivors*. Match the appositives with the words or ideas they explain. There are three extra appositives.

_____ 1. conditions that change

_____ 2. ptarmigan

_____ 3. camouflage

_____ 4. summer outfit

_____ 5. Caribbean flounder

a. a bird about the size of a pigeon that lives in Europe and North America

b. a fish whose flat body is the color of the ocean floor

c. a bird that preys on moths

d. speckled grey and brown feathers

e. a sea creature from the Atlantic Ocean

f. availability of food and water, temperatures, the presence of predators both animal and human

g. a disguise that helps the ptarmigan hide from predators by matching the color of its environment

h. rocks, moss, and wildflowers

 **B.** Go online for more practice recognizing appositives that explain.

LISTENING 2 | Caught Off Guard

UNIT OBJECTIVE ▶▶▶▶ Researchers study deception in many areas, from photographs to strategies of war. You are going to listen to a history lecture from a Massive Open Online Course (MOOC) about deception in warfare, or catching an enemy off guard. As you listen to the lecture, gather information and ideas about how the eyes can deceive the mind.

PREVIEW THE LISTENING

A. **PREVIEW** Write down two or three examples you know about (from history or fiction) in which one side tried to deceive an enemy. Compare your examples with a partner and then listen to see if any of them are mentioned in the lecture.

_____

_____

_____

B. **VOCABULARY** Read aloud these words from Listening 2. Check (✓) the ones you know. Use a dictionary to define any new or unknown words. Then discuss with a partner how the words will relate to the unit.

accurate *(adj.)* 🔑	distract *(v.)*	objective *(n.)* 🔑
adversary *(n.)*	enhance *(v.)*	operation *(n.)* 🔑
capability *(n.)*	illusion *(n.)*	revolution *(n.)* 🔑
catch off guard *(phr.)*	manipulate *(v.)*	utilize *(v.)*

🔑 Oxford 3000™ words

C. Go online to listen and practice your pronunciation.

WORK WITH THE LISTENING

A. **LISTEN AND TAKE NOTES** Complete the graphic organizer with details you hear in the lecture. Feel free to add more branches to the diagram.

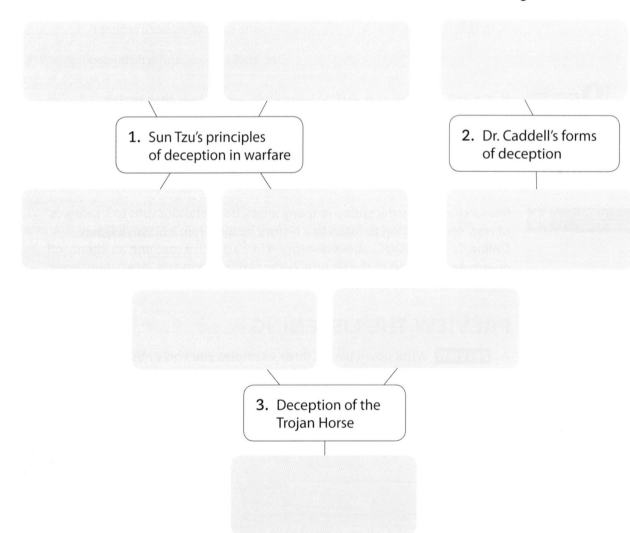

1. Sun Tzu's principles of deception in warfare

2. Dr. Caddell's forms of deception

3. Deception of the Trojan Horse

4. George Washington's illusions

5. D-Day WWII

B. Use your notes to summarize Sun Tzu's and Dr. Caddell's ideas on deception in warfare. Include examples from the lecture. Then explain them to your partner.

Tip for Success

Discourse markers help speakers gain time to think and allow listeners to show they are following a discussion, acknowledge an idea, or hedge while thinking of a response. Some common discourse markers in Listening 2 are *so, in fact, uh, well,* and *actually.*

1. Sun Tzu: ways to deceive an enemy

_____

_____

2. Dr. Caddell: passive deception and examples on the class website

_____

_____

3. Dr. Caddell: active deception and examples on the class website

_____

_____

C. Read these questions. Then listen again. Circle the correct answers.

1. What was Sun Tzu's profession?
   a. He was a famous Chinese historian.
   b. He was a famous Chinese general.

2. What do the examples used by the lecturer show about deception in nature and everyday life?
   a. In both situations, the objective is to distract or confuse.
   b. In nature, the objective is to attract attention.
   c. In everyday life, the objectives might be to enhance and manipulate.

3. According to Dr. Caddell, which type of deception is designed to convince the enemy that you have something you do not really possess?
   a. active deception
   b. passive deception

4. What attitude does the lecturer seem to have about the Trojan War?
   a. It is purely an event in Greek mythology.
   b. It is a good fictional example of active deception.
   c. It may be based on real battles in Greek history.

5. The lecturer uses the example of George Washington to
   a. prove the belief in Washington as the president who "never told a lie."
   b. show the class the best way to win a battle.
   c. explain the importance of deception in fighting a stronger opponent.

6. Which of the three examples discussed by the lecturer received the least number of comments by students?
   a. the Greeks and Trojans in the Trojan War
   b. George Washington in the Revolutionary War
   c. the Allies in World War II

7. Which two groups used the most similar strategies of deception?
   a. the Greeks and the British
   b. George Washington and the Allies
   c. the Trojans and the Germans

8. With which statement do you think the lecturer would agree?
   a. Sun Tzu's teachings on warfare continue to be relevant over time.
   b. Sun Tzu's teachings are valuable only in studying ancient historical battles.
   c. Sun Tzu's teachings are no longer worth examining in the 21st century.

D. Match the examples with the type of deception. Compare answers with a partner.

Examples

_____ 1. sound mimicry

_____ 2. clothing and makeup

_____ 3. when near, appear far

_____ 4. pretending to sail home in defeat

_____ 5. small items in big boxes

_____ 6. ordering extra supplies for a small army

_____ 7. false radio signals and messages

_____ 8. uniforms that blend into the environment

Type of Deception

a. deception in advertising

b. Greek strategy of passive deception

c. common military deception

d. Washington's strategy of active deception

e. Sun Tzu's deceptive warfare

f. manipulation by attracting attention

g. WWII deception

h. distraction

E. Work with a partner. Take turns asking and answering these questions.

1. From the professor's comments, could you infer that he was satisfied or dissatisfied with his students' participation in this online discussion? Why?

2. Which of the three historical examples in the lecture provided the clearest examples of armies being caught off guard?

3. If you were a student in this class, how would you reply to the final question, "With the modern technology that we have today in the 21st century, do you think battles are still fought using such deceptive devices?"

F. **VOCABULARY** Use the new vocabulary from Listening 2. Read the sentences. Circle the answer that best matches the meaning of each bold word or phrase.

1. Is deception ever **utilized** for a good purpose, or is it always intended to play a trick on others to have an advantage over them?
   a. made use of
   b. made fun of

2. When we asked him why he had made that decision, we could see the question surprised him and he was **caught off guard**.

   a. expecting a situation or result

   b. unaware of what was coming next

3. During warfare, military **operations** often involve covering machines with trees so they are invisible from the sky.

   a. medical procedures involving repairing a damaged body part

   b. organized activities involving many parts

4. Because **adversaries** were ready to cut down his theories, the biologist was careful to trace the steps that led to his conclusions.

   a. enemies

   b. supporters

 Tip for Success

When learning new words, make a note of the prepositions that go with them. For example, *notice a link <u>between</u> two events* and *manipulate someone <u>into</u> doing something.*

5. The general was able to **manipulate** the enemy into believing what he wanted them to without their even realizing it.

   a. threaten or force someone to take a particular action

   b. control or influence someone in a skillful way

6. Certain people have an amazing **capability** to remain calm while enduring high levels of stress.

   a. having qualities or resources necessary to do something

   b. not having the power to represent a true image

7. Even when we have **accurate** information, we sometimes make a mistake because our mind influences us to see what we want to see.

   a. interesting and careful

   b. correct and true

8. People traveling in deserts sometimes think they see a pool of water in the distance that isn't really there. This is an optical **illusion** created by the intense heat.

   a. visual trick

   b. strong wish

9. It's dangerous to use a cell phone while driving because it can **distract** you, and you might not notice other cars or people in the road.

   a. remind; help you recall information

   b. take your attention away from something

10. His **objective** was to persuade his sister to clean the kitchen so he could finish watching a special program on television.
    a. planned purpose or goal
    b. lack of personal opinion

11. It is not a good idea to **enhance** your résumé by listing companies you haven't worked for, because the truth often comes out in the end.
    a. improve the quality of
    b. avoid the benefits of

12. That Web site has caused a **revolution** in how we believe animal camouflage relates to species survival.
    a. imaginary or unimportant actions
    b. a complete change in methods

 G. Go online for more practice with the vocabulary.

H. Go online to listen to *The Career of Harry Houdini* and check your comprehension.

 SAY WHAT YOU THINK

A. Discuss the questions in a group.

1. How might Sun Tzu respond to the question "How can the eyes deceive the mind?"

2. The lecturer presents three examples of deception in warfare. Which do you think was the most successful in catching the enemy off guard?

 Critical Thinking **Tip**

The questions in Activity B ask you to **extend** the information you have learned by applying it to a new situation.

B. Think about the unit video, Listening 1, and Listening 2 as you discuss the questions.

1. In what ways do the ideas of passive and active deception apply to camouflage and mimicry in nature?

2. In what ways do the visual effects in science fiction movies make battles between humans or between humans and animals seem more or less realistic?

3. Did the examples in the documentary, lecture, or video convince you that the eyes really can deceive the mind? Why or why not?

A **suffix** is a group of letters at the end of a word. A suffix can show the part of speech of a word. For example, -*ary* often signals an adjective, and -*tion* indicates a noun. Sometimes when you add a suffix, there are spelling changes to the original word root. For example, when you add a suffix to a word ending in silent -*e*, you usually delete the -*e*.

Children **imagine** all sorts of wonderful stories.
verb

He believed in lots of **imaginary** places.
adjective

He had a very vivid **imagination**.
noun

Learning related forms of words helps build your vocabulary. When you learn one new word, you can also learn its related forms. This can also help you understand unfamiliar words. When you see a word that is related to a word you know, you can sometimes guess its meaning.

Here are some common suffixes that usually indicate nouns, verbs, adjectives, and adverbs.

Suffixes that show . . .			
Nouns	**Verbs**	**Adjectives**	**Adverbs**
-ance/ence	-ate	-able/ible	-ly
-tion	-ify	-al/ical	-ward
-ee	-ize	-ary/ory	
-er/or		-ent/ant	
-ian		-ese	
-ism		-ful	
-(i)ty		-ive	
-ment		-less	
-ology		-ous	

A. Work with a partner. Complete the chart with correct word forms. Sometimes there is more than one noun or adjective form. Write *X* if there is no related word form. Check the dictionary to make sure your word forms are correct.

Noun	Verb	Adjective	Adverb
1. imagination	imagine	imaginative	imaginatively
2.		adaptive	
3.	deceive		
4.			capably
5.	differ		
6.			individually
7. maturity			
8.		predatory	
9.	revolt		

B. Choose the correct word forms from the chart in Activity A to complete these sentences. Use the context and the position of the word in the sentence to help you.

1. Sun Tzu believed that _____ was an important part of warfare.

2. When a _____ is hunting for food, it stays quiet and tries to blend in with the background.

3. It may be hard to tell the _____ between lying and deception.

4. The development of new technology caused a _____ in the normally very traditional field of education.

5. Animal species that cannot _____ to changes may not survive for many more generations.

6. As we _____, it is not so easy for others to fool us.

iQ ONLINE   **C.** Go online for more practice with word forms and suffixes.

At the end of this unit, you will give a group presentation on the uses of visual deception. In order to discuss examples of visual deception, you will need to be able to clarify information.

Grammar | Relative clauses

Relative clauses identify, define, or comment on the noun, noun phrase, or pronoun they follow. They can make your sentences more varied, interesting, and informative.

You can think of a sentence with a relative clause as a combination of two sentences.

The conductor walked onto the platform. + He was wearing a blue cap.

relative clause

The conductor, **who was wearing a blue cap**, walked onto the platform.

noun · relative pronoun

Relative clauses usually begin with a relative pronoun: *who, whom, whose, that, when, where,* or *which.* The relative pronoun refers to the same person or thing as the noun or noun clause being modified. So in the example above, "who" refers to "the conductor."

Relative clauses are dependent clauses. They must connect to a main clause. They cannot stand alone as sentences.

Relative clauses can be either **subject relative clauses** or **object relative clauses**.

Relative pronoun	Use	Example
who who(m)	subject/object pronoun for people (Informally, many people use "who" instead of "whom.")	The leaders **who planned the operation** tried to avoid conflict. The historian **whom I respect most** specializes in Greek history.
whose	possessive pronoun for people, animals, or things	The bird **whose feathers I found** was a ptarmigan.
that	subject /object pronoun for people, animals, or things	The paper **that I read** was too difficult to understand.
which	subject/object pronoun for things; can refer to a previous clause	The evidence did not convince him, **which surprised me**.

Subject relative clauses

In subject relative clauses, the relative pronoun takes the place of the subject of the clause. It is followed by a verb. The verb agrees with the noun that the clause modifies.

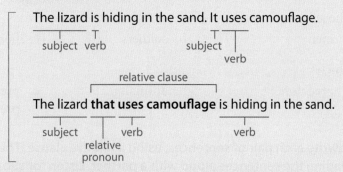

The lizard is hiding in the sand. It uses camouflage.

The lizard **that uses camouflage** is hiding in the sand.

Object relative clauses

In object relative clauses, the relative pronoun takes the place of the object of the clause. It is followed by a subject and a verb. The verb agrees with the subject.

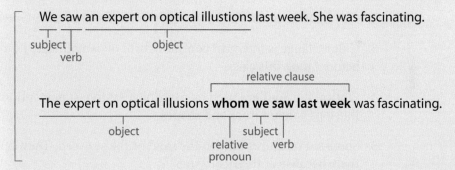

We saw an expert on optical illusions last week. She was fascinating.

The expert on optical illusions **whom we saw last week** was fascinating.

You can omit the relative pronoun in object relative clauses. This is common in everyday speech.

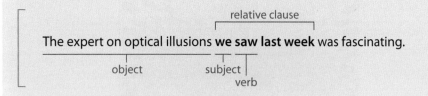

The expert on optical illusions **we saw last week** was fascinating.

🔊 **A. Listen to the sentences. For each one, circle the noun or pronoun that the relative clause modifies.**

1. that =
   a. events
   b. dates
   c. confusion

2. whom =
   a. China
   b. we
   c. general

3. that =

    a. river   b. troops   c. army

4. that =

    a. sounds   b. nature   c. radios

5. whose =

    a. men   b. soldiers   c. horse

6. which =

    a. predators   b. animals   c. predators are also prey

B. Rewrite each pair of sentences, using a relative clause. Then take turns reading the sentences aloud with a partner. Listen for subject-verb agreement or pronoun problems.

1. Sun Tzu lived during the 5th century BCE. His teachings are still important today.

2. Odysseus designed the Trojan Horse. He was a famous Greek warrior.

3. Color change is the most common form of camouflage. I didn't know that before I took this class.

4. Optical illusions are used by psychologists to test perception. Optical illusions contain lines and shapes.

5. Some sea creatures hide in the sand or the seaweed. They can't be seen there because of their coloring.

an optical illusion

 C. Go online for more practice with relative clauses.

D. Go online for the grammar expansion.

Changing a word to a different form by adding a suffix can sometimes cause the primary word stress to change. Although deciding where to stress words of more than one syllable can be difficult, there are a few rules you can follow. When in doubt, always check a dictionary.

Listen to the examples in the chart below.

Rules	Suffixes	Examples
1. Put the primary stress on these suffixes.	*-ee, -eer, -ese, -ier, -ique*	re-TIRE / re-tir-**EE** CHI-na / Chi-N**ESE** cash / ca-SH**IER**
2. Keep the syllable stress from the base word when adding these suffixes.	*-al, -ment, -ness, -ous, -or, -y, -ism, -ly*	pro-FESS-ion / pro-FESS-ion-**al** e-QUIP / e-QUIP-**ment** e-FFECT-ive / e-FFECT-ive-**ness** sub-JECT-ive / sub-JECT-ive-**ly**
3. Put the primary stress on the syllable just before these suffixes.	*-ial, -ian, -ion, -ic(s), -ical, -ient, -ious, -ify, -itive, -ity, -graphy, -logy, -ual*	CA-pa-ble / ca-pa-BI-li-**ty** psy-CHO-**lo-gy** / psy-cho-LO-**gi-cal**
4. Put the primary stress two syllables before these suffixes.	*-ary, -ate, -ize*	VO-cab / vo-CAB-u-**la-ry** CER-ti-fy / cer-TIF-i-**cate** lo-CA-tion / LO-cal-**ize**

A. For each pair of words, predict where the stress should go and circle that syllable. Then listen and check your answers.

1. a. manipulate   b. manipulation

2. a. alternate   b. alternative

3. a. deceive   b. deception

4. a. image   b. imaginary

5. a. technique   b. technically

6. a. mystery   b. mysterious

7. a. popular   b. popularity

8. a. psychology   b. psychological

9. a. terrify   b. terrific

10. a. visual   b. visualize

B. Work with a partner. Take turns reading these sentences. Listen for correct word stress on the underlined words.

1. Some children are <u>terrified</u> by airplanes, but others think they're <u>terrific</u>.

2. Teachers use different <u>techniques</u>, but <u>technically</u> their goals are the same.

3. The <u>mystery</u> of nature is revealed in <u>mysterious</u> ways.

4. The <u>objective</u> of this exercise is to move the <u>object</u> from point A to point B.

5. The <u>images</u> in the book helped the children visualize the <u>imaginary</u> places.

6. They did <u>psychological</u> tests to understand the <u>psychology</u> behind optical illusions.

 C. Go online for more practice with stress shifts with suffixes.

Speaking Skill | Clarifying information

In a conversation, there are a number of ways to ask someone to clarify something that he or she has said.

Restating speaker's point
Do you mean that . . . ?
So are you saying that . . . ?
Let me see if I understand . . .
Am I correct in assuming that . . . ?

Asking speaker for clarification
Could you clarify that last concept?
Could you give an example?
Could you explain how that works?

Asking speaker to rephrase what was said
What do you mean by . . . ?
Could you explain that another way?
I'm not sure what that means.
Can you rephrase that?

In this example, a student in the class restates the lecturer's idea and then asks him/her for clarification.

In your lecture, you hinted that there is some evidence that the Trojan Wars were not just mythological. Can you give an example?

To clarify a point in response to a question, or to rephrase a difficult idea without being asked, a speaker often uses phrases like these.

What I mean to say is . . .	To make myself clear, . . .
In other words, . . .	Sorry, let me rephrase that.
That is, . . .	Just to clarify, . . .
Let me explain . . .	

A. Work with a partner. Use phrases from the Speaking Skill box to complete this conversation. Then practice the conversation aloud. Take turns playing the tutor and the student.

Tutor: So you have a quiz on mimicry and camouflage tomorrow. Do you have any questions?

Student: I get camouflage, but _____ mimicry?
                                                  1

Tutor: Well, the technical definition for mimicry is when one organism can share characteristics and imitate sounds or actions of another.

Student: _____?
                         2

Tutor: Sure. An example would be a moth that makes a clicking sound to make it sound like something dangerous to bats so they won't come near. Remember, mimicry is part of a bigger concept called *crypsis*.

_____, mimicry falls into a larger category of
                3
behavior along with evasion, camouflage, and just plain hiding.

Student: _____ running away from something and
                              4
hiding are considered in the same category as camouflage and mimicry?

Tutor: Exactly. So _____, they are all part of the
                                        5
same protective behavior.

B. Work with a partner. Role-play an interview between a reporter and a scientist explaining one or more of the concepts below. Use phrases from the skill box. Then practice the conversation aloud and present it to the class.

camouflage	distract	illusions	manipulate

Unit Assignment Give a group presentation on the uses of visual deception

---

 In this assignment, you are going to deliver a group presentation on how different forms of visual deception are used. As you prepare your presentation, think about the Unit Question, "How can the eyes deceive the mind?" Use information from Listening 1, Listening 2, the unit video, and your work in this unit to support your presentation. Refer to the Self-Assessment checklist on page 84.

CONSIDER THE IDEAS

Look at these images from a lecture on optical illusions. In a group, discuss the questions below.

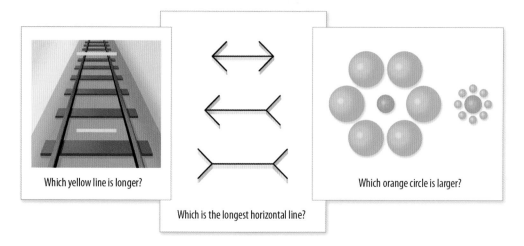

Which yellow line is longer?

Which is the longest horizontal line?

Which orange circle is larger?

1. In each illusion, one object appears longer or bigger than the others, but they are the same size. What creates the illusion in each case?

2. Do we always see what is really there, or do we sometimes see only what we want to see? Do you think some people can resist being fooled?

3. Do you think the study of optical illusions is important? Why or why not?

PREPARE AND SPEAK

A. **GATHER IDEAS** Work in a group. Brainstorm some ways illusions and forms of visual deceptions like the ones presented in this unit are or could be used in each of the following fields. Take notes in the chart on page 83.

Field	Uses
Fashion	
Art	
Architecture	
Advertising	
Psychology	
Computer Science	
Theater/ Film/TV	
Other	

B. ORGANIZE IDEAS **Plan your group presentation.**

1. Choose one of the fields above or one of your own. As a group, discuss examples of visual deception in the field you have chosen. The examples can be ones you have seen or ones you imagine. Be creative.

2. Plan the report on your findings. Your presentation should include these parts:
    - a description of the field you chose and the reasons why
    - a description of three or four examples of visual deception that are or could be used and how they work (If possible, collect pictures from the Internet or magazines, or create your own.)
    - a response to the question, "How easily do you think people are deceived by this illusion?"
    - a conclusion that addresses implications of using visual deception in this field

3. Divide the points and/or examples among the members of your group. Use a note card for each part of the report you will give, and write essential points to remind yourself what to say.

4. Practice presenting your information to your group. Use relative clauses to describe each optical illusion figure or picture and explain how it is used in a particular field.

This optical illusion shows two lines that are the same length but don't appear that way.

People who want to look taller might wear a V-neck sweater rather than one with a round neck.

C. **SPEAK** Present your ideas to the class. Answer questions from the audience at the end. When you listen to other presentations, ask questions to clarify information if you are not sure of the meaning. Refer to the Self-Assessment checklist below before you begin.

 Go online for your alternate Unit Assignment.

CHECK AND REFLECT

A. **CHECK** Think about the Unit Assignment as you complete the Self-Assessment checklist.

SELF-ASSESSMENT		
Yes	**No**	
☐	☐	I was able to speak fluently about the topic.
☐	☐	My partner, group, and class understood me.
☐	☐	I used relative clauses correctly.
☐	☐	I used vocabulary from the unit to express my ideas.
☐	☐	I emphasized the correct syllable in words to indicate the word form.
☐	☐	I asked for clarification as necessary and clarified my speech for others when asked.

 B. **REFLECT** Go to the Online Discussion Board to discuss these questions.

1. What is something new you learned in this unit?

2. Look back at the Unit Question—How can the eyes deceive the mind? Is your answer different now than when you started this unit? If yes, how is it different? Why?

TRACK YOUR SUCCESS

Circle the words you have learned in this unit.

Nouns
adversary
camouflage
capability AWL
illusion
objective 🔑 AWL
operation 🔑
predator
prey
revolution 🔑 AWL
survival AWL

verbs
adapt 🔑 AWL
distract
enhance AWL
manipulate AWL
mature AWL
mimic
resemble
utilize AWL

Adjectives
accurate 🔑 AWL
elaborate
infinite AWL
obvious 🔑 AWL

Adverb
virtually 🔑 AWL

Phrase
catch off guard

🔑 Oxford 3000™ words
AWL Academic Word List

Check (✓) the skills you learned. If you need more work on a skill, refer to the page(s) in parentheses.

NOTE TAKING ■	I can use prior knowledge to prepare and organize notes. (p. 61)
LISTENING ■	I can recognize appositives that explain. (p. 66)
VOCABULARY ■	I can use word forms and suffixes. (p. 74)
GRAMMAR ■	I can use relative clauses. (pp. 76–77)
PRONUNCIATION ■	I can shift word stress with suffixes. (p. 79)
SPEAKING ■	I can clarify information. (pp. 80–81)
UNIT OBJECTIVE ▶▶▶▶ ■	I can gather information and ideas to give a group presentation on the uses of visual deception.

NOTE TAKING ▶ using a T-chart to take notes on problems and solutions
LISTENING ▶ listening for facts and figures
VOCABULARY ▶ collocations
GRAMMAR ▶ reported speech
PRONUNCIATION ▶ linking with final consonants
SPEAKING ▶ citing sources

UNIT QUESTION

What does it mean to be a global citizen?

A Discuss these questions with your classmates.

1. Which of these concerns get the most attention: short-term disasters, such as hurricane relief, or long-term problems, such as world hunger? Why?

2. Look at the photo. How do each of us act as global citizens?

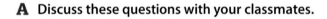

B Listen to *The Q Classroom* online. Then answer these questions.

1. How does Marcus define a global citizen? Do you agree with his definition?

2. What examples does Yuna give to show ways good global citizens help others? What can you add?

 C Go to the Online Discussion Board to discuss the Unit Question with your classmates.

D Look at the photos. What problems do you see? Talk with a partner and write your ideas. Then think of four more problems you think the world faces today.

Problems the world faces today

_____

_____

_____

_____

E Work with a group. For each problem in Activity D, decide who is primarily responsible for solving the problem. (There may be more than one answer.) Write the problem next to the correct heading.

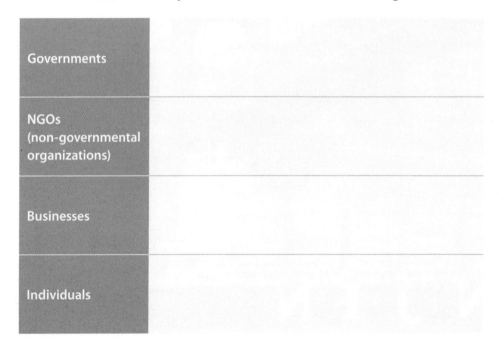

Governments	
NGOs (non-governmental organizations)	
Businesses	
Individuals	

Recognizing organizational patterns helps you understand information as you listen. When a speaker introduces problems and the solutions to them, a T-chart is a good tool to use to take notes and organize the ideas. For example, if you are going to listen to a report on how society can solve world hunger, you can expect the speaker to provide facts about the problems caused by hunger, followed by some possible solutions.

Remember that in a lecture you might hear some of the information out of order. However, if you note problems in one column and solutions in the other, you can reorder them later when you revise your notes. If you hear a detail that you don't have time to write down, such as the solution for a specific problem, draw a line to remind you to ask a classmate later. Sometimes, an instructor may intentionally leave out a solution and ask students to research the missing information or come up with their own ideas later.

Here are some key phrases to listen for:

Problems	Solutions
One problem is . . .	People should/must . . .
The group worries about the . . .	One suggestion is to . . .
The trouble is that . . .	We can solve this by . . .
They are concerned about . . .	They need to . . .
Another obstacle we face is . . .	We've figured out that . . .

It is a good strategy to try to prepare a graphic organizer before a lecture. If your instructor tells you to read a chapter about environmental disasters for the next class, for example, you might prepare a T-chart to get ready for the lecture.

A. So far, you have learned to organize notes using a timeline, a Venn diagram, and a T-chart. Match the following lectures with the best graphic organizer for taking notes.

____ 1. Similarities and differences between two global organizations

____ 2. Concerns about childhood disease and UN actions

____ 3. Summary of natural disasters over the past 50 years

a. a timeline

b. a Venn diagram

c. a T-chart

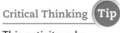 **B.** Listen to students talking about humanitarian organizations. Write the problems and solutions they discuss. Then compare notes with a partner.

Critical Thinking **Tip**

This activity asks you to **identify** the problems and solutions you hear the speakers talk about. Identifying ideas is one way to show you understand the information.

Problems	Solutions
1.	
2.	
3.	
4.	

 C. Go online for more practice using a T-chart to take notes on problems and solutions.

| The Campaign to Humanize the Coffee Trade

You are going to listen to a report, "The Campaign to Humanize the Coffee Trade," by Daniel Zwerdling for American RadioWorks. It addresses an issue of global concern for a product consumed in almost every country. As you listen to the report, gather information and ideas about what it means to be a global citizen.

PREVIEW THE LISTENING

A. PREVIEW Check (✓) your predictions of what the speaker will say about humanizing the coffee trade, which means improving the conditions for the workers.

☐ Coffee production in small villages is usually not controlled by the farmers themselves.

☐ Products that come from socially responsible businesses that protect workers and the environment cost less because they come from small companies.

☐ Coffee farmers earn less than one-tenth of the money from their beans that are sold in other countries.

B. VOCABULARY Read aloud these words from Listening 1. Check (✓) the ones you know. Use a dictionary to define any new or unknown words. Then discuss with a partner how the words will relate to the unit.

activist *(n.)* 🔑	intermediary *(n.)*
afford *(v.)* 🔑	massive *(adj.)* 🔑
commodity *(n.)*	processor *(n.)*
co-op *(n.)*	roughly *(adv.)* 🔑
devise *(v.)*	speculation *(n.)*
guarantee *(v.)* 🔑	transform *(v.)* 🔑

🔑 Oxford 3000™ words

 C. Go online to listen and practice your pronunciation.

WORK WITH THE LISTENING

A. **LISTEN AND TAKE NOTES** Listen to the report on the coffee trade. From the title, you can predict that the problem is unfairness in the coffee trade and that the solution will be a campaign to improve, or humanize, the situation. Use this T-chart to take notes on the problems and solutions you hear.

Farmers' problems	Fair trade solutions

B. Match each statement with the person who would say it.

___ 1. I learned that everyone was making a profit on the coffee except the growers.

___ 2. I believe I pay a fair price for the coffee beans that we then sell to the processors.

___ 3. I know that helping farmers become independent of the intermediaries is the main goal.

___ 4. I might pay 10% more for coffee if I were sure it came directly from the farmers.

___ 5. I don't know how much this coffee is sold for at stores in the U.S.

a. a coyote

b. a coffee farmer

c. a coffee consumer

d. the American RadioWork reporter

e. a Fair Trade organizer

C. Use your notes to write a sentence for each topic to express the main idea.

1. The lives and homes of the coffee farmers

_____

2. The role of the coyote, or middleman

_____

3. The goal of the Fair Trade system

_____

D. Read the statements. Then listen again. Write *T* (true) or *F* (false). Correct the false statements.

_____ 1. The coffee farmers introduced here say they send their coffee into town on trucks.

_____ 2. The coyotes, or middlemen, buy the coffee beans for 50 cents or less per pound.

_____ 3. Zwerdling says that in Washington, D.C., he spends less than $9.00 per pound for coffee.

_____ 4. Coffee is not a highly traded commodity.

_____ 5. Fair Trade was started by Europeans.

_____ 6. At the time of the report, about 300 groups of farmers around the world had joined the Fair Trade system.

_____ 7. Large corporate plantations can join Fair Trade if they promise to follow fair business practices.

_____ 8. Guillermo Denaux explains that under Fair Trade, farmers are basically guaranteed to earn enough money for food, education, clothes, and health care.

E. Who sells coffee to whom? Number the people in the order that they purchase coffee after the farmer offers it for sale. Then check your answers with a partner.

_____ a coffee shop

__1__ a coyote, or middleman

_____ a processor

_____ a roaster

_____ the consumer

_____ an exporter

Vocabulary
Skill Review

In Unit 3, you
reviewed suffixes
that change the part
of speech. Find four
words with noun
suffixes in the bold
vocabulary words.

F. **VOCABULARY** Here are some words from Listening 1. Read the
sentences. Then write each bold word next to the correct definition.

1. Many celebrity **activists** worked together to bring attention to the effects
   of the tsunami and to raise money for countries affected by it.

2. If a local community effort, or grassroots campaign, gets a lot of media
   attention, it might **transform** into a national or even a global fight for change.

3. Many farmers are forced to find other jobs because they cannot **afford** the
   high costs of producing food.

4. Some businesspeople who like risk base their investments on **speculation**
   and luck rather than on past performance history.

5. There was a **massive** demand for sugar, but because of agricultural
   problems, the supply was very low.

6. Coffee is a popular **commodity** that is traded in many parts of the world.

7. The grower sells his product to a **processor**, who then gets it ready for
   the market.

8. Human rights groups spend a lot of their energy trying to **devise** ways to
   improve labor laws around the world.

9. **Roughly** 884 million people worldwide have unsafe drinking water, and
   according to the humanitarian group Save the Children, this estimate is low.

10. In order to avoid the obstacles that can prevent small businesses from
    succeeding, some people prefer to join a **co-op** and work together with
    other small business owners.

11. The United Nations Global Compact wants businesses to **guarantee** that
    they will reduce their environmental impact, not just say they hope it
    will happen.

12. The importer didn't have a license to do business in that country, so she
    needed an **intermediary** to buy the products for her.

a. _____ (*n.*) the activity of guessing that an investment will
   make a profit but with the risk of a bad result

b. _____ (*v.*) to change completely

c. _____ (*adv.*) more or less; approximately

d. _____ (*v.*) to give a promise

e. _____ (*n.*) a product or raw material that can be bought
   and sold

f. _____ (n.) someone who passes on information;
    a middleman

g. _____ (n.) something or someone that handles, treats, or
    changes materials before they can be used or sold

h. _____ (v.) to come up with or develop a plan or system

i. _____ (n.) people who work to achieve social change

j. _____ (v.) to be able to pay for something

k. _____ (adj.) very big; great amount

l. _____ (n.) a community organization of people working
    together toward a shared goal

 G. Go online for more practice with the vocabulary.

 ## SAY WHAT YOU THINK

Discuss the questions in a group.

1. Would you be willing to pay extra for Fair Trade products? Why or why
   not? How much more would you pay (than you do now) for a cup of
   coffee? A chocolate bar? A cotton T-shirt?

2. Zwerdling says that "consumers have to help, too." In what ways can
   consumers help in the development of the Fair Trade network?

3. Who should determine prices of luxury commodities (such as coffee
   or chocolate)? Who should determine the prices of necessities (such as
   vegetables)? What might happen if farmers were allowed to charge as much
   as they wanted for their products?

Tip for Success

Develop your own set of note-taking abbreviations and symbols, such as *b/c* (because), *e.g.* (for example), ↑↓ (increase/decrease), and > < (greater/less than).

Reporters use personal stories to make a point. Lectures present theories and examples to support them. Many fields rely on facts, dates, and statistics for evidence. It is important to know what type of presentation you will be listening to in order to know what to listen for. It is common for many speakers today to use presentation software to show graphs and charts summarizing data. Make sure to look at the big picture so you understand the purpose of the chart before just copying everything in your notes. Listen to what the speaker is saying; don't just read the statistics. In any presentation that relies on statistical facts and figures, it is important to write down overall ideas and important trends as well as specific data that the speaker emphasizes. When you are taking notes and hear a fact or number that you think is important, write it down with some key words. If you miss something, add a question mark (?) to remind yourself to find out the information later.

Phrases that introduce facts and figures:

before/after 1900	roughly
in the early/late 1990s	it costs over
from . . . to . . .	fewer/more than
in recent years/recently	research shows that
a(n) decrease/increase in	data show that
it is estimated that	the percent/number/amount of

A. Listen to this report on coffee consumption. Take notes on the facts and figures. Write down the numbers you hear, even if you have to add the details later.

B. Use your notes to answer these questions.

1. What percent of the coffee is produced in developing countries?

2. Roughly how much coffee do people drink per year?

3. According to the reporter, what is the current number of families that work cultivating coffee?

4. How much of the world's coffee is grown in Brazil?

 C. Go online for more practice listening for facts and figures.

LISTENING 2 | The UN Global Compact

UNIT OBJECTIVE ▶▶▶▶

You are going to listen to a professor of a course in international trade introduce two videos on the UN Global Compact, one of the many subgroups of the United Nations that work on international cooperation. The first video describes the formal agreement, or compact, between concerned businesses; the second is on the current state of the compact. As you listen to the clips, gather information and ideas about what it means to be a global citizen.

PREVIEW THE LISTENING

A. **PREVIEW** Check (✓) the issues you expect to hear discussed in the report.

☐ corruption   ☐ cost of products

☐ import and export prices   ☐ worker safety

☐ pollution   ☐ climate change

☐ treatment of employees   ☐ consumer spending

The United Nations building

B. **VOCABULARY** Read aloud these words from Listening 2. Check (✓) the ones you know. Use a dictionary to define any new or unknown words. Then discuss with a partner how the words will relate to the unit.

confidence of investors *(phr.)*	ethical goods *(phr.)*	labor standards *(phr.)*
core strategies *(phr.)*	exploit *(v.)*	proactive *(adj.)*
corporate responsibility *(phr.)*	household expenditure *(phr.)*	social impact *(phr.)*
emerging economy *(phr.)*	intangible assets *(phr.)*	sustainable market *(phr.)*

 C. Go online to listen and practice your pronunciation.

WORK WITH THE LISTENING

🔊 **A.** **LISTEN AND TAKE NOTES** As you listen to the clips, use the T-chart to take notes on the problems businesses face and the solutions the UN Global Compact offers.

Problems	Solutions

B. Use your notes to answer these questions. Compare your answers with a partner.

1. What problem did the *Exxon Valdez* oil spill reveal that helped lead to the development of the UN Global Compact?

2. If a bad reputation can hurt business, what solution is presented here?

3. What are some of the problems that Kell feels still remain in 2014?

4. At the Oslo summit, Georg Kell asks, "Can we envision a day, hopefully not in the too distant future, where the majority of business acts responsibly and in a sustainable manner?" In what ways does Kell show that the problem of corporate irresponsibility is being solved by the Global Compact?

C. Circle the answer that best completes each statement.

1. Expansion into the global market brings more risk to the public because
   a. emerging markets have weaker regulations.
   b. emerging markets will increase competition.

2. In order to participate in the UN Global Compact, companies must promise to
   a. take responsibility for their own actions.
   b. report irresponsible actions by other businesses.

3. Two of the ten areas that the Global Compact is intended to safeguard are
   a. labor standards and business reputations.
   b. human rights and the environment.

4. Evidence of changes in public attitudes includes findings that people are
   a. spending more money on ethical goods.
   b. more concerned about the cost of a product than the reputation of the company that produced it.

5. Ban Ki-Moon's hopes for the future of the Global Compact include
   a. limiting global expansion and development.
   b. creating sustainable markets.

6. In his speech at the Business for Peace summit in Oslo, Kell says he believes the state of the union between business and society is
   a. at a crossroads in progress.
   b. at a point where old problems have been solved.

D. Read this list of supporting details. Then listen again. Complete the chart with the correct facts and figures as you listen. Check your answers with a partner.

Details	Facts/Figures
1. The year of the *Exxon Valdez* disaster	
2. The number of gallons of crude oil spilled into the water by the *Exxon Valdez*	
3. The year the UN started the Global Compact	
4. The number of Global Compact principles the participating companies agree to uphold	
5. The percentage of a company's market value that is determined by its reputation and intangible assets	
6. The share price of Enron before its bad reputation caused the price to fall to less than 50 cents in 2001	
7. The percentage of CEOs who report doing more now to incorporate environmental, social, and political issues into their core strategies	
8. The number of companies in the Global Compact when it first started	
9. The number of corporate participants, or businesses, in the Global Compact that Kell reports at the Oslo summit	
10. The number of countries in the Global Compact in 2014	

Tip for Success

The field of business has many noun phrases that are collocations such as the words in bold here. See the Vocabulary Skill on page 102 for more information on collocations.

E. **VOCABULARY** Here are some words and phrases from Listening 2. Read the sentences. Then write each bold word or phrase next to the correct definition.

1. India is recognized as a key **emerging economy** in the world. There is some risk in investing there, but potential for enormous profits and growth, too.

2. Many organizations try to ensure that proper **labor standards** exist so that employees have safe conditions at their jobs.

3. Businesses worry about the **confidence of investors** because if people don't invest, there won't be money to innovate and expand, or perhaps even to stay in business.

4. Institutions such as the World Bank provide loans to developing countries to improve their **social impact** in the world.

a. _____ laws that protect workers

b. _____ the effects of an organization or agency on others

c. _____ a region that is experiencing rapid growth and industrialization

d. _____ a feeling or belief by people with money that it is safe to spend it in order to make a future profit

5. Businesses have easily identifiable assets, or property. They also have **intangible assets**, like a good reputation, that are not easily visible.

6. Consumers can show they care about **corporate responsibility** by not buying products that have a negative impact on the environment.

7. In tough economic times, families need to reduce unnecessary **household expenditures** such as eating in restaurants.

8. I am only interested in buying **ethical goods** for people as gifts this year. I don't want to support any businesses that don't treat workers fairly.

e. _____ the costs of taking care of a home and family

f. _____ the requirements for a business to abide by laws and ethical practices

g. _____ products that are judged to be morally acceptable and not harmful to society or the workers who produce them

h. _____ things of value that cannot be seen, such as knowledge

9. Even though countries want to **exploit** their own natural resources, they have to consider the environmental impact of using those resources too quickly.

10. In recent years, businesses have tried to find ways of being **proactive** with problems so they can take action before being criticized.

11. The principles, or basic beliefs, of a company determine its **core strategies**.

12. The country's economic policies are focused on creating a **sustainable market** to attract and keep foreign investors.

i. _____ a system that can operate continuously while still meeting global economic, environmental, and social needs

j. _____ to use something well in order to gain as much from it as possble

k. _____ controlling a situation by making things happen rather than waiting for things to happen and then reacting to them

l. _____ primary or fundamental plans of action for a business

F. Go online for more practice with the vocabulary.

G. Go online to listen to *Teaching Chinese* and check your comprehension.

SAY WHAT YOU THINK

A. Discuss the questions in a group.

1. What do you think are the most serious problems caused by businesses and corporations that the Global Compact should force them to address?

2. Do you think corporations that follow the Global Compact are motivated more by the desire for profits, the desire to be better global citizens, or something else?

B. Before you watch the video, discuss these questions in a group.

1. Do you think the support of famous celebrities makes a real difference in gathering help in a national or international crisis?

2. Who should pay for the global aid following a natural disaster, such as a tsunami or the destruction following an oil spill?

C. Go online to watch the video about hurricane relief efforts. Then check your comprehension.

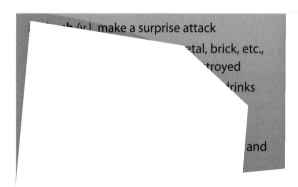

_____ (v.) make a surprise attack

...tal, brick, etc., ...troyed

...rinks

...and

D. Think about the unit video, Listening 1, and Listening 2 as you discuss these questions.

1. Did the two reports change your mind about global citizenship and cooperation, or did they confirm views you already had? In what ways?

2. Can volunteers and businesses do enough to make a difference in global problems, or is it necessary for governments to step in and help more?

3. What kinds of local or national problems would you be willing to volunteer time to?

Vocabulary Skill | Collocations

To increase your fluency and expand your vocabulary, it is important to know about **collocation**, or the way two or more words are commonly combined when written or spoken. Compound words, idioms, lexical phrases, and phrasal verbs, as well as adjective-noun combinations, are examples of collocations.

Collocations are based on common usage and not usually on grammatical rules.

We say . . .	but not . . .
crude oil	rough oil
Fair Trade products	Kind Trade products
climb the corporate ladder	climb the business ladder

Learners' and collocations dictionaries are good tools for finding out which word collocates with another. A thesaurus might lead you in the wrong direction, however, because even though two words are synonyms, they will probably not collocate with the same words.

Synonyms	global	international
Collocations	global warming	international borders

Tip for Success

One way to check for common collocations is to use the Internet to search for a phrase in quotations. For example, "emerging market" gives over two million hits, but "emerging economy" fewer than 200,000.

A. Choose the phrase that has the correct collocation. Check a collocations dictionary if necessary.

1. Agencies like Amnesty International help protect (personal rights / human rights) around the world.

2. We need to write the (final draft / end draft) of our proposal.

3. The (prices rose / prices ascended) when the corporation took over.

4. They carried the coffee (down and up / up and down) the mountain.

5. The (short supply of / little supply of) that commodity affected prices.

6. My favorite charity is one that brings (disaster comfort / disaster relief) to victims of hurricanes.

7. We need to (make some research / **do some research**) on that project before we invest in it.

8. (Startup markets / **Emerging markets**) are those in developing countries where businesses see the possibility for growth and are making new investments.

9. The (**coffee shop** / coffee store) buys most of its coffee from Fair Trade organizations.

10. Businesses that abuse the environment are partly responsible for the problem of (weather change / **climate change**).

B. Work with a partner. Circle the two words or phrases that collocate with the bold word or expression. Check a learners' or collocations dictionary if necessary.

1. **business**   a. run a . . .   b. make a . . .   c. go into . . .

2. **money**   a. make . . .   b. spend . . .   c. afford . . .

3. **costs**   a. get rid of . . . b. run up . . .   c. cover . . .

4. **confidence**   a. grow . . . in   b. have . . . in   c. lose . . . in

5. **responsibility**   a. take . . . for   b. discover   c. have . . . for
                                               . . . for

6. **chief . . . officer** a. financial   b. executive   c. management

C. With your partner, write at least six sentences using collocations from Activity B.

_____

_____

_____

_____

_____

_____

 D. Go online for more practice with collocations.

At the end of this unit, you are going to report on a global problem. In order to report on the problem, you will need to cite sources and use reported speech.

Grammar   Reported speech

In **reported speech** (or indirect speech), you restate what someone else has said or written. It is often used to incorporate information from another source into a presentation. In reported speech, it is important to keep the same meaning as the original source, although it is not necessary to use the exact words.

Reported speech . . .	Examples

requires a backshift in verb tense when talking about things said in and about the past.
 	
  simple present → simple past
  present continuous →
    past continuous
  simple past → past perfect
  present perfect → past perfect
  will → would
  can → could
  may → might
	The farmer said, "We <u>need</u> to get a higher price."
	The farmer said that **they needed** to get a higher price.
	
	The board said, "We <u>will invest</u> more in emerging markets in the future."
	The board said **they would invest** more in emerging markets.

keeps the same verb tense if the speaker's words involve a timeless or current situation or event.	He said, "Climate change <u>is</u> a reality." He said (that) climate change **is** a reality.
uses statement word order, even if the original source is a question.	The executive asked, "<u>What's the agenda?</u>" The executive asked **what the agenda was**.
starts with a reporting verb such as *say, tell, ask, add, assert, point out, state, remark, respond,* and *warn;* has an optional *that* for statements.	"The environmental crisis is a global problem." (Barry Commoner) Barry Commoner **asserts (that)** the environmental crisis is a global problem.
may require a change in pronoun from *I/we/you* to clarify the reporter's relationship to what is said.	I told her, "<u>You and I</u> can do more." I told her **she and I** could do more.

uses *if* or *whether* to introduce a *Yes/No* question, or an infinitive to introduce a command.	The UN speaker asked, "<u>Are you</u> ready to make a global commitment? Then <u>do</u> it." The UN speaker asked **whether** they were ready to make a global commitment and told them **to do** it.

A. Work with a partner and take turns. One person reads the quotation, and the other changes it to reported speech. Remember to begin with a reporting verb.

1. The farmer, about growing coffee: "It's a lot of work, and sometimes we can't even cover our costs."

   The farmer stated that growing coffee was a lot of work, and . . .

2. Deborah Amos, to the radio audience: "Do you ever think about the farmers who grew that coffee?"

3. Georg Kell, about the Global Compact: "Initially we started off with a moral core."

4. Ban Ki-Moon, UN Secretary General: "Together we can achieve a new face of globalization."

5. Dan Zwerdling, about the coffee farmers: "These farmers are the poorest and most powerless part of the global coffee trade."

6. Daniel Zwerdling, about Fair Trade: "Still, the Fair Trade network can't raise all the money that farmers need just by cutting out middlemen. Consumers have to help, too."

B. Work in a group. Sit in a circle. Share a fact or ask a question about a global issue. The person to your right will report what you said and then add another fact or question. Continue around the circle until everyone has had a chance to share and report.

> *A: In Cambodia last year, heavy rains caused flooding, and many farmers' crops were destroyed.*
>
> *B: Student A reported that in Cambodia last year, heavy rains had caused flooding and many crops had been destroyed. Do any international organizations help farmers in different countries?*
>
> *C: Student B asked if any international organizations help farmers in different countries. I think the United Nations . . .*

C. Go online for more practice with reported speech.

D. Go online for the grammar expansion.

| Pronunciation | Linking with final consonants |

In order to improve fluency, it is important to connect the final sound of one word or syllable to the initial sound of the next, especially in the same thought group. If you say each sound perfectly, but in isolation, your speech will sound unnatural.

It is important not to drop final consonants, or your speech will be unclear because one word may be confused with another. *Time is money* should *not* sound like *Tie is money*.

Do not link a word that ends with a consonant to one that begins with another consonant by inserting a vowel sound between them. This will cause you to add an extra syllable that will confuse your listener. *The date began with a three* should *not* sound like *The data began with a three*.

Read the principles of linking with final consonants and study the examples in the chart. Then listen to the example sentences.

Principles of linking	Examples
1. Join a final consonant sound to the vowel sound at the beginning of the next word.	They sold items made in Africa thousands of miles away.
2. When the same consonant ends one word and begins the next, do not insert a vowel sound. Hold the consonant longer instead of repeating it.	They want to take control of production.
3. When a word ends in the consonant sounds *t, k, d, p, g,* or *b,* do not release the first sound, but say the second one right away.	They grow some of the best coffee you can drink.

A. Link the final consonants in these phrases. Write ⌣ where the sounds are joined, __ where the same sound is held longer, and) where the final consonant sound is not released. Then listen and repeat to check your work. Practice saying the phrases aloud with a partner.

1. an economist
2. growing coffee
3. special label
4. stuck in poverty
5. can't cover costs

6. basic commodity
7. household expenditure
8. global expansion
9. climate change
10. environmental issues

B. Mark the places where sounds should be linked. Then ask and answer the questions with a partner. Help each other improve linking sounds by listening carefully and pointing out problems.

1. What time is the conference on the global economy?

2. What kind of help does a refugee camp provide?

3. How can countries demonstrate international unity?

4. What are some ways to help earthquake victims?

5. How can companies promise to reduce their environmental impact?

6. What are some nonprofit organizations that collect food donations for the hungry?

7. What are some ways you take care of the people in your community?

8. How might an economist describe fair trade?

 C. Go online for more practice linking with final consonants.

When giving academic presentations, you need to tell the audience where your information comes from. Giving credit to authorities or outside sources will make your presentation more believable and informative. You can show that you have studied background information and up-to-date material.

In speaking, you can cite information by:

- introducing the person who wrote or said something important about your topic.
- telling where and when it was published or said.
- using reported speech to restate the speaker's idea.

When citing a speaker's words from a specific point in the past, related to past activities or ideas, use a reporting verb in the past form (he *stated*, she *explained*, they *claimed*).

When citing written material, a quotation that is closely related in time to the speaker, or a statement of a universally accepted idea, it is common to use either the present perfect form (he *has asserted*) or the citational present (the report *proves*; research *shows*).

Here are some common phrases for citing sources:

According to X, . . .

As X says / explains / reports, . . .

X's article shows . . .

In [year], X proved that . . .

In a survey published in [year], the results showed . . .

At a conference on [date], X explained how . . .

A. Add a different opening for each sentence to introduce the source provided in parentheses. Read your sentences to a partner and compare your choices.

1. _____ Fair Trade is a social movement that has been organized to give power to developing countries. (Wikipedia)

2. _____ the Heifer Foundation has provided an orphanage in Vietnam with an animal farm, so children learn how to raise and care for animals. (Rose Tran Bach Yen, orphanage director, Vietnam)

3. _____ more than 90 percent of CEOs are doing more about environmental, social, and political issues now. (2007, McKinsey survey)

4. _____ "My fellow Americans, people all over the world, we need to solve the climate crisis. It's not a political issue; it's a moral issue." (Al Gore, award acceptance speech, February 2007)

5. _____ colleagues at Doctors Without Borders treated more than 150,000 children suffering from hunger around the world. (Susan Shepherd, pediatrician, *The New York Times*, January 30, 2008)

B. Work with a partner. Read these descriptions of organizations that have made a difference. Take turns asking questions about them and citing the information.

1. Save the Children is the leading independent organization creating lasting change for children in need in the United States and around the world. For more than 75 years, Save the Children has been helping children survive and thrive by improving their health, education and economic opportunities and, in times of acute crisis, mobilizing rapid life-saving assistance to help children recover from the effects of war, conflict and natural disasters. (Save the Children, Causecast.org, http://www.causecast.org)

2. More than 1,400 people, both specialized staff and delegates, are currently on field missions for the [International Federation of Red Cross and Red Crescent Societies] across the globe. This work is backed up by some 11,000 local employees and supported and coordinated by around 800 staff at its Geneva headquarters. (International Federation of Red Cross and Red Crescent Societies, http://www.ifrc.org)

C. Go online for more practice with citing sources.

UNIT OBJECTIVE ▶▶▶▶ In this assignment, you are going to deliver a group presentation on a global problem. As you prepare your presentation, think about the Unit Question, "What does it mean to be a global citizen?" Use information from Listening 1, Listening 2, the unit video, and your work in this unit to support your presentation. Refer to the Self-Assessment checklist on page 112.

CONSIDER THE IDEAS

In a group, discuss this campus flyer that introduces students to ways they can get involved in grassroots campaigns and become better global citizens on their own campus.

Informed Students ▶▶▶ **Global Citizens**

New students! Welcome to this month's edition of *Informed Students* ▶▶▶ **Global Citizens**

You're in college now, and doors are open to the following organizations! Join up and make a difference.

Greenpeace: You've probably seen Greenpeace volunteers and recruiters around campus. They're here to encourage you to sign petitions to protect the whales and other endangered species. If you want to do more, why not sign up to be a volunteer yourself?

Habitat for Humanity: Although spring break is months away, check out a Habitat for Humanity working vacation to an area where hurricane victims get needed homes.

Humanities Out There: No need to go far from home to lend a hand. Underprivileged students nearby need tutors in English and math. Volunteer to help!

Campus Recyclers: Work at the recycling center collecting plastic bottles and paper and helping to raise awareness on campus about the need to recycle. Every little bit helps!

1. Discuss the issues these groups are involved in and the problems they are working to solve. What solutions do they offer?

2. Many grassroots organizations like these try to raise money, write letters to political leaders, or work on small projects that help people in need. What kind of work would you be willing to volunteer to do? How could an organization persuade others to volunteer?

PREPARE AND SPEAK

A. GATHER IDEAS Work in a group. Think about the global problems and solutions discussed in this unit. Choose an issue related to the environment, health, education, energy, poverty, or a similar topic. Complete the chart with your group's ideas.

What is the problem or issue?	
What are some of the causes of the problem?	
What are some of its effects?	
What are some possible solutions?	
What solutions or suggestions can your group offer?	

B. ORGANIZE IDEAS Plan your group presentation.

Tip for Success

To make sure points are not lost in a long discussion, signal importance by using introductory phrases and numbering points. *"Here's how it worked: First, they signed up volunteers. Second, they . . . "*

1. Divide the following parts of your presentation among your group members:

   a. Introduce and explain the problem

   b. Explain possible causes

   c. Discuss effects

   d. Present possible solutions

2. If possible, use information from outside sources in your presentation (you can research outside of class or use information from this unit).

3. Make note cards to remind you of what to cover during the presentation.

4. Practice your presentation. Time yourselves so that you keep to the limit set by your instructor. Give each other feedback on your sections of the presentation, and exchange suggestions for improvement.

C. **SPEAK** Give your presentation to the class. Refer to the Self-Assessment checklist below before you begin.

 Go online for your alternate Unit Assignment.

CHECK AND REFLECT

A. **CHECK** Think about the Unit Assignment as you complete the Self-Assessment checklist.

SELF-ASSESSMENT		
Yes	**No**	
☐	☐	I was able to speak fluently about the topic.
☐	☐	My partner, group, and class understood me.
☐	☐	I used vocabulary and collocations from the unit to express my ideas.
☐	☐	I used reported speech to cite information from others.
☐	☐	I linked final sounds to make my speech more fluent and understandable.
☐	☐	I cited sources appropriately and effectively.

 B. **REFLECT** Go to the Online Discussion Board to discuss these questions.

1. What is something new you learned in this unit?

2. Look back at the Unit Question—What does it mean to be a global citizen? Is your answer different now from when you started this unit? If yes, how is it different? Why?

TRACK YOUR SUCCESS

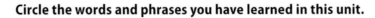

Circle the words and phrases you have learned in this unit.

Nouns
activist 🔑
commodity AWL
co-op
intermediary
processor
speculation

Verbs
afford 🔑
devise

exploit AWL
guarantee 🔑 AWL
transform 🔑 AWL

Adjectives
massive 🔑
proactive

Adverb
roughly 🔑

Phrases
confidence of investors
core strategies
corporate responsibility
emerging economy
ethical goods
household expenditure
intangible assets
labor standards
social impact
sustainable market

🔑 Oxford 3000™ words
AWL Academic Word List

Check (✓) the skills you learned. If you need more work on a skill, refer to the page(s) in parentheses.

NOTE TAKING ■	I can use a T-chart to take notes on problems and solutions. (p. 89)
LISTENING ■	I can listen for facts and figures. (p. 96)
VOCABULARY ■	I can use collocations. (p. 102)
GRAMMAR ■	I can use reported speech. (pp. 104–105)
PRONUNCIATION ■	I can understand and use linking with final consonants. (p. 106)
SPEAKING ■	I can cite sources. (p. 108)
UNIT OBJECTIVE ▶▶▶ ■	I can gather information and ideas to give a group presentation on a global problem.

UNIT **5**

Sociology

NOTE TAKING	▷	organizing notes into a formal outline
LISTENING	▷	recognizing organizational cues
VOCABULARY	▷	words with multiple meanings
GRAMMAR	▷	conditionals
PRONUNCIATION	▷	thought groups
SPEAKING	▷	giving advice

UNIT QUESTION

How do you make a space your own?

A Discuss these questions with your classmates.

1. What places or spaces do you have that you consider "yours"? How do other people know that these spaces belong to you?

2. What are some differences in the way different groups—such as males, females, adults, or children—personalize their space?

3. Look at the photo. How would you personalize this space?

◗ B Listen to *The Q Classroom* online. Then answer these questions.

1. What does Yuna cover her walls with and why?
   Pictures ecologic, friend, love people around me

2. What in Marcus's room drives his mother crazy? Do your parents or roommates have any complaints about the way you define your personal space?
   a lot of book around *Sport, poster, ronning shoes, coleccion balls.* *Sofi...*

iQ ONLINE **C** Go online to watch the video about the architect Frank Gehry. Then check your comprehension.

alter ego *(n.)* a person whose personality is different from your own but who shows or acts as another side of your personality

basket case *(n.)* a person who is slightly crazy and who has trouble dealing with problems

pilgrimage *(n.)* a journey to a place that is connected with someone or something that you admire or respect

rumpled *(adj.)* messy or not smooth and neat

iQ ONLINE **D** Go to the Online Discussion Board to discuss the Unit Question with your classmates.

A
- family
- Enjoyable
- Summer

B
- Estudent
- Organice
- Library

C
- Clean
- Businessman
- Perfectionist

D
- Social media
- marketing
- fields

E Look at the pictures of different kinds of space. What does each space tell you about the person? Share your ideas with a partner.

A

B

C

D

F Work in a group. Think of one of your personal spaces. Take turns describing your space and explaining what it shows about you.

My room is usually a little messy, but it is filled with things I really enjoy. In one corner is a pile of sports equipment: my tennis racket, some balls, a Frisbee, and a baseball glove. I've got a lot of DVDs on the shelves. There's a plant on my windowsill.

One of the most conventional ways to organize information and relationships between points is an outline. The key advantage of any outline is that main ideas and supporting details can be easily identified: main ideas (people, theories, events, etc.) stand out along the left margin, while supporting details and examples are clearly indented beneath them. A formal outline labels the main topics with Roman numerals (I., II.), the major points under each main topic with capital letters (A., B.), examples with regular numbers (1., 2.), and any explanations of the examples with small letters (a., b.).

Notice the differences between an informal and a formal outline:

Informal	Formal
Traditional Psychology	I. Traditional Psychology
Definition	A. Definition
Branches	B. Branches
clinical psychology	1. clinical psychology
developmental psychology	2. developmental psychology
childhood stages	a. stages of childhood

It would be impossible to create a formal outline as you take notes, although you can create a preliminary one based on the main topics you might know about in advance. For example, if your professor was going to lecture on three famous psychologists—Freud, Jung, and Piaget—you could start the rough draft of an outline of their names and leave room for notes under each name:

   I. Freud
  II. Jung
 III. Piaget

Formal outlines are most useful as study guides that you create by organizing your notes after a lecture. Arranging the key points in a logical way helps you understand the relationships between ideas and summarize the main points and explanations. Formal outlines are important tools for writers as they structure essays and for speakers as they make plans for presentations. Many lecturers even provide this graphic organizer on a software presentation slide so listeners can follow along more easily. Remember, however, to pay attention to what the speaker is saying because you may miss important information if you are too busy just copying what you see on the screen.

During a lecture, listen for key words and phrases, such as the ones below, to help you create an outline:

Today I am going to talk about
    two theories, X and Y.
The research on X was done by . . .
Next, we have . . .

Another important theory was . . .
Following in X's footsteps, Y introduced . . .
One of his important ideas was that . . .

A. You are going to listen to a short talk on personal space. Before you listen, read the notes below. Then listen to the lecture and organize the notes into a formal outline.

RFID tags	RFID readers give information on
Edward Hall—anthropologist	shopping habits
burglars robbing you while you're away	police tracking a potential criminal
personal space bubble equals 2.5 to	technology and personal space
4 feet	parents knowing where children are
proxemics—the study of personal space	from phones
GPS devices	entering personal space = an invasion
information on price and manufacturer	

I.

   A.

   B.

      1.

II.

   A.

      1.

      2.

   B.

      1.

      2.

      3.

 **Tip for Success**

Remember to review your notes soon after class, share them with a classmate, and use them as study guides.

 B. Go online for more practice organizing notes into a formal outline.

LISTENING 1 | Environmental Psychology

 UNIT OBJECTIVE You are going to listen to an excerpt from a lecture by Dr. Traci Craig, a psychology professor at the University of Idaho. It will introduce you to the field of environmental psychology. As you listen to the lecture, gather information and ideas about how you make a space your own.

PREVIEW THE LISTENING

A. **PREVIEW** *Behavioral psychology* is the study of how humans react to stimuli from outside and within themselves. *Educational psychology* is the study of how humans learn. Look at the pictures below. What do you think *environmental psychology* is? Write a short definition.

_____

_____

_____

Tip for Success

Learning the special vocabulary of academic fields will help you understand discussions and lectures and make you more comfortable communicating at school. Keep lists of vocabulary you learn in different subjects.

B. **VOCABULARY** Read aloud these words from Listening 1. Check (✓) the ones you know. Use a dictionary to define any new or unknown words. Then discuss with a partner how the words will relate to the unit.

adjacent *(adj.)* adyacente	gender *(n.)* genero	radius *(n.)* radio
affiliate with *(phr. v.)* afiliadoa	ingrained in *(phr.)* arraigado	refrain from *(phr. v.)* abstenerse de
belongings *(n.)* pertenencias	invade *(v.)* invadir	remarkable *(adj.)* 🔑 notable
engage in *(phr. v.)* 🔑 participar en	moderately *(adv.)* moderadamente	suburban *(adj.)* suburbano

🔑 Oxford 3000™ words

 iQ ONLINE **C.** Go online to listen and practice your pronunciation.

WORK WITH THE LISTENING

A. **LISTEN AND TAKE NOTES** Listen to the lecture. Take notes to complete the ideas in the formal outline.

Critical Thinking (Tip)

In Activity A, you will complete an outline. **Outlining** is one way of breaking down information into its component parts.

I. Environmental psychology *inter*

A. Definition: *area realions invaornent with human behavior*

B. Areas the lecture will focus on:

1. *eye ontact / gender*

2. *Caracteristic behav*

3. *need for privacy*

II. Male and female _____*espace*_____ behavior

A. Feelings of invasion

1. Face-to-face invasion (males)

2. *adjacent* invasion (females) *??*

B. Placement of belongings

1. The _____*Jacket*_____ study

2. Placement of *desks, offices space*

C. Exploring territories on bikes

1. Smaller territories for girls

2. Larger territories for boys

D. Touching _____*plates*_____ in _____*the rest*_____

III. Eye contact: Post office experiment

A. _____*less*_____ likely to make eye contact in a _____*city / philadelphia*_____

B. _____*most*_____ likely to make eye contact in a *Parksford / small twoun rural area*

120   UNIT 5 | How do you make a space your own?

IV. Visual intrusion and privacy—stressful places

    A. Visual intrusion—to see and be seen

        1. Restaurants   *does not decrese*

        2. __*Officess*__

    B. Privacy—dorm rooms

B. Use your notes from the outline in Activity A to write answers to these questions.

1. What is environmental psychology?

_____

2. In what ways does Dr. Craig believe males and females are similar or different in their territorial behavior?

_____

3. According to Dr. Craig, what is the connection between eye contact and personal space?

_____

4. What effects can a feeling of lack of privacy have on an individual?

_____

C. Read the statements. Then listen again. Write *T* (true) or *F* (false). Correct the false statements.

_F_ **1.** Males are more offended by someone sitting adjacent to them than someone sitting across from them.

_____

_T_ **2.** The statement "Females are expected to affiliate" means females feel they have to make contact with someone they sit next to.

_____

_T_ **3.** In a large lecture class, the majority of students sit in the same seat all semester.

_____

___F___ **4.** Visitors to a male's office will touch his belongings displayed on the desk more freely than they would if the office belonged to a female.

_____

___T___ **5.** In the jacket study, people tended to move a jacket that clearly belonged to a female, but refrained from moving one that belonged to a male.

_____

___F___ **6.** Territorial behavior does not begin until we are teenagers. ?

_____

___F___ **7.** Even at a young age, females explore larger territories than males.

_____

___T___ **8.** Touching your plate in a restaurant is a sign of marking the plate as your own.

_____

___F___ **9.** It is more acceptable and expected for people to make eye contact in a post office in a large city than in a small town.

_____

D. Match the points in Column A with the examples in Column B.

A	**B**
____ **1.** a built environment	**a.** making less eye contact
____ **2.** an ingrained behavior	**b.** a school
____ **3.** a way to maintain a sense of privacy	**c.** refraining from touching a plate in a restaurant
____ **4.** an invasion of personal space	**d.** sitting next to someone
____ **5.** a non-territorial behavior	**e.** preventing face-to-face invasion

E. Use your notes from Activity A to summarize one of the experiments Dr. Craig used to support her ideas.

_____

_____

_____

_____

_____

F. **VOCABULARY** Here are some words and phrases from Listening 1. Read the sentences. Circle the answer that best matches the meaning of each bold word or phrase.

1. **Gender** differences between boys and girls can be seen at an early age.
   a. classification by age
   b. classification by whether you are male or female
   c. classification by name

2. To work with your partner on this dialog, sit in chairs that are face-to-face or in ones that are **adjacent** so you can communicate easily.
   a. next to each other
   b. away from the door
   c. far from each other

3. People usually **affiliate with** others who are similar to themselves. They like to feel that they belong to a group of like-minded friends.
   a. connect to
   b. are curious about
   c. are afraid of

4. The teachers are going to **engage in** a discussion on social psychology, so I'd like to stay and hear what they have to say.
   a. schedule
   b. take part in
   c. call off

5. He keeps all of his **belongings**, including his books and clothes, in one small cabinet in his dorm room.
   a. things you want
   b. things you don't want
   c. things you own

6. It's **remarkable** how often people will choose to sit at the same table in a restaurant, even when better tables are available.
   a. very interesting
   b. very difficult to believe
   c. very uncomfortable

7. Territorial behavior, or wanting to protect a personal space, is **ingrained in** us, and it is hard to change our attitude.
   a. all around
   b. unfamiliar to
   c. deeply a part of

8. When my little sister **invades** my room, she throws her toys all over my bed.
   a. forgets about; ignores
   b. protects; takes good care of
   c. marches into; enters by force

9. Most pizza places only deliver within a three-mile **radius**.
   a. circular area
   b. city center
   c. diameter

10. Please **refrain from** using your cell phone in class because it distracts other students.
    a. think about
    b. continue
    c. avoid

11. They prefer to commute to work in the city every day but live in a **suburban** area, because life is less stressful there.
    a. in a city
    b. near a city
    c. very far from a city

12. Although visitors are not likely to enter a house without knocking, they are **moderately** likely to stop by for a visit without being invited. It happens sometimes.
    a. always
    b. a little
    c. very

 G. Go online for more practice with the vocabulary.

H. Go online to listen to *Maps and Privacy* and check your comprehension.

SAY WHAT YOU THINK

Discuss the questions in a group.

1. Look back at Activity C on pages 121–122. How do the details that you marked as true fit your own actions or your observations of others? Do you always choose to sit in the same chair in class, for example?

2. Has Dr. Craig convinced you that males and females have very different reactions to personal space? Why or why not?

3. In what ways do you think the rules for respecting personal space and personalizing territories vary in different countries and cultures?

Listening Skill | Recognizing organizational cues

Organizational cues are words or phrases a speaker uses to signal the type of information that follows. Recognizing organizational cues can help you predict what speakers will say next.

Organizational cues	What they signal	Examples
most importantly, in fact, actually, what we will focus on here is, I want to stress	importance, emphasis	*What we will focus on here is a definition of territoriality.*
for example, such as, for instance, specifically, in particular, that is	examples, illustrations	*There are many ways to invade someone's space. For example, if you . . .*
furthermore, in addition, moreover, besides, additionally, also	additional support or evidence	*Women try to talk to those sitting next to them. In addition, they feel they have to affiliate with them.*
now let's turn to, moving on, let's now look at, related to that	shifting topics	*Now let's turn to the statistical evidence.*
in short, to sum up, in conclusion, we've seen that, in the end	conclusions	*In short, gender affects our sense of space.*

A. Listen to this excerpt from Listening 1 and write down the six organizational cues that you hear. Then work with a partner and discuss the reasons the lecturer used them in each case.

1. _____

2. _____

3. _____

4. _____

5. _____

6. _____

B. Listen to the beginnings of these sentences and circle the correct ending for each, based on the organizational cues that you hear.

1. a   students who take the time to put up pictures feel more at home.
   b. their attendance in class is better and their grades are higher.

2. a. we found some posts by teenagers about how they got out of doing some school assignments.
   b. we found some detailed résumés of businessmen.

3. a. women don't usually consider their cars as a personal space to spend time on.
   b. it is believed that most men would rather watch football on their day off than go out to eat.

4. a. our car is just one piece of evidence of who we are.
   b. a car is enough information on which to base an opinion of a person.

5. a. eye contact does not appear to be a gender-related issue.
   b. men usually put a jacket on a seat in front of them rather than next to them.

6. a. staring at people makes them feel uncomfortable and is considered inappropriate.
   b. psychologists use all of this information to help people understand why they behave the way they do

iQ ONLINE   **C.** Go online for more practice recognizing organizational clues.

UNIT OBJECTIVE ▶▶▶ You are going to listen to part of a radio interview and call-in show from NPR's *Talk of the Nation*.[1] On the show, Dr. Sam Gosling, a psychology professor, discusses his book, *Snoop: What Your Stuff Says About You*. As you listen to the interview, gather information and ideas about how you make a space your own.

[1] "What Your Stuff Says About You" originally broadcast on NPR's *Talk of the Nation*® on May 26, 2008. Used with the permission of NPR®.

PREVIEW THE LISTENING

A. **PREVIEW** Dr. Gosling says that he looks for information about people in many places—and that he uses the word *places* very broadly, to refer not only to physical areas. Talk with a partner. What kinds of places or things do you think Dr. Gosling might be interested in?

B. **VOCABULARY** Read aloud these words from Listening 2. Check (✓) the ones you know. Use a dictionary to define any new or unknown words. Then discuss with a partner how the words will relate to the unit.

clarify *(v.)*	domain *(n.)*	introvert *(n.)*	propose *(v.)* 🔑
clue *(n.)*	extrovert *(n.)*	modify *(v.)*	tentatively *(adv.)*
crucial *(adj.)* 🔑	framework *(n.)*	profile *(n.)* 🔑	trait *(n.)*

🔑 Oxford 3000™ words

iQ ONLINE **C.** Go online to listen and practice your pronunciation.

WORK WITH THE LISTENING

🔊 **A.** **LISTEN AND TAKE NOTES** Listen to the interview. Take notes in this graphic organizer.

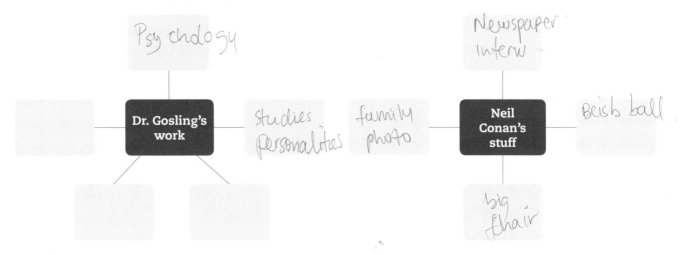

(handwritten notes on diagram)
familiar photos · personal items and what they reveal
Sentimental meaning · introvertido · using clues to build a picture · apretar manos · face people · Extrovertido

B. Turn your notes into a formal outline. Compare your outline with a partner.

C. Listen again. Complete these statements.

1. Two personal objects the host, Neal Conan, has on the wall in his office are

   _____.

2. In addition to the actual objects people display, Dr. Gosling says it is

   important to notice _____.

3. The objects Dr. Gosling indicates as revealing the most about people are

   _____.

4. One example of a virtual environment would be

   _____.

5. The two personality types the psychologist often refers to are

   _____.

6. The experiment mentioned in the interview that affected people's

   impressions of others involved _____.

7. When we are asked, "What does this stuff say about someone?"
   Dr. Gosling believes that the mistake we make is that we might

   _____.

8. In the end, Dr. Gosling decides that the adjective he would use to describe

   the host, Neal Conan, is _____

D. Answer the questions. Compare your ideas with a partner.

1. What are some places Dr. Gosling snoops around and why do they reveal so much about people?

2. Does Dr. Gosling believe that people are always correct in the conclusions they come to about the possessions and actions of others? Why or why not?

3. How does psychology play a role in figuring out "what your stuff says about you"?

E. Choose the correct phrase to complete the sentence.

1. Neil Conan has an (autographed Giants / unsigned) baseball on his desk.

2. A family photo turned (away from / toward) the owner of a desk shows a desire to impress others.

3. Dr. Gosling believes (we are all / most of us are) natural-born snoops.

4. Dr. Gosling is an associate professor of psychology and a (detective / writer).

5. Listeners to this program can ask questions by (calling in and going on Facebook / blogging and emailing).

Vocabulary Skill Review

In Unit 4 you learned about collocations. Find the words that collocate with *personality, human, eye, personal,* and *get* in these paragraphs.

F. VOCABULARY Here are some words from Listening 2. Read the paragraphs. Then write each bold word next to the correct definition.

Each of our actions and all of the spaces within our **domain** say something about us, whether we make those statements on purpose or not. Our personality **traits** are revealed by the ways we behave and the things we use to define our spaces. Anyone who spends time with us usually can walk away with a **profile** of us based on the things we own and the way we act with others. Although this information may provide **clues** to help others judge our personalities, it can also mislead them if one action or object makes them jump to the wrong conclusion. Then they have to **modify** their perception and try again to figure us out.

Two traits of the human personality that psychologists use as a **framework** to study human behavior are *introversion* and *extroversion*. Through observations and experiments, they try to **clarify** the differences between groups with these traits. An **introvert** generally prefers not to make eye contact and prefers to be alone, while an **extrovert** seeks opportunities to invite people in and start up a conversation. An introvert does not want to make eye contact because he wants to maintain his own personal space. He enters a room **tentatively** and might stand in the corner observing others before talking to them. Privacy is **crucial** to him. In contrast, an extrovert invites people to learn more about her; she may quickly **propose** getting together for some kind of activity even if she has just met someone.

1. _____ (v.) to change slightly

2. _____ (v.) to suggest a plan or an action

3. _____ (n.) a quiet person not interested in spending time with others

4. _____ (n.) pieces of information that help solve a puzzle

5. _____ (v.) to make something clear and easy to understand

6. _____ (n.) a description of somebody or something that gives useful information

7. _____ (adv.) without confidence or certainty

8. _____ (n.) qualities of a person's character

9. _____ (n.) a lively, confident person who enjoys being with others

10. _____ (n.) an area owned, controlled, or ruled by a person or government

11. _____ (adj.) extremely important

12. _____ (n.) a system of ideas or rules

 G. Go online for more practice with the vocabulary.

 ## SAY WHAT YOU THINK

A. Discuss the questions in a group.

1. Do you agree with Dr. Gosling that we are all natural-born snoops? Why or why not? Use examples from your own life to support your opinion.

2. Look around your classroom. What conclusions might Dr. Gosling draw from what he could see there?

B. Think about the unit video, Listening 1, and Listening 2 as you discuss these questions.

1. What different answers might Dr. Gosling and Dr. Craig have to this question that was sent in to *Talk of the Nation*: "What would you say about people who do not include personal items in their offices or cars?"

2. What do you think Dr. Gosling would have to say about Gehry's buildings?

3. In what fields might the findings of psychologists about personal space, privacy, possessions, and personalities be of interest?

Vocabulary Skill | Words with multiple meanings

Many words in English have more than one meaning, so you cannot assume that the one definition you know will fit every situation. For example, the following definitions can be found in the dictionary for the word *chair*.

chair /tʃɛr/ noun, verb
* **noun** **1** [C] a piece of furniture for one person to sit on, with a back, a seat, and four legs: *a table and chairs* • *Sit on your chair!* • *an old man asleep in a chair* (= an ARMCHAIR) ➲ picture on page 235 ➲ see also ARMCHAIR, DECK CHAIR, EASY CHAIR, HIGH CHAIR, MUSICAL CHAIRS, ROCKING CHAIR, WHEELCHAIR **2** [C] = CHAIRMAN, CHAIRPERSON **3** [C] the person in charge of a department in a university: *He is the chair of philosophy at Stanford.* **4** **the chair** [sing.] (*informal*) = THE ELECTRIC CHAIR
* **verb** ~ **sth** to act as the chairman or chairwoman of a meeting, discussion, etc.: *Who's chairing the meeting?*

The dictionary can help you choose the correct definition if you:
1. check the part of speech to eliminate any definitions that do not fit the grammar of the sentence.
2. check the first definition, which is usually the most common definition.
3. look at the sample sentences to determine which best fits the context.

The third step would confirm that the best definition of *chair* in the sentence "She is the chair of the psychology department" is the third definition listed, "the person in charge of a department in a university."

All dictionary entries are from the *Oxford Advanced American Dictionary for learners of English* © Oxford University Press 2011.

A. Read the sentences and write the letter of the correct definition of the underlined words. Use the context and a dictionary to help you. You will not use all of the definitions.

____ 1. They didn't understand that the jacket was a <u>marker</u> to save a seat.

____ 2. She bought a <u>marker</u> to write her name in her books.

a. (*n.*) a type of pen that draws thick lines

b. (*n.*) an object or sign that shows the position of something

c. (*n.*) a sign that something exists or that shows what it is like

____ 3. In the video game <u>Space</u> Invasion, players engage in wars between the planets.

_____ 4. We try to respect the desk, office <u>space</u>, and seating arrangements.

_____ 5. Can you <u>space</u> the chairs so that they don't touch one another?

    d. *(n.)* an area or room

    e. *(n.)* an unused or empty area

    f. *(n.)* the universe beyond Earth's atmosphere

    g. *(n.)* a period of time

    h. *(v.)* to arrange things with areas or gaps between

_____ 6. Did you <u>mean</u> to leave your jacket on my desk?

_____ 7. The <u>mean</u> number of students who take that psychology class each year is 75.

_____ 8. Radius can <u>mean</u> one-half of a diameter or an area surrounding a point.

    i. *(v.)* to intend to say or do something

    j. *(v.)* to have something as a meaning

    k. *(adj.)* average

    l. *(adj.)* (of people or their behavior) unkind

_____ 9. She couldn't <u>refrain</u> from trying to make eye contact with him.

_____ 10. The teacher said the same <u>refrain</u> again and again: "Keep your eyes to yourself."

    m. *(n.)* a part of a poem or chant that is repeated

    n. *(n.)* a comment or complaint that is often repeated

    o. *(v.)* to stop yourself from doing something

B. Use your dictionary to look up the definitions for one of these words. Copy three definitions and label them *a*, *b*, and *c*. Then write three sentences that reflect the different definitions for each of your words, as in Activity A.

contact	place	stress	stuff	type

Word: _____

Definitions:

a. _____

b. _____

c. _____

Sentences:

a. _____

_____

b. _____

_____

c. _____

_____

C. Take turns reading one of your sentences from Activity B to a partner. See if your partner can choose the correct definition of the word for that sentence.

 D. Go online for more practice with words with multiple meanings.

At the end of this unit, you are going to role-play a talk show focused on conflicts of personal space. In order to role-play the discussion, you will need to be able to give advice.

Grammar | Conditionals

The verbs in conditional sentences show:

- the time frame (present, present/future, or past).
- whether the conditions are real (true) or unreal (not true; imaginary).

Present/future real conditionals: There is a real possibility the condition will happen, or it can, should, or might happen.

If clause = present tense form
Result = *will, can, might, should* + base verb

> If he **wants** to make friends, he **should join** a club.
> He **will not enjoy** large events if he **is** an introvert.

Present/future unreal conditionals: The condition is not true now, so the results are not true either.

If clause = past tense form
Result = *would, might* + base verb

> If she **wanted** to reveal more about her personality, she **would display** photos.
> He **might sit** at the front of the classroom if he **weren't** so shy.

Past unreal conditionals: The condition was not true before; the result in the past or the present is not true either.

If clause = past perfect form
Result = *would, could, might* + base verb (present results)
      would have, could have, might have + past participle (past results)

> If they **had asked** everyone about painting the room, no one **would be** angry now.
> If everyone **had contributed** some money, we **could have redecorated**.

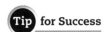 **Tip** for Success

In present unreal conditionals, the form *were* is used instead of *was* for all speakers: *If I **were** rich, I'd give more money to charity.* However, in informal situations, you may hear people use *was*.

A. Read the conditional sentence. Then circle the correct conclusion that you can draw.

1. If I'd seen him, I would've said "hello."
   a. I saw the man.
   b. I didn't say "hello."

2. She will probably be standing in a crowd of friends if she is an extrovert.
   a. She isn't standing in a crowd of friends now.
   b. She may be an extrovert, but I'm not sure.

3. If privacy had been so important to her, she wouldn't have left the door open.
   a. Privacy was important to her.
   b. She left the door open.

4. Shouldn't you label your stuff if you want us to know it's yours?
   a. We know it's your stuff.
   b. Your stuff is not labeled.

5. If he weren't so afraid of making new friends, he'd hang out in the library more.
   a. He doesn't hang out in the library much now.
   b. He isn't afraid of making new friends.

6. I would be sitting on that chair if he hadn't left his coat on it.
   a. I am sitting on the chair.
   b. He left his coat on the chair.

B. Complete the sentences. Then compare them with a partner. Check each other's verb forms.

1. If I had known you were an extrovert, _____.

2. If I could redecorate my room, _____.

3. If I am going into a new classroom for the first time, _____.

4. If I didn't want to share my space, _____.

5. _____ he might lock the door.

6. _____ I would get a roommate.

7. _____ I wouldn't have gone home early.

8. _____ I would have been angry.

C. Go online for more practice with conditionals.

D. Go online for the grammar expansion.

Thought groups are meaningful phrases (groups of words) or clauses (sentence parts that have a subject and a verb) that express an idea. Just as writers use punctuation to separate sentence elements, speakers use intonation and pauses to help listeners process what they are hearing.

If listeners make the wrong connections between your words, this can lead to an error in understanding.

For example, read and listen to these two sentences. Notice how the different thought groups (indicated with slashes /) change the meaning.

The psychologist / said the lecturer / tries to understand social behavior.
"The psychologist," said the lecturer, "tries to understand social behavior."

The psychologist said / the lecturer / tries to understand social behavior.
The psychologist said, "The lecturer tries to understand social behavior."

To make effective thought groups, remember to:

- divide sentences into meaningful units (don't separate an adjective and a noun, for example).
- put the most stress on the final key word in each thought group.
- end a thought group with a slight fall or a fall-rise in intonation.
- pause slightly at the end of each thought group.
- not drop your pitch too low until the end of a sentence.

A. Listen to this excerpt from Listening 2. Mark the thought groups you hear by drawing lines between them. Compare your work with a partner. The first sentence is done for you.

Dr. Gosling: That's right / because it's really important / you know / if I had one wish / one wish in the world / it would be that one clue / told you something / about a person. If you had a stuffed teddy on your bed it meant something you know. But the world is more complicated than that. So unfortunately it doesn't work like that because there are many reasons why we might have say a stuffed animal on our bed or something like that. And so really you can't use a codebook approach where *x* means *y*. What you have to do is you have to build up a picture piece by piece and sometimes you only have a very little piece and you have to hold your view very tentatively. But that will that will guide your search for more information.

Tip for Success

As you become a more proficient speaker, try to make your thought groups longer so your speaking is less choppy and more fluent.

B. With your partner, take turns reading one of the following sentences in each set. See if your partner can identify which sentence, *a* or *b*, you are reading.

1. a. So if we really wanted to understand kids, that's the question we would ask.

    b. So, if we really wanted to understand, kids, that's the question we would ask.

2. a. "The lecturer," said the students, "couldn't explain environmental psychology very well."

    b. The lecturer said, "The students couldn't explain environmental psychology very well."

3. a. This is a way of maintaining space. In a rural area, you often feel you have enough space.

    b. This is a way of maintaining space in a rural area. You often feel you have enough space.

4. a. "The psychologist," claims my sister, "is an extrovert," but I don't believe it.

    b. The psychologist claims my sister is an extrovert, but I don't believe it.

iQ ONLINE   **C.** Go online for more practice with thought groups.

Speaking Skill Giving advice

Knowing how to make suggestions and give advice without sounding pushy or demanding is an important conversational skill.

In each column in the chart, the expressions are listed from the weakest to the strongest forms of advice.

Advice with modals in the present/future	Advice with modals in the past	Advice using *if*	Other expressions
You might want to . . .	You could have . . .	If I were you, I would . . .	Why don't you . . . ?
You can/could . . .	You might have . . .	(Notice that we use *if I were you* to show that the speaker is not really that person.)	Have you thought about . . . ?
You should . . .			Whatever you do, don't . . . !
You ought to . . .	You should have . . .		
You had better (You'd better) . . .	You had to . . .		Whatever you do, make sure to . . . !
You must (not) . . .			

 **Tip** for Success

Suggest and *recommend* are followed by *that* + the person you are giving advice to + a base verb: *I suggested that he move in. She recommended that he talk more.*

A. **Work in a group. Take turns reading the problems below and giving advice to the speaker according to the situation. Share and discuss your sentences in a group.**

> *A: My brother thinks I'm a slob because I don't wash or clean my car.*
> *B: I think you should clean it if you want to change his attitude.*
> *C: Yeah, if I were you, I'd clean it. Otherwise he won't want to go anywhere with you.*
> *D: Why don't you ask a couple of friends to help you clean it?*

1. People make fun of me for wearing crazy clothes.

2. My room is so full of stuff I can't get any work done.

3. Our neighbors are going to build a tall fence around their property.

4. I'd like to ask my instructor for help, but I feel too shy.

5. I sat next to someone on the subway this morning, and he gave me a terrible look.

6. My roommate is always using my computer.

B. **Work with a partner. Role-play a conversation with a friend who is moving into an empty office space for his or her first job. Take turns asking for and giving advice on ways to personalize the space and mark it as his or her own.**

 C. Go online for more practice giving advice.

 Oral presentation 11/29

In this assignment, you are going to role-play a talk show on conflicts about personal space. As you prepare your role-play, think about the Unit Question, "How do you make a space your own?" Use information from Listening 1, Listening 2, the unit video, and your work in this unit to support your role-play. Refer to the Self-Assessment checklist on page 140.

CONSIDER THE IDEAS

🔊 Listen to this excerpt from a radio call-in show, in which a psychologist helps two college roommates who need advice about sharing a space. Discuss the questions below in a group.

1. What is the main issue that is causing the problem between the roommates? What kind of advice do you think Dr. Hill will offer?

2. Talk about a time when your own feelings about personal space caused you to come into conflict with someone else. What happened? How did you resolve the conflict? What did you learn from it?

PREPARE AND SPEAK

A. **GATHER IDEAS** In a group, talk about the kinds of conflicts that can develop when people live together. Brainstorm different types of relationships, the conflicts that might come up between people regarding personal space, and solutions. Write your ideas in the chart.

_10 %_

Relationship	Conflict	Advice / Solution
① Grandauther's friend and Granparents	- the friend can't stay late in the house	manage the time.
② Sisters in the same room	- old sister study until midnight with light on.	- Buy a small lamp
③ Couple	- Go out with friend from work	- Going out with friends and girlfriend together / respect the time

Dan and Jason
middle school
Jason's people on la room
no puede usar
Dan:hasta q' de to. q' estudia
- Radio : noice
- puedes estudiar o unirte

B. **ORGANIZE IDEAS** In pairs or groups of three, write a script for a role-play of a talk show, using one of the conflicts you came up with in Activity A. One or two of you will play the role(s) of someone with a problem related to space. One of you will be the expert who offers advice and solutions. Follow these steps.

1. Introduce yourselves and describe your situation and relationship.

2. Explain the problem or conflict over personal space.

3. Offer solutions and advice, both real and imaginary.

4. Give your reactions to the advice.

30%
Script example
guion ¿

 **Tip for Success**

In order to avoid monotone intonation or flat speaking, make sure to show enthusiasm and interest by stressing key words so they stand out.

C. **SPEAK** Practice your role-play in your group, and then present it to the class. Ask the class if they can think of any other solutions to the problem you presented. Refer to the Self-Assessment checklist below before you begin.

iQ ONLINE Go online for your alternate Unit Assignment.

CHECK AND REFLECT

A. **CHECK** Think about the Unit Assignment as you complete the Self-Assessment checklist.

		SELF-ASSESSMENT
Yes	No	
☐	☐	I was able to speak fluently about the topic.
☐	☐	My partner, group, and class understood me.
☐	☐	I used conditionals correctly.
☐	☐	I used vocabulary from the unit to express my ideas.
☐	☐	I phrased my sentences in thought groups to help my speech sound more natural.
☐	☐	I was able to give advice.

 iQ ONLINE **B.** **REFLECT** Go to the Online Discussion Board to discuss these questions.

10% -

1. What is something new you learned in this unit?

2. Look back at the Unit Question—How do you make a space your own? Is your answer different now than when you started this unit? If yes, how is it different? Why?

después de la presentación

TRACK YOUR SUCCESS

Circle the words and phrases you have learned in this unit.

Nouns
belongings
clue
domain AWL
extrovert
framework AWL
gender AWL
introvert
profile 🔑
radius
trait

Verbs
clarify AWL
invade
modify AWL
propose 🔑

Adjectives
adjacent AWL
crucial 🔑 AWL
remarkable 🔑
suburban

Adverbs
moderately
tentatively

Phrases
ingrained in

Phrasal Verbs
affiliate with
engage in 🔑
refrain from

🔑 Oxford 3000™ words
AWL Academic Word List

Check (✓) the skills you learned. If you need more work on a skill, refer to the page(s) in parentheses.

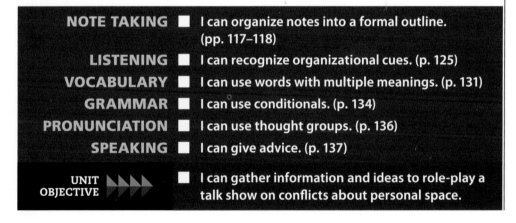

NOTE TAKING ■	I can organize notes into a formal outline. (pp. 117–118)
LISTENING ■	I can recognize organizational cues. (p. 125)
VOCABULARY ■	I can use words with multiple meanings. (p. 131)
GRAMMAR ■	I can use conditionals. (p. 134)
PRONUNCIATION ■	I can use thought groups. (p. 136)
SPEAKING ■	I can give advice. (p. 137)
UNIT OBJECTIVE ▶▶▶▶ ■	I can gather information and ideas to role-play a talk show on conflicts about personal space.

UNIT QUESTION

Where do new ideas come from?

A Discuss these questions with your classmates.

1. How do you come up with new ideas or solve problems? Where do you look for inspiration?

2. What do you think have been some of the best inventions in the past ten years?

3. Look at the photo. What are some different ways of coming up with an idea?

B Listen to *The Q Classroom* online. Then answer these questions.

1. What does Marcus do when he gets stuck while working on a problem?

2. Why does Felix think talking to other people is a good way to solve a problem? Do you agree?

 C Go to the Online Discussion Board to discuss the Unit Question with your classmates.

D Complete the survey. Then share and explain your responses in a group. Give specific examples where you can. Discuss what your answers show about your personality.

When you . . ., . . . what do you do?

1. want to decide what book to read
   ☐ read the newspaper or a magazine
   ☐ talk to friends
   ☐ read online reviews

2. are sick
   ☐ use traditional or folk remedies
   ☐ rely on mainstream medicine
   ☐ try a new-age or alternative therapy

3. prepare a meal for friends
   ☐ make a favorite family dish
   ☐ try a new recipe from a magazine
   ☐ check the refrigerator and use what's there

4. imagine where you'll live in the future
   ☐ imagine a house like where you grew up
   ☐ imagine a home like one you have visited or seen on TV
   ☐ imagine a futuristic home

5. need a new cell phone
   ☐ get a similar model to the one you have
   ☐ carefully research new phones and their features
   ☐ buy a popular model or one your friends recommend

6. fail at a task
   ☐ give up on the task and do something else instead
   ☐ ask someone for help
   ☐ rethink your plan and start over

7. are faced with a problem
   ☐ use a solution that worked in the past
   ☐ think up a new solution
   ☐ brainstorm several possible solutions

E A fad is an activity, game, style, or idea that becomes popular very quickly but usually lasts for just a short period of time. In a group, discuss fads you know of. Discuss why some fads come back years later and remain a part of our culture while others don't.

LISTENING 1 | Alternative Ideas in Medicine

UNIT
OBJECTIVE

You are going to listen to two reports: "Doc-in-a-Box?" from WorldVision.org and "Bee Sting Therapy" from North Carolina Public Radio. They present innovative ideas to solve health problems. As you listen to the reports, gather information and ideas about where new ideas come from.

PREVIEW THE LISTENING

A. **PREVIEW** With a partner, look at the photos. In the chart, list some typical uses of bees and of shipping containers. Then brainstorm some unconventional uses for them. Write down your ideas, and then share them with another pair.

	Conventional uses	Unconventional uses
1. Shipping containers		
2. Bees		

B. **VOCABULARY** Read aloud these words from Listening 1. Check (✓) the ones you know. Use a dictionary to define any new or unknown words. Then discuss with a partner how the words will relate to the unit.

anecdotal evidence *(phr.)*	convert *(v.)* 🔑	periodically *(adv.)*	reluctant *(adj.)*
compound *(n.)*	convince *(v.)* 🔑	protocol *(n.)*	shortage *(n.)*
container *(n.)* 🔑	deny *(v.)* 🔑	prototype *(n.)*	verify *(v.)*

🔑 Oxford 3000™ words

 C. Go online to listen and practice your pronunciation.

WORK WITH THE LISTENING

🔊 **A.** LISTEN AND TAKE NOTES Listen to the reports. Use the chart to take notes. Then compare notes with a partner and add any missing information.

	Report 1: Doc-in-a-Box	Report 2: Bee Sting Therapy
1. Meaning of the term and how it came to be used		
2. Problem the idea is trying to solve		
3. Two steps in the process		
4. Analysis of the solution: Benefits		
5. Analysis of the solution: Obstacles		

B. Ask and answer the questions in pairs. Use your notes from Activity A to help you.

Report 1: Doc-in-a-Box?

1. What is the meaning of *Doc-in-a-Box*?

2. What is the next step in the process of making this type of portable medicine a reality?

3. What problem is the Doc-in-a-Box program trying to solve? How is the program trying to solve it?

Report 2: Bee Sting Therapy

4. What is apitherapy and why does it work?

5. Why are the speakers so enthusiastic about this type of therapy?

6. What is one step that might make bee sting therapy more widely acceptable?

Both Reports:

7. What are the main obstacles faced by those who try to present alternative ideas in medicine to the medical community?

C. Read the statements. Then listen again. Write *T* (true) or *F* (false). Correct the false statements.

Report 1

____ 1. Laurie Garrett, founder of the Doc-in-a-Box idea, works for the Ministry of Health.

_____

____ 2. Doc-in-a-Box medical centers could only offer medical care to poor people in cities near ports where ships could unload the containers.

_____

____ 3. Ministries of Health or non-governmental agencies would operate the Doc-in-a-Box clinics.

_____

____ 4. Garrett hopes that the Doc-in-a-Box clinics will mostly be staffed by doctors and paramedics from famous hospitals around the world.

_____

____ 5. Garrett believes the container price could eventually go down from $5,000 to $1,500.

_____

Report 2

____ 6. Frederique Keller is a nurse and an acupuncturist.

_____

____ 7. It is difficult to travel with the bees.

_____

_____ 8. The idea behind apipuncture is to use the venom of dead bees to treat pain or discomfort.

_____

_____ 9. Andrew Cokin, a pain management doctor, says that the use of bee products already has a strong tradition in Asia and South America.

_____

_____ 10. According to former state legislator Fountain Odom, alternatives such as bee therapy are inexpensive and worth supporting.

_____

D. **Discuss these questions in a group. See if you can reach a consensus for each response.**

1. Which is less expensive to put into action, Doc-in-a-Box or Bee Sting Therapy?

2. Which alternative use of something that already exists is more creative?

3. Which of the two ideas will help the most people?

E. **Write a tweet to WorldVision.org or wunc.org (North Carolina Public Radio) stating your reaction to their interview. (Remember: You only have 140 characters!)**

_____

_____

Vocabulary
Skill Review
_____

In Unit 5, you learned about words that can have more than one meaning, such as *play* (a theater performance or to participate in an athletic activity). Find at least five words with multiple meanings in the sentences in Activity F.

F. **VOCABULARY** **Here are some words and a phrase from Listening 1. Read the sentences. Cross out the word or phrase with a different meaning from the bold word or phrase.**

1. Housing prices have increased because of the **shortage** of wood and other raw materials.
   a. poor quality   b. scarcity   c. lack

2. The appliances were packed in a large **container** for shipping.
   a. box   b. carton   c. house

3. Before you travel to France, you should **convert** your dollars to euros.
   a. change   b. preserve   c. transform

4. The space center built a **prototype** of the spacecraft to test it in a controlled environment.
   a. model   b. diagram   c. example

5. I'm **reluctant** to spend any more money on this failing project.
   a. hesitant   b. excited   c. unwilling

6. Please take a minute to **verify** the correct spelling of your name and address.
   a. confirm   b. check   c. hide

7. After adding two simple elements together, the scientist told us she had discovered a new **compound** that would cure a common cold.
   a. chemical   b. alternative medicine   c. bonded mixture

8. You must follow the proper **protocol** for your experiment to be valid.
   a. procedure   b. set of rules   c. trend

9. My cousin applied for a visa, but unfortunately, he was **denied**.
   a. rejected   b. refused   c. reminded

10. I've heard **anecdotal evidence** that vitamin E helps cuts heal faster, but I've never read any research that supports that.
    a. scientific proof   b. personal reports   c. individual observations

11. It's important to review your investments **periodically**; my advisor recommends that I check every three or four months.
    a. occasionally   b. constantly   c. regularly

12. All of his clever arguments still didn't **convince** me to change my mind.
    a. persuade   b. prevent   c. influence

 G. Go online for more practice with the vocabulary.

 ## SAY WHAT YOU THINK

Discuss these questions in a group.

1. In both of the reports in Listening 1, people have come up with a new use for something that has been around a long time. Can you think of any other inventions or therapies that are examples of the same principles?

2. Would you go to a doctor whose office was in a shipping container? Would you trust a bee to cure your pain? Why or why not?

3. In each of the two reports, do you feel that the narrator is taking a neutral position, or is he or she trying to persuade the listeners to accept or reject the idea? Explain your reasons.

A **fact** is something that is known to be true or that can be proven or disproven. An **opinion** is someone's personal belief. It cannot be proven or disproven. The ability to distinguish between facts and opinions helps you analyze the strength of a speaker's argument. It also allows you to determine if the information provided is reliable. For example, we expect speakers to offer *support* for their opinions through their use of logic, examples, or facts.

Noticing certain words or phrases while you listen can help you identify whether a statement is a fact or an opinion.

Words or phrases identifying facts

- **Verbs that signal information or research:** *show, prove, verify, support, cause*
- **Numbers, statistics, or time periods to introduce facts:** *40 percent of, 15 students, for 200 years, since the early 20th century*
- **Expressions to introduce factual support:** *studies conducted, eyewitness reports, from the evidence, data reveal, studies have shown*

Words or phrases identifying opinions

- **Expressions to signal a belief, perception, or interpretation:** *I think, we believe, it seems, it appears*
- **Modals to signal advice, certainty, or possible solutions:** *should, must, could, might*
- **Adjectives that express judgments:** *best, worst, most important*
- **Adverbs and other words that show uncertainty:** *likely, probably, possibly, maybe, perhaps*

 Listen to these examples from Listening 1.

Facts: Bee venom has been used as a treatment since the time of the Greeks and for at least 2,000, 3,000 years in Chinese medicine.

Opinions: We believe that there are tremendous opportunities for the beekeepers of this state to develop some of the ancient modalities for medical treatment of pain and other uses. These are some alternatives that are very, very inexpensive.

A. Listen to the sentences. Identify them as *F* (fact) or *O* (opinion). Write the word or phrase that helps you decide. Then compare answers with a partner. The first one is done for you.

Sentence	Fact or Opinion?	Words / Phrases
1	O	I think, unreliable
2		
3		
4		
5		
6		
7		
8		
9		
10		

B. Listen to this advertisement for an alternative medicine and complete the sentences with the words and phrases the speakers use. With a partner, talk about whether the ad relies mostly on fact or opinion to convince the audience. Then explain why you would or wouldn't buy the product.

Go-Cream

Speaker: Have you noticed that your legs get tired in the middle of the day?

Do you wish you could keep going when your body wants you to sit down?

Do you have trouble keeping up with other people—or with life in general?

Our _____ product, Go-Cream, is the answer you've been
₁

looking for. It offers the _____ solution for tired legs and
₂

low energy. After just one application of this energizing leg cream, you

_____ convinced. Made from the oils of the Brazil nut and
₃

sand from the beaches of Hawaii, Go-Cream soothes and energizes at the

same time. _____ of people suffer from tired legs, but now
₄

there is relief. Listen to what some of our satisfied customers have to say.

Customer 1: I'm a busy mother of four, and I've been using this product

_____. I've tried vitamins and other alternative therapies,
₅

but nothing worked—until Go-Cream. It's definitely _____
6

product out there and a deal at only $9.99 a jar.

Customer 2: _____ Go-Cream is for people of all ages.
7

My friends and I are students, and we're always on the go. We've all

tried Go-Cream and noticed a big difference in our energy. And it

_____ even helps make your skin smoother and
8

healthier, too.

Speaker: Don't get left behind. Order your Go-Cream today!

 C. Go online for more practice distinguishing between facts and opinions.

Note-taking Skill | Taking notes on process and development

The topics of many lectures, presentations, and reports in the fields of science, engineering, and business focus on the development of a product or project. Understanding the order in which things develop is a critical thinking skill. It requires focusing on *how* an idea turned into a product; the information on *who* and *why* may be secondary. Taking notes on this information can be difficult because you are not going to hear a short step-by-step process; the time between steps may take months or years. The development of an idea will also probably not follow a 1-2-3 order of instructions that will always be the same.

A simple timeline may not work in this situation either, because unlike history, the progression of ideas is not always linear. Rather than specific years, you might hear a progress marker related to where someone was at the time an idea came to mind. Sometimes it is necessary for inventors to go backwards and try something a different way. Other times a long break is needed to raise money or rethink a design, and new experts may take the project in a different direction.

Words and phrases to listen for include those for chronological order and step-by-step processes, such as:

| In 2000, . . . | Between 1999 and 2006, . . . |
| After that, . . . | First, second, next, finally, last |

In addition, you should listen for phrases such as:

Before that, . . .	In the meantime, . . .
While she was working on that idea, . . .	Eventually, . . .
A few years later, . . .	We went back to the drawing board and . . .

A. Listen to this speaker explain how one young man turned something small into something big. Use the first column of the T-chart to take notes on any key steps you hear in the process. Don't worry about putting them in the correct order.

Process development	Time markers

B. Listen again. Add these time markers to the T-chart in Activity A. Write them in the second column next to the corresponding key step in the process.

over a year later (2006)	for a few months	for over a year	in the future
today	in 2005	in his childhood	first
a year before	after a while	a few years later	eventually
two days later			

C. Compare your notes with a partner and rewrite them in the correct order.

 D. Go online for more practice taking notes on process and development.

You are going to listen to a *Colorado Matters* radio interview with Tim Carlin, the executive director of a program called "Freiker." Carlin describes the idea he and his partner came up with to encourage children to ride bikes to school and updates us on how the program has changed since then. As you listen to the interview, gather information and ideas about where new ideas come from.

PREVIEW THE LISTENING

A. **PREVIEW** Check (✓) the ways you think kids could be encouraged to bike to school. Then listen to find out if any of them are mentioned as part of Carlin's plan.

☐ get praised by teachers and parents

☐ get an iPod

☐ get a water bottle

☐ get a certificate from the school

☐ get stickers

☐ get extra credit in a school class

☐ get healthy

☐ get a cash gift

B. **VOCABULARY** Read aloud these words from Listening 2. Check (✓) the ones you know. Use a dictionary to define any new or unknown words. Then discuss with a partner how the words will relate to the unit.

bar code *(n.)*	grant *(n.)* 🔑	incentive *(n.)*	propel *(v.)*
buzzword *(n.)*	implement *(v.)*	infrastructure *(n.)*	submit *(v.)*
consistently *(adv.)*	impromptu *(adj.)*	outrageous *(adj.)*	substantial *(adj.)* 🔑

🔑 Oxford 3000™ words

 C. Go online to listen and practice your pronunciation.

WORK WITH THE LISTENING

🔊 **A.** **LISTEN AND TAKE NOTES** Use the graphic organizer on page 155 to take notes as you listen to the development of the Boulder Bike-to-School Program. Fill in the people *who* started the program, *why* they started it, *how* the partners made changes to the product, *why* they changed the name, and *what* the program is like now.

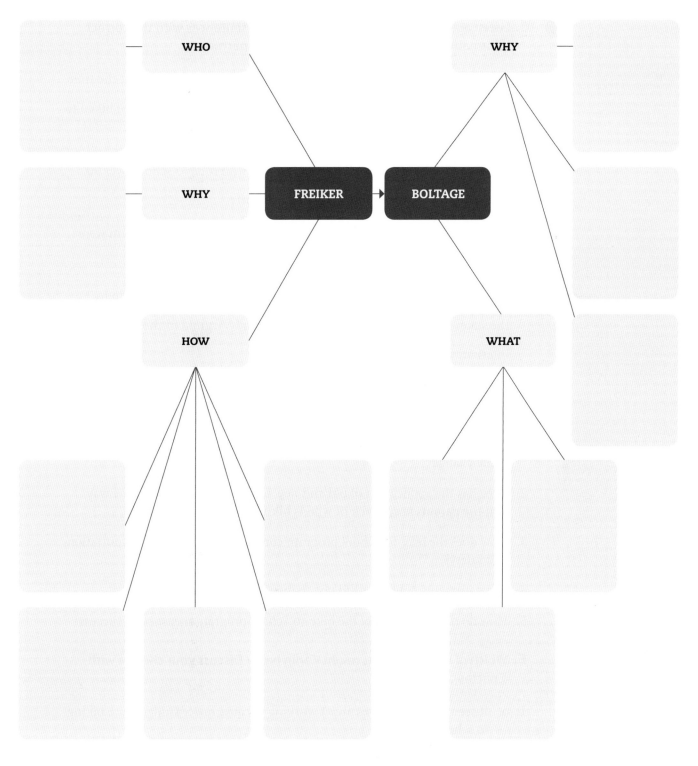

B. Work with a partner. Use your notes to number the following features of the program in the order they were developed.

____ RFID readers   ____ grab bags   ____ bar codes

____ incentives   ____ walkers   ____ punch cards

C. Listen again for the facts and complete the sentences with the correct information. Compare your answers with a partner.

1. The Freiker program at Crestview was started by two dads, and at the time of the interview, about _____ of the schoolchildren biked to that school.

2. The incentive offered to children in Boulder who rode to school over 90 percent of the days was the chance to win a(n) _____.

3. The three main sources of funding for the original Freiker program were

   _____.

4. The Boulder Bike-to-School program has expanded from Colorado to the states of California, Texas, Wisconsin, and Virginia in the U.S., and internationally to _____.

D. Use your notes to write short answers to these questions. Then discuss them with a partner.

1. What is the significance of the names *Freiker* and *Boltage* and why did the name change?

2. How has the application of old and new technologies improved the way that the parents keep track of who is biking to school?

3. How does the bike-to-school program connect health, active transportation, and safety?

4. What elements of Freiker did not change under the new program?

5. How do the developers of the bike-to-school program measure its success?

E. Which of these opinions might Carlin have? Discuss your choices with a partner.

1. a. It seems the incentives aren't working because fewer students are biking to school.
   b. The Freiker program has been successful because technology has made it easier.

2. a. The name of the company should have remained Freiker.
   b. Boltage has continued the Freiker tradition of helping kids exercise.

F. Label each statement as *F* (fact) or *O* (opinion).

____ 1. All children definitely need to exercise more.

____ 2. Freiker is a strange-sounding name for this program.

____ 3. Active transportation is the buzzword for using your own energy to get somewhere.

____ 4. Kids in the bike-to-school program have burned over 78 million calories.

____ 5. Incentives are the best way to get kids motivated.

G. **VOCABULARY** Here are some words from Listening 2. Read the sentences. Then write each bold word or phrase next to the correct definition. Write each word in its singular or base form.

1. I ride a bike to school occasionally, but my doctor says I really need to exercise **consistently** to improve my health.

2. When you have to give an **impromptu** speech, it's easy to make mistakes and forget to cover all the crucial information.

3. The **incentive** for trying out acupuncture is one month of free treatments.

4. Some supermarkets have self-checkouts, where you scan the **bar codes** on your groceries yourself.

5. The organization made a **substantial** donation to our school, so we were able to buy 500 new computers.

6. The marketing department made some **outrageous** claims about the product that could not be proven.

7. What's the latest **buzzword** to get young adults excited about a new product?

8. A motor **propels** a car, but a bike is propelled by foot power.

9. Land in the countryside is cheaper to buy, but there is no existing **infrastructure**, such as water pipes and electric cables.

10. The committee **submitted** several plans to encourage children to participate in healthy activities.

11. The school district tried to get a **grant** to pay for bikes for children who couldn't afford one.

12. Before we can **implement** the new plan, we must get approval from management.

a. _____ (n.) a pattern of lines that contains information read by a computer

b. _____ (n.) the basic systems and services necessary for a country or city to run

c. _____ (v.) to give to somebody in authority for consideration; to hand in

d. _____ (v.) to move, drive, or push forward

e. _____ (adj.) large in value or importance

f. _____ (adj.) very unusual and slightly shocking

g. _____ (v.) to make something start to happen

h. _____ (adv.) repeatedly and in the same way

i. _____ (n.) a sum of money to be used for a specific purpose

j. _____ (n.) something that encourages somebody to do something; a reward

k. _____ (adj.) done without preparation or planning

l. _____ (n.) an expression or phrase that has become popular

H. Go online for more practice with the vocabulary.

I. Go online to listen to *Putting Garbage to Good Use* and check your comprehension.

SAY WHAT YOU THINK

A. Discuss these questions in a group.

1. What are some advantages and disadvantages of offering children incentives to improve their health? What are some other ways to achieve the same goal?

2. Do you think it is possible to implement a bike-to-school program in every type of community? In what types of communities would it be easier? More difficult?

B. Before you watch the video, discuss these questions in a group.

1. Why is it challenging for some people to give up traditional methods for newer, innovative ones? What are some reasons others find it easy to make those changes?

2. Steve Jobs built the first Apple computer in his garage. Do you think people with big ideas need special places to work on them?

C. Go online to watch the video about a company called Inventionland. Then check your comprehension.

> **assembly line** *(n.)* a system for making things in a factory
>
> **churn out** *(phr. v.)* produce something quickly and in large amounts
>
> **gadget** *(n.)* a small tool or device that does something useful
>
> **retailer** *(n.)* a person or business that sells goods to the public
>
> **wonderland** *(n.)* an imaginary or exciting place filled with interesting t̲

D. Think about the unit video, Listening 1, and Listening 2 as you discuss these questions.

1. Where should the money come from to encourage alternative ideas and inventions? How can people raise money or support for these projects?

2. Did any of the reports in this unit remind you of a gadget or crazy idea you have heard of? Share it with the group and discuss why it succeeded or failed.

Vocabulary Skill | Idioms and informal expressions

Informal expressions can enrich your language when used correctly. However, informal language also affects the tone of the conversation or speech, and you should be very careful not to use informal language in the wrong situation. Here are some reasons people use informal language.

- to show that they belong to a certain group, such as young people or a certain club
- to show other people they are friendly, relaxed, or approachable
- to make a serious subject seem easier to understand

Most dictionaries indicate when words have an informal meaning (**kid** ▪ noun, *informal*) or are considered **slang** (**dude** ▪ noun, *slang*), meaning too informal and used only in conversation. Many **idioms** or set expressions are considered informal and are usually labeled (**IDM**) and listed in learners' dictionaries in a separate section at the end of an entry. Check the meaning of idioms and informal or slang expressions carefully before using them.

You can find an idiom by looking up the keyword—usually a noun or a verb—such as *think* in *think outside the box*. The keyword may not always be the first word in the expression. In addition, the idiom or informal expression may not always be the first meaning listed for a word. Look at these examples of idioms using the keyword *think*.

> *nothing of walking thirty miles a day.* **think on your feet** to be able to think and react to things very quickly and effectively without any preparation **think outside (of) the box** to think about something, or how to do something, in a way that is new, different, or shows imagination **think straight** to think in a clear or logical way **think twice about sth/**

All dictionary entries are from the *Oxford Advanced American Dictionary for learners of English* © Oxford University Press 2011.

A. Circle the keywords of these expressions. Then write a more formal expression for each one.

Informal expression	More formal alternative
1. the (buzz)	news; rumors
2. just around the corner	
3. the deal is / here's the deal	
4. to catch on	
5. to get (something) off the ground	
6. a cut above (something)	
7. to wrap (something) up	
8. wild about (something)	

B. Listen to these excerpts from Listening 1 and Listening 2. Complete the sentences with the idiom or informal expression you hear. Discuss the meanings of each expression with a partner. Check a dictionary if necessary.

1. **Rose Hoban:** But now Odom's a true believer. He says getting stung is the only thing that helps him with his pain. He's also convinced his wife, and that's _____, since she's the state secretary for Health and Human Services.

   Meaning: _____

2. **Rose Hoban:** Keller was here for the annual meeting of the American Apitherapy Society in Durham a couple of weeks ago. She demonstrated

bee venom therapy during a session for about a dozen people who

practically _____ excitement as they waited to get stung.

Meaning: _____

Tip for Success

If you search the
Internet for "business
idioms" you will
find many lists that
include expressions
such as *plug an idea,
sell like hotcakes,
cut a deal,* and *get
off to a flying start.*

3. **Fountain Odom:** They might look at you askance or say, "Uh, you know,

you're kind of _____, aren't you? I mean, why would you

want to be stung by a bee?"

Meaning: _____

4. **Laurie Garrett:** There was a description of a place called "Container

City" in London in which shipping containers, painted in primary

colors, had been stacked in unusual ways to create apartment buildings.

And I, I simply thought of it at that moment and a little sort of "bingo"

_____ in my head.

Meaning: _____

5. **Narrator:** Laurie Garrett, who now works with the Council on Foreign

Relations, hopes governments and aid organizations will take her idea and

_____. She believes the container clinics, ultimately, could

make portable medicine a reality for people in countries that need it most.

Meaning: _____

6. **Tim Carlin:** So, once we felt that we had a really good day-to-day tracking

system, we, um, well, Rob, the guy who, ah, really started the program,

decided that, um, "Why don't we _____

and offer a crazy incentive?" And, ah, his crazy incentive was an iPod.

Meaning: _____

iQ ONLINE   **C.** Go online for more practice with idioms and informal expressions.

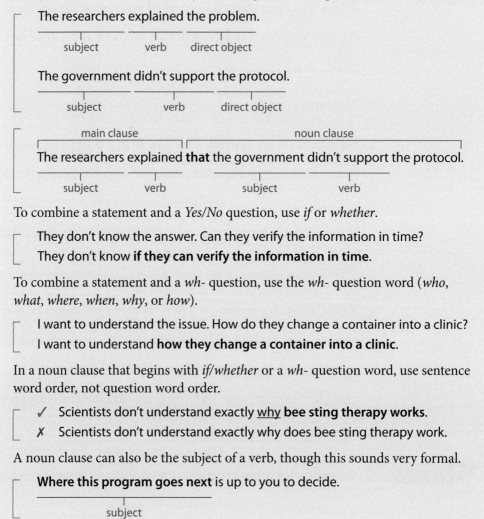

UNIT OBJECTIVE At the end of this unit, you are going to develop a marketing presentation to sell a new invention or idea. In your presentation, you will need to assess how and when to use formal or informal language to market your idea.

Grammar Noun clauses

A **noun clause** is a group of words that functions as a noun. Like a noun, it can be a subject or a direct object in a sentence. A noun clause is a dependent clause and cannot stand alone as a sentence.

Noun clauses can combine two clauses, showing a connection between the ideas. To combine two statements, use *that*. Notice how the entire noun clause in the second sentence functions in the same way as the simpler noun *the problem* in the first sentence:

The researchers explained the problem.
subject   verb   direct object

The government didn't support the protocol.
subject   verb   direct object

main clause   noun clause
The researchers explained **that** the government didn't support the protocol.
subject   verb   subject   verb

To combine a statement and a *Yes/No* question, use *if* or *whether*.

They don't know the answer. Can they verify the information in time?
They don't know **if they can verify the information in time**.

To combine a statement and a *wh-* question, use the *wh-* question word (*who, what, where, when, why,* or *how*).

I want to understand the issue. How do they change a container into a clinic?
I want to understand **how they change a container into a clinic**.

In a noun clause that begins with *if/whether* or a *wh-* question word, use sentence word order, not question word order.

✓ Scientists don't understand exactly <u>why</u> **bee sting therapy works**.
✗ Scientists don't understand exactly why does bee sting therapy work.

A noun clause can also be the subject of a verb, though this sounds very formal.

Where this program goes next is up to you to decide.
subject

A. Underline the noun clause in each sentence.

1. She believes the container clinics, ultimately, could make portable medicine a reality for people in countries that need it most.

2. I've had patients in the last 20 years who told me that relatives of theirs, older relatives working in the garden, had accidently got stung on their hands by a bee, and their arthritis got better.

3. And I might also add that we also include walkers now, um, as part of the program.

4. We see no reason why, if retrofitting is done on a mass scale . . . , these containers couldn't come in for well under $1,500 apiece.

5. Some compounds in bee venom might affect how the body transmits pain signals to the brain, but it's hard to know for sure.

6. He told me how this grew from a handful of kids at Crestview Elementary School in Boulder into an international program.

Tip for Success

It is common to delete the word *that* before noun clauses in speaking, but not in writing. *Garrett says [that] the cost of the clinics could be less.*

B. Work with a partner. Take turns reading the sets of two short sentences and combining them by using a noun clause.

> *A: Should I invest in that new product? I'm not sure.*
> *B: I'm not sure if I should invest in that new product.*

1. He thought that his coworker had stolen his idea. He told his boss.

2. Do we want to sell it online? We aren't sure.

3. Where did they develop the prototype? I need to find out.

4. How did they raise enough money to give away iPods? It's not clear.

5. Why can't we convince people to get stung by bees? I don't understand.

6. Can they convince the public to buy it? They are trying to decide.

7. When was the product featured on the air? We are trying to find out.

8. The incentive could be seen as too outrageous. The group was worried.

C. Go online for more practice with noun clauses.

D. Go online for the grammar expansion.

The auxiliary verb *have* in conditional modal expressions such as *could have*, *would have*, and *should have* has a weakened **reduced form** when spoken. You may hear only the /v/ sound or what sounds like the word *of*.

In addition, in the negative contracted forms *couldn't have*, *wouldn't have*, and *shouldn't have*, the /t/ sound is not said distinctly. Therefore, it can be difficult to know whether you have heard *could have* or *couldn't have*!

To tell the difference, listen for the number of syllables (beats). *Could have*, even when the *have* is reduced, has two syllables. *Couldn't have* has three syllables.

Listen and repeat these sentences.

I could have told her.
I couldn't have told her.
You should have come on Sunday.
You shouldn't have come on Sunday.
We would have been happy with that answer.
We wouldn't have been happy with that answer.

A. Listen to the sentences. For each, circle *A* (affirmative) or *N* (negative).

1. A N   5. A N

2. A N   6. A N

3. A N   7. A N

4. A N   8. A N

B. Practice the conversations with a partner. Pay attention to the modal expressions. Then listen to check your pronunciation.

1. **A:** Did you read about that woman who tried bee sting therapy? That's crazy! I wouldn't have done something like that. Would you?

    B: Well, I'm not sure. I would have researched it first, of course. I wouldn't have dismissed it without finding out about it, though.

    A: I wonder if it helped her at all. Perhaps she should have gone to a conventional doctor.

    B: But the article said that her arthritis was completely cured. Maybe you should have finished reading it.

2. **A:** I went to an amazing conference on alternative medicine yesterday. You should have been there. You would have loved it.

B: I know, but I had a big test to study for. If I hadn't studied, I wouldn't have passed. What did I miss?

A: Well, the best part was this guy who talked about using shark fin extract to help boost your immune system. I wouldn't have imagined that was possible. But he convinced me and even gave out some free samples.

B: Really? Maybe if I had been there, I could have tried one of those shark fin samples. I think I'm getting a cold.

 C. Go online for more practice with affirmative and negative conditional modals.

Speaking Skill | Using formal and informal language

Deciding when to use formal and informal language, or appropriate **register**, is an important speaking skill. Register is reflected in the words, expressions, and pronunciation that speakers use.

Different situations and different audiences determine the register you should use. For example, it is too informal to use words like *stuff* and *awesome* when giving an academic presentation. However, it is too formal to try to convince a friend to look at your new cell phone by saying, "I would like you to examine this phone." You would probably just say, "Hey, check this out!"

In general, English speakers use more formal language with people they don't know or people of a higher social status and more informal language with friends or family members. However, the situation itself is also important. You might use informal language with an older, unfamiliar person in a relaxed social situation such as a picnic. You might use more formal language if you were asking a close friend for a large favor or delivering some difficult or bad news.

Formal register uses . . .	Informal register uses . . .
uncontracted forms such as *cannot, did not, he would*	more contractions such as *can't, didn't, he'd*
discourse markers such as *I see, Yes, Actually, Exactly*	discourse markers such as *OK, Yeah, Sure, Well, Oh*
more passive voice	more active voice
standard English vocabulary	idioms, informal expressions, and slang
more one-word verbs	more phrasal verbs
longer, more complex sentences	shorter sentences

A. In what ways would your use of formal or informal language differ in these three situations? Discuss your points with a partner.

1. Explaining to your friend how you damaged his car in an accident / Reporting an accident in your friend's car to your insurance company

2. Explaining to your sister or brother why you had to buy the latest technology gadget / Explaining to your parents why you need money for a new technology device

3. Telling your friend about a new online chat site you found / Giving a report to your class about an online chat site

B. Work with a partner. Choose one of the situations in Activity A or a similar one. Write a conversation. Make sure you use appropriately formal or informal language. Practice your conversation, and then present it to another pair or the class.

 **C.** Go online for more practice with using formal and informal language.

Unit Assignment Market a new idea

 In this assignment, you are going to prepare a short presentation to "sell" a new invention or idea. As you prepare your presentation, think about the Unit Question, "Where do new ideas come from?" Use information from Listening 1, Listening 2, the unit video, and your work in this unit to support your presentation. Refer to the Self-Assessment checklist on page 168.

CONSIDER THE IDEAS

A. Listen to these two marketing presentations for a new product, the Vibrating Wallet. One presentation is for an audience of businesspeople looking to invest in a new product. The other is for an audience of young adult consumers. Take notes on types of language the speakers use in each presentation. Listen for formal and informal expressions, facts and opinions, and reduced forms. Compare notes with a partner.

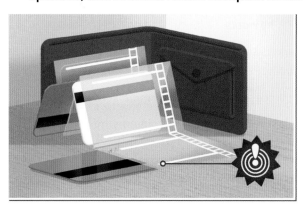

B. Discuss these questions in a group.

1. What problem is this invention trying to solve?

2. Does this product recycle old ideas, demonstrate alternative thinking, or combine old and new ideas?

3. How does each marketing presentation attempt to appeal to the two different audiences? Are the presentations effective? What other suggestions might you offer to help sell this product to these audiences?

4. Would you buy this product? Why or why not?

PREPARE AND SPEAK

Critical Thinking (Tip)

In this Unit Assignment, you will discuss possible inventions that can solve a problem. When you **invent** solutions, even in your imagination, you are applying knowledge to create something new.

A. GATHER IDEAS Work with a partner. Discuss possible inventions or solutions to these problems or one of your own. Be creative.

Problem	Invention / Solution
1. remembering to take back your credit card	
2. losing your cell phone or MP3 player	
3. forgetting all of your Internet passwords	
4. not having enough time to clean your house	
5. spending too much money for public transportation	
6. (your own idea) _____	

B. ORGANIZE IDEAS Follow these steps to organize your ideas.

1. Work with your partner. Choose one problem and invention or solution from Activity A or suggest one of your own. You will make a presentation to a large group of business investors or a small gathering of young customers. Decide whether your presentation will be formal or informal.

2. Write an outline with notes for your presentation. Use this format.

    I. Introduction

    II. Problem / existing situation

    III. Description of invention / solution

    IV. Benefits or advantages of invention / solution

    V. Conclusion

3. Write note cards with your key ideas and any special language you want to use. Divide the presentation material so that each partner speaks for about the same amount of time.

C. **SPEAK** Practice your presentation a few times. Then give it to a group or the whole class. Refer to the Self-Assessment checklist below before you begin.

 Go online for your alternate Unit Assignment.

CHECK AND REFLECT

A. **CHECK** Think about the Unit Assignment as you complete the Self-Assessment checklist.

SELF-ASSESSMENT		
Yes	No	
☐	☐	I was able to speak fluently about the topic.
☐	☐	My partner, group, and class understood me.
☐	☐	I used noun clauses correctly.
☐	☐	I used vocabulary to talk about innovations, problems, and solutions.
☐	☐	I pronounced affirmative and negative conditional modals correctly.
☐	☐	I distinguished between facts and opinions and used them appropriately.
☐	☐	I used formal and informal language correctly.

 B. **REFLECT** Go to the Online Discussion Board to discuss these questions.

1. What is something new you learned in this unit?

2. Look back at the Unit Question—Where do new ideas come from? Is your answer different now than when you started this unit? If yes, how is it different? Why?

TRACK YOUR SUCCESS

Circle the words and phrases you have learned in this unit.

Nouns
bar code
buzzword
compound AWL
container 🔑
grant 🔑 AWL
incentive AWL
infrastructure AWL
protocol AWL
prototype
shortage

Verbs
convert 🔑 AWL
convince 🔑 AWL
deny 🔑 AWL
implement AWL
propel
submit AWL
verify

Adjectives
impromptu
outrageous

reluctant AWL
substantial 🔑

Adverbs
consistently AWL
periodically AWL

Phrase
anecdotal evidence

🔑 Oxford 3000™ words
AWL Academic Word List

Check (✓) the skills you learned. If you need more work on a skill, refer to the page(s) in parentheses.

LISTENING ☐	I can distinguish between facts and opinions. (p. 150)
NOTE TAKING ☐	I can take notes on process and development (p. 152)
VOCABULARY ☐	I can use idioms and informal expressions. (pp. 159–160)
GRAMMAR ☐	I can use noun clauses. (p. 162)
PRONUNCIATION ☐	I can pronounce affirmative and negative conditional modals. (p. 164)
SPEAKING ☐	I can use formal and informal language appropriately. (p. 165)
UNIT OBJECTIVE ▲▲▲▲ ☐	I can gather information and ideas to develop a marketing presentation designed to sell a new invention or idea.

UNIT QUESTION

How do people react to change?

A Discuss these questions with your classmates.

1. Have you or your family moved for work, education, or other reasons? How many times has your family moved?

2. List a few major changes in your life. Are you a person who welcomes new opportunities or one who avoids change?

3. Look at the photos. How does each photo show a reaction to change?

B Listen to *The Q Classroom* online. Then answer these questions.

1. Who has a more positive attitude toward change, Felix or Marcus, and why?

2. Who does Sophy agree with and what proof does she give?

 C Go online to watch the video about people changing careers. Then check your comprehension.

beleaguered *(adj.)* experiencing a lot of difficulties

a knee-jerk reaction *(phr.)* a quick decision made without thought

sector *(n.)* an area of the economy

went bust *(phr.)* went to pieces; failed

 D Go to the Online Discussion Board to discuss the Unit Question with your classmates.

E According to recent United Nations statistics, people are migrating more than ever. Look at the statistics and discuss the question.

Percentage of population that are immigrants			
Kuwait	69.2	United States	14.3
Hong Kong	38.9	United Kingdom	12.4
Saudi Arabia	31.4	Republic of Congo	9.7
Australia	27.7	Japan	1.9
Canada	20.7	China	0.1

Do these statistics surprise you? In a group, discuss why you think so many people move.

F Read this blog post written by a university student who moved from China to Canada as a child. Then work in a group. Discuss the questions below.

Good News, Bad News
By Huang Yubin   Wednesday, May 5 at 11:22 a.m.

In China we have a story about a farmer whose theme is "Good news, bad news—I don't know." What we sometimes think is bad news may turn out to be good news. When my parents decided to move to Canada, I was angry. I was just 12 years old. We lived in a big house with all of our family around us. I was considered a good student in my school, and I had lots of friends. I was a ping-pong champion and spent weekends playing with friends or competing in tournaments. Suddenly, my parents wanted me to give up the life I loved. Bad news.

I hated my new life. Even though I had studied English in my home country, I felt lost. My accent made it hard for people to understand me, and everyone spoke so fast I could barely understand them. I had to work twice as hard, and I was still not considered a good student. I made it worse by staying by myself; I didn't have any friends. I was a very unhappy person.

Looking back today, I wonder when all the bad news changed to good news. I am now at a prestigious university. I play on a club ping-pong team and have more friends than I have time for. I speak perfect English, and my parents are proud of me. When I graduate, I'll be able to take care of them. The change has done me good, and I'll probably stay where I am.

Comments (2) | Write a Comment | Email to a Friend

PREVIOUS REVIEW   NEXT REVIEW

1. Would you consider a move like the one described here as good news or bad news? Why do you think the writer's feeling about his situation eventually changed?

2. Do you want to live and work in the same city where you were born?

3. Have you always had the same plan for your future career, or has it changed?

Anecdotal evidence consists of personal reports, stories, and explanations that are not based on research or facts. For this reason, this type of information is not always considered reliable; its truth cannot be proven. However, anecdotal evidence is important in many fields such as education, sociology, and psychology. When enough anecdotal evidence is collected to support a theory in these fields, the theory may be considered more valid.

Taking notes on anecdotal evidence requires that you listen to a story. A speaker has chosen anecdotal evidence because he or she considers it to be valuable support for a point he or she is trying to make. Most effective stories and anecdotes include information related to the six main question words: *who, what, where, when, why,* and *how.* Asking yourself questions with each of these words as they relate to the anecdote is often a good way to take notes on anecdotal evidence.

One of the biggest problems in taking notes on anecdotal evidence is eliminating unnecessary details. As people tell stories, they often include irrelevant information. If you keep in mind the purpose of the anecdote and ask yourself broad-based questions with each of the main question words, it will help you focus on what is most important. You don't want to miss an important point while you are making note of an insignificant detail.

After you have listened to and taken notes on anecdotal evidence, make sure to review your notes and do the following:

- Write down the main point the speaker wants to make and the purpose the anecdotes serve.
- Make notes of what is fact and what is opinion.
- Look over your notes and cross out anything that you realize wasn't important.
- Organize your notes in a way that will be useful, such as a chronological or otherwise logical order.

You may want to leave your notes in an informal outline or timeline, or you may want to convert them into a short summary that can be incorporated into a report you have to present.

A. Go online to watch the unit video on attitudes toward new jobs again. Take notes on the two main anecdotes in the chart on page 174. As you listen, ask yourself questions based on the question words in the chart to try to capture the main points of each person's story.

Who . . . ?		
What . . . ?		
Where . . . ?		
When . . . ?		
Why . . . ?		
How . . . ?		

B. Review your notes and use them to complete this summary. Present the anecdotal evidence from the video in a logical and concise way.

According to a BBC report, a lot of people have to change
jobs because of the economy and unemployment.
They have different reactions. For example, Mike Portsmouth _____

_____

_____

On the other hand, Drew Murley _____

_____

_____

 C. Go online for more practice using notes to summarize anecdotal evidence.

LISTENING 1 | The Reindeer People

You are going to listen to a radio documentary, *The Reindeer People*, produced for the nonprofit organization Worlds of Difference. It is about a nomadic group that travels around the regions of Mongolia in order to find food for their animals. As you listen to the documentary, gather information and ideas about how people react to change.

PREVIEW THE LISTENING

A. **PREVIEW** How do you think nomads would react to opportunities to settle down and give up their life as herders? Check (✓) your prediction.

☐ They would welcome the government's help to relocate.

☐ They would fight to maintain their traditional culture.

☐ They would want to keep their nomadic life for themselves, but encourage their children to change.

B. **VOCABULARY** Read aloud these words from Listening 1. Check (✓) the ones you know. Use a dictionary to define any new or unknown words. Then discuss with a partner how the words will relate to the unit.

contemplate *(v.)*	make a living *(phr.)*
cope *(v.)* 🔑	nomad *(n.)*
critical *(adj.)* 🔑	obligation *(n.)*
elder *(n.)*	settle *(v.)* 🔑
elite *(adj.)*	subsidy *(n.)*
embrace *(v.)*	sustain *(v.)*

🔑 Oxford 3000™ words

C. Go online to listen and practice your pronunciation.

WORK WITH THE LISTENING

◉ **A.** **LISTEN AND TAKE NOTES** Listen to the report. Use the chart to take notes on the reactions to change from the elder Sanjeem, Yudoon, and his wife Uyumbottom.

Interviewees	Traditional Mongolian life	Facing changes
Sanjeem		
Yudoon		
Uyumbottom		

B. Use the anecdotal evidence from your notes in Activity A to write a short summary of how the nomadic reindeer herders feel they are caught between two worlds.

◉ **C.** Listen again and complete the sentences. Compare your answers with a partner.

Traditional Mongolian life

1. The reindeer eat _____.

2. There are _____ people living in Sanjeem's group in the Taiga region.

3. Some of the staples, or main foods, in the Taiga diet that reindeer provide are _____, _____, and _____.

4. Uyumbottom went to the government for support for the traditional culture by pleading for _____.

Facing changes

5. With the end of government subsidies, nomadic life was threatened

   because herders lost free _____ care for their reindeer.

6. Because of _____ and attacks by

   _____, the size of the reindeer herd is decreasing.

D. Use your notes from Activity A and the details from Activity C to answer these questions. Then discuss them with a partner.

1. In what ways have the nomads been fighting to preserve their culture?

2. Why does the elder Sanjeem not want to settle?

3. What proof does the narrator give that other Mongolians support the herders?

4. One American NGO working with the reindeer people is called *Itgel*. What does this word mean, and why is it significant?

E. Identify the person who made these comments: Sanjeem (*S*), Yudoon (*Y*), or Uyumbottom (*U*).

____ 1. Increasing numbers of families are trying to leave the Taiga.

____ 2. There was less poverty under communism.

____ 3. Our culture will survive if we can continue earning our living by the ways of the reindeer.

____ 4. We were able to speak for our culture during our visit to the capital of Mongolia.

____ 5. I'm not sure we can expand our herd enough to support our families.

____ 6. The environment and the climate are perfectly suited to our culture.

F. The American biologist Morgan Kay uses the anecdotal evidence provided by Sanjeem, Yudoon, and Uyumbottom to reach the conclusion that we can learn something from these nomads. Write two to three sentences summarizing her beliefs.

_____

_____

_____

G. **VOCABULARY** Here are some words from Listening 1. Read the paragraphs. Then write each bold word next to the correct definition. (One definition under each paragraph will not be used.)

Some people feel sorry for groups of **nomads**. They must change environments during different times of the year in order to make sure their animals have enough food. It is not easy for outsiders to understand how these people feel close to their animals, the land, and nature. However, these groups choose not to **settle** in one place, despite government threats to remove any financial **subsidies** they receive that help them continue their lifestyle. With each new cycle of nature, nomadic tribes pack up and move on to a different area to **sustain** their herds of animals—and their way of life.

1. _____ (v.) to make a place your permanent home

2. _____ (n.) money provided to help individuals or groups reduce costs of services or goods

3. _____ (n.) members of a community that moves with its animals from place to place

4. _____ (v.) to provide enough of what somebody or something needs in order to live or exist

5. _____ (v.) to develop or create a close relationship or connection with somebody or something

The 21st century will be a **critical** time for nomads and other indigenous groups. While the **elders** feel an **obligation** to preserve their customs and rituals and keep the beliefs of the culture alive, some members of the younger generation are ready to **embrace** change.

6. _____ (adj.) extremely important because a future situation will be affected by it

7. _____ (n.) something which you must do

8. _____ (n.) stories from ancient times, especially one that was told to explain natural events to describe the early history of a people

9. _____ (n.) older people, usually with a special status

10. _____ (v.) to accept an idea or proposal with enthusiasm

> Many of these young people **contemplate** how different life would be if they went away to college or moved to a city to get a job and **make a living**. It's not that they dream of an **elite** lifestyle; they just don't want to **cope** with the hardships their parents endured.

11. _____ *(v.)* to deal successfully with a difficult matter

12. _____ *(v.)* to think about whether you should do something, or how you should do it

13. _____ *(adj.)* unnecessarily expensive; more costly that the value of the object

14. _____ *(adj.)* powerful, influential; wealthy or of high status

15. _____ *(v.)* to earn money to buy the things you need

 H. Go online for more practice with the vocabulary.

SAY WHAT YOU THINK

Discuss these questions in a group.

1. Why do you think some elders in many cultures resist change? Why do you think younger people embrace change?

2. What are some reasons others in Mongolia might think the nomads should settle in permanent homes?

3. Do you think that these Mongolian nomads will be able to survive in the 21st century? Why or why not?

Intonation is a tool speakers can use to indicate their attitude or emotions without stating them directly.

It is useful to recognize common intonation patterns because people do not always express their true attitude or feeling through their words alone. You can use their intonation and tone of voice to make inferences about what they really mean.

Intonation pattern	This can convey . . .
flat mid-pitch, low fall	sadness, regret
varied pitch	excitement, interest, or pleasure
very high, rising pitch	disbelief or surprise
sharp rise with a sharp fall	disagreement or denial

Listen to the intonation and attitude in these examples.

1. **Sadness or regret**

   The future of the reindeer herders sounds pretty uncertain.

2. **Excitement or interest**

   The female nomads have a lot to say about this issue.

3. **Disbelief or surprise**

   The number of reindeer is decreasing?

4. **Disagreement or denial**

   Personally, I think the herders are going to survive.

A. Listen to the sentences. Check (✓) the box for the attitude you can infer.

Sentence	Sadness	Excitement or interest	Disagreement	Disbelief or surprise
1	☐	☐	☐	☐
2	☐	☐	☐	☐
3	☐	☐	☐	☐
4	☐	☐	☐	☐
5	☐	☐	☐	☐
6	☐	☐	☐	☐
7	☐	☐	☐	☐
8	☐	☐	☐	☐

B. Listen to these statements from Listening 1 and Listening 2. Circle the best inference for each one. With a partner, discuss how you made your choice.

1. a. The speaker feels that the world should respect the life the nomads have chosen, even if others cannot understand their choice to live such a difficult life.

   b. The speaker feels the government should protect the nomads from the forces of nature that are ruining a culture that cannot survive.

   c. The speaker feels that the nomads should settle in one place and adopt a western lifestyle.

2. a. The speaker admires and envies the members of the group he is describing.

   b. The speaker seems surprised and fascinated by this group of frequent travelers.

   c. The speaker criticizes the members of this group for wanting to travel so much.

 C. Go online for more practice recognizing attitudes.

LISTENING 2 | High-Tech Nomads

UNIT OBJECTIVE ▶▶▶▶ You are going to hear Rudy Maxa, host of the radio show *The Savvy Traveler*, interview reporter Joel Garreau about his research on a special group of businesspeople called *high-tech nomads*. As you listen to the interview, gather information and ideas about how people react to change.

PREVIEW THE LISTENING

A. **PREVIEW** Check (✓) the descriptions you think would apply to a high-tech nomad.

☐ a self-employed businessperson

☐ a cyberspace traveler, rather than a plane traveler

☐ a worker who changes offices frequently

☐ a computer "geek"

☐ an employee who can't keep one job

☐ a worker who has an email address but no business address

☐ a businessperson who works from home

B. **VOCABULARY** Read aloud these words from Listening 2. Check (✓) the ones you know. Use a dictionary to define any new or unknown words. Then discuss with a partner how the words will relate to the unit.

accomplish *(v.)*	marginal *(adj.)*
attention span *(n.)*	mundane *(adj.)*
breakthrough *(n.)*	payoff *(n.)*
evolved *(adj.)*	psyche *(n.)*
intrepid *(adj.)*	roots *(n.)* 🔑
irony *(n.)*	stability *(n.)*

🔑 Oxford 3000™ words

 C. Go online to listen and practice your pronunciation.

WORK WITH THE LISTENING

A. **LISTEN AND TAKE NOTES** Listen to Joel Garreau describe high-tech nomads and share anecdotal evidence. Think about answers to *Wh-*questions as you take notes in the T-chart.

General characteristics	Anecdotal evidence

B. Based on the anecdotes, summarize Joel Garreau's description of the character of high-tech nomads in a few sentences.

_____

_____

_____

C. Listen again. Check (✓) the details that are supported by Garreau's anecdotal evidence. Compare your answers with a partner.

☐ 1. Both men and women are members of this high-tech nomad group.

☐ 2. Some high-tech nomads have million-dollar incomes.

☐ 3. One high-tech device that these businesspeople no longer have use for is the cell phone.

☐ 4. Even though these nomads like to travel for business, most have one specific home where they spend weekends, do laundry, and get mail.

☐ 5. The woman who swims every day does so because she needs exercise after the long plane rides.

☐ 6. Some high-tech nomads take their families with them when they travel on business.

D. Write short answers. Then discuss them with a partner.

1. According to Garreau, why do these business travelers choose this nomadic life?

   _____

   _____

2. What do high-tech nomads give up for their lifestyle?

   _____

   _____

3. Garreau asks, "If these guys are so plugged in, and they can communicate from anywhere, why bother [to] travel at all?" How does he answer his own question?

   _____

   _____

E. Read the statements. Write *T* (true) or *F* (false). Then correct the false statements.

High-tech nomads:

____ 1. don't have enough stability for Garreau.

   _____

____ 2. figure out ways to deal with the tasks of everyday life.

   _____

____ 3. don't have short attention spans.

   _____

____ 4. have homes in more than one city.

   _____

____ 5. hope that one day they won't need face-to-face meetings.

   _____

____ 6. have common jobs, but just do them in uncommon ways.

   _____

Vocabulary
Skill Review

In Unit 6, you learned
about idioms and
informal expressions.
Find three idioms
in the sentences
in Activity F.

F. **VOCABULARY** Here are some words from Listening 2. Complete each
sentence with the correct word or phrase. Use the plural form of a word
when necessary.

accomplish *(v.)*	**intrepid** *(adj.)*	**payoff** *(n.)*
attention span *(n.)*	**irony** *(n.)*	**psyche** *(n.)*
breakthrough *(n.)*	**marginal** *(adj.)*	**roots** *(n.)*
evolved *(adj.)*	**mundane** *(adj.)*	**stability** *(n.)*

1. Labeling people according to their income level, ethnic background, or
   language can lead to discrimination because it makes it sound like they are
   _____ groups.

2. Those who want to investigate their _____ and learn about
   their culture often go back to the country where their parents were born.

3. Those who have signed up for a trip on a spaceship are certainly
   _____ travelers.

4. Something about the human _____ makes us need to define
   our own space.

5. Scientific _____ such as high-tech devices help business
   travelers stay plugged in to work.

6. The parents felt the children needed more _____ and didn't
   want to move from one city to another too frequently.

7. He found _____ in the idea that the city dwellers really
   believed they were giving freedom to the nomads by making them move to
   the city.

8. It drives the boss crazy when his workers can't _____ their
   goals in an eight-hour day.

9. The _____ for working so hard was that she earned enough
   money to buy a new computer.

10. Some people complain about _____ jobs, but others like having a set, predictable routine, even if it gets boring after a while.

11. Traditional societies that choose to resist change are sometimes criticized as being less _____ than those that jump on the bandwagon of every new modern technological advancement.

12. People with a short _____ jump from project to project so they don't get bored.

G. Go online for more practice with the vocabulary.

H. Go online to listen to *Restoring Famous Landmarks* and check your comprehension.

SAY WHAT YOU THINK

A. Discuss these questions in a group.

1. What do the speakers seem to think of the high-tech nomads? Do you agree with them? Why or why not?

2. Do you have the type of personality required to be a high-tech nomad? Do you have any interest in that sort of lifestyle? Why or why not?

3. In what ways do you try to be "wired" to the outside world? How much has your use of high-tech devices changed your daily life?

B. Think about the unit video, Listening 1, and Listening 2 as you discuss these questions.

1. The reports described changes in the world around us (e.g., a decrease in natural resources; an increase in technology; economic downturns). What other changes in today's world can you think of that could change the way some groups of people live, work, or study?

2. What types of individuals embrace change while others resist it? Can you give any personal examples?

Phrasal verbs, made up of a verb followed by a **particle**, are a common type of collocation. The particle (usually a preposition or an adverb) following the verb changes the meaning. For example, *take on* does not have the same meaning as *take* or *take over*. Phrasal verbs are listed separately in learners' dictionaries and are marked with a symbol.

> ˌtake sth/sb↔'on **1** to decide to do something; to agree to be responsible for something or someone: *I can't take on any extra work.* ◆ *We're not taking on any new clients at present.* **2** (of a bus, plane, or ship) to allow someone or something to enter: *The bus stopped to take on more passengers.* ◆ *The ship took on more fuel at Freetown.*

Some phrasal verbs take an object. A phrasal verb is **separable** if the object can be placed between the verb and the particle (*take* something *on*) as well as after it (*take on* something).

> That group **took over** the meeting and discussed their changes to the plan.
> We had contemplated **taking** the new project **on**, but decided not to.
> **Taking** it **on** would have been too much work.

Phrasal verbs are often less formal and more conversational than one-word verbs with a similar meaning.

> We decided to *take on* the new project. = more informal
> We decided to *undertake* the new project. = more formal

Over time, some phrasal verbs join together to become nouns; examples from Listening 2 include *breakthrough* and *payoff*.

All dictionary entries are from the *Oxford Advanced American Dictionary for learners of English* © Oxford University Press 2011.

A. Use a dictionary to complete the phrasal verbs with particles from the box. Then write *S* if the phrasal verb is separable and *I* if it is inseparable.

at	in
away	out
away	up
back	up
back	up on
down	up with

_____ 1. give _____: to give something as a gift

_____ 2. give _____: to stop trying to do something

_____ 3. give _____: to return something to its owner

_____ 4. keep _____ (something): to continue working
or doing something

_____ 5. keep _____: to avoid going near something or someone

_____ 6. keep _____ _____: to stay in contact with someone; to stay
informed about a situation

_____ 7. pick _____: to choose or select something

_____ 8. pick _____: to collect something

_____ 9. pick _____ _____: to return to a point already discussed

_____ 10. turn _____: to return the way you have come

_____ 11. turn _____: to reject or refuse something

_____ 12. turn _____: to go to bed / go to sleep

B. Complete the sentences with a phrasal verb from Activity A. If the verb is separable, rewrite the sentences using a pronoun. If the verb is not separable, put an *X* on the line.

1. The group submitted an application for a government subsidy, but unfortunately, the government _____turned down_____ the application.

   _The government turned it down._____

2. It's important to _____ from the edge of the cliff. You could fall!

   _____

3. I know that it's unhealthy to consume a lot of sugar, so I'm trying to _____ soda.

   _____

4. High-tech nomads have no central place to _____ their mail.

   _____

5. I'm not sure I understand what you mean. Can we _____ the point you raised earlier about subsidies?

   _____

6. It's getting very late. I'm going to _____ soon.

   _____

7. If you receive something you can't use and don't want, I think it's OK to _____ that item _____.

   _____

iQ ONLINE **C.** Go online for more practice with phrasal verbs.

At the end of this unit, you are going to interview a classmate about his or her attitudes about change and report back to the class. In order to report back, you will need to be able to paraphrase.

Grammar | Gerunds and infinitives

Gerunds are formed with a verb + -*ing*.

Infinitives are formed with *to* + base form of the verb.

Gerunds and infinitives are both nouns, even though they may look like verbs. They take the same position in a sentence as other nouns, such as subjects, direct objects, and objects of prepositional phrases.

1. Both gerunds and infinitives can be used as sentence subjects; this can make a sentence seem more formal.

2. Both gerunds and infinitives are used as direct objects; whether you use a gerund or an infinitive sometimes depends on the main verb in the sentence.

3. Only gerunds can be used as objects of prepositional phrases.

4. Gerunds are used as objects of verb phrases with *have* + noun.

5. Infinitives are also used in sentences whose subjects are noun phrases with *It* + adjective.

Study the examples in the chart.

	Infinitive	Gerund
1. Subject	**To meet people face-to-face** is important.	**Meeting people face-to-face** is important.
2. Object	High-tech nomads like **to meet people face-to-face**.	High-tech nomads like **meeting people face-to-face**.
3. Object of a prepositional phrase	✗	He is interested in **meeting people face-to-face**.
4. Object of a verb phrase with *have* + noun	✗	He has difficulty **meeting people face-to-face**.
5. Object of a noun phrase with *it* + adjective	It is important **to meet people face-to-face**.	✗

Here are some common verbs and phrases that are followed by gerunds or infinitives.

	Infinitive	Gerund
avoid, dislike, enjoy, finish, mind, practice, quit		✓
agree, decide, expect, force, hope, intend, plan, promise	✓	
continue, hate, like, love, prefer, start	✓	✓
have difficulty / fun / a problem / a hard time / trouble		✓
it is easy / hard / important / necessary	✓	

A. Complete each sentence with the gerund or infinitive form of the verb in parentheses. Check your answers with a partner. In some cases, more than one answer is possible.

1. Many Mongolian nomads would prefer _____ (maintain) their traditional lifestyle.

2. It appears that the Mongolian nomads don't have trouble _____ (move) as the seasons change.

3. Mongolia's geography forces people _____ (embrace) the nomadic life.

4. Still, it is not easy _____ (cope) with so many changes.

5. High-tech nomads avoid _____ (stay) in any one place or job for too long.

6. They don't have a problem _____ (use) an airport as their office.

7. Some of them intend _____ (travel) for just a few years, and others choose it for their entire career.

Tip for Success

Learners' dictionaries list object forms needed after main verbs. If you look up *deny* you'll see *doing sth*, so you know the verb that follows *deny* should use the gerund form: *He denied **taking** it.*

B. Work with a partner. Discuss the questions. Use verbs and expressions from the chart on page 191, followed by gerunds and infinitives.

1. Think about your life now and then how it might change in the future. What do you enjoy doing now? What do you dislike doing? What do you intend to change in the future? What are some things you hope to do?

2. Think about a career you are interested in. Do you hope to get a job in that field? How do you plan to prepare or train for that? Will it be easy or difficult to find a job? Could it be necessary to move to another city or country? Would you mind moving?

iQ ONLINE

C. Go online for more practice with gerunds and infinitives.

D. Go online for the grammar expansion.

Pronunciation | Consonant variations

Consonant sounds may change according to their position in a word and the other sounds around them. This chart summarizes some of the important variations in English consonant sounds.

 Listen to and repeat the examples.

Consonant variation	Explanation	Conditions	Examples
Aspiration of /p/, /t/, /k/	add an extra puff of air after the voiceless sounds /p/, /t/, /k/	when /p/, /t/, /k/ come at the beginning of a stressed syllable (except when preceded by *s*)	*poor* *appeal* *tech* *return* *cope* *account*
Flap or tap /t̬/	use a quick flick or tap /t̬/ of the tongue on the roof of the mouth for *t* and *d*	when a *t* or *d* comes between a stressed vowel and an unstressed vowel (American English)	*leader* *matter* *subsidy*
Palatalization	pronounce *d* like /dʒ/ and *t* like /tʃ/, creating friction rather than a stop	when *d* or *t* combines with a following /y/ sound	*question* *nature* *situate* *gradual*

A. Listen to these pairs of words and repeat them.

1. Feel the extra puff of air with your hand when you say the second word in each pair.

   open – opinion

   atom – atomic

   intern – turn

2. Feel how the quick tap /t̬/ is substituted for /t/ or /d/ in the second word in each pair.

   master – matter

   lender – leader

   invitation – invited

3. Feel how your tongue creates friction with the roof of your mouth in the second word instead of just stopping the sound.

   grader – gradual

   native – natural

   captive – capture

B. Circle the three words in each set that have these features. Then listen and check your answers.

1. aspirated /p/

   a. cope   b. expand   c. payoff   d. policy

2. aspirated /k/

   a. connection   b. crazy   c. accomplish   d. cycle

3. aspirated /t/

   a. routine   b. elite   c. attention   d. tourist

4. flap /t̬/

   a. critical   b. material   c. ability   d. letter

5. flap /t̬/

   a. media   b. pleaded   c. nomadic   d. advisor

6. palatalized /tʃ/

   a. century   b. future   c. fifty   d. culture

7. palatalized /dʒ/

   a. gradual   b. reindeer   c. schedule   d. individual

C. Listen to these sentences and circle the words with an aspirated, flap, or palatalized *t*.

Welcome to the world of the high-tech nomad. Writer Joel Garreau investigated this unique breed of traveler for *The Washington Post*, and he sat down with us recently to tell us what he learned.

D. Go online for more practice with consonant variations.

Speaking Skill | Paraphrasing

To **paraphrase** is to repeat an idea in a way that keeps the same meaning but uses different words. Speakers paraphrase for emphasis or to make a meaning clearer or easier to understand. Sometimes we paraphrase what we have heard a speaker say just to clarify our own understanding.

Listen to the way the Rudy Maxa paraphrases some of Joel Garreau's words in his interview.

> Garreau: One of the great ironies of this lifestyle is that, you know, you ask yourself, well if these guys are so plugged in, and they can communicate from anywhere, **why bother travel at all**?
>
> Maxa: Exactly. **Why do you even move?**

Here, Maxa shows that he has understood the question that Garreau is asking; also, by repeating it, he emphasizes the question for the listening audience.

Here are some techniques that you can use to paraphrase.

☐ Original sentence: Discovering the nomads was a surprising experience for us.

Use synonyms

> Paraphrase: The reporter said that finding the nomads was an astonishing experience.

Vary word forms

☐ Paraphrase: The discovery of the nomadic group surprised them.

Change positive to negative forms

☐ Paraphrase: The discovery of the nomads was not expected.

When paraphrasing, it is also common to:

Combine sentences and ideas

Original sentences: We were at least listened to . . . I'm encouraged by this.

Paraphrase: Uyumbotton said that she felt encouraged because at least the government listened to them.

Break a long idea or sentence into two

Original sentence: Mongolia's geography, a boundless wilderness with soil that can't sustain agriculture, forces people to embrace the nomadic life.

Paraphrase: The narrator explains that Mongolia has vast lands, but it is impossible to grow food there. As a result, a nomadic life is necessary.

When paraphrasing in a conversation, use expressions such as *in other words*, *what I'm/you're saying is . . .*, and *so what I/you mean is . . . .*

A. Listen to your partner read a sentence below. Paraphrase the sentence using the techniques in the Speaking Skill box. Ask your partner to confirm that you paraphrased the ideas accurately.

A: *These guys tend to have very short attention spans on average.*

B: *So you mean most high-tech nomads don't have long attention spans?*

A: *Yes, exactly / Yes, that's right / Indeed.*

1. The economic advisor to Mongolia's president did not have encouraging words.

2. And the great irony is that the reason they are nomads is for face-to-face contact.

3. Well it's only been in the last ten years that we've had enough wired technology to make this barely possible.

4. When Mongolia's communist government was toppled by a democratic revolution in the 1990s, his state salary was withdrawn.

B. Work with a partner. Role-play a conversation between one of the people in the recordings and an interviewer who paraphrases the speaker's words.

A: *Mr. Garreau, do you believe that high-tech nomads are crazy?*

B: *No, I couldn't live that nomadic lifestyle, but these people are successful.*

A: *In other words, even though the life of a nomad isn't for you, their success shows that they aren't crazy.*

Possible topics:

Ask Sanjeem what would happen if his people moved closer to the city.

Ask Uyumbottom why she went to the capital or what the results of the trip were.

Ask Dyson why she swims every day.

Ask Garreau what he thinks high-tech nomads miss most.

Ask Maxa what he learned from his interview with Garreau.

 C. Go online for more practice with paraphrasing.

Unit Assignment Conduct a personal interview

 In this assignment, you are going to interview a classmate to find out whether she or he resists or embraces change and then report on your findings. As you prepare your report, think about the Unit Question, "How do people react to change?" Use information from Listening 1, Listening 2, the unit video, and your work in this unit to support your report. Refer to the Self-Assessment checklist on page 198.

CONSIDER THE IDEAS

The topic of change has fascinated many great thinkers, writers, and leaders. In a group, read and discuss the following quotations about change. Take turns paraphrasing the ideas and explaining your reactions to them. Which ones seem positive? Which are negative?

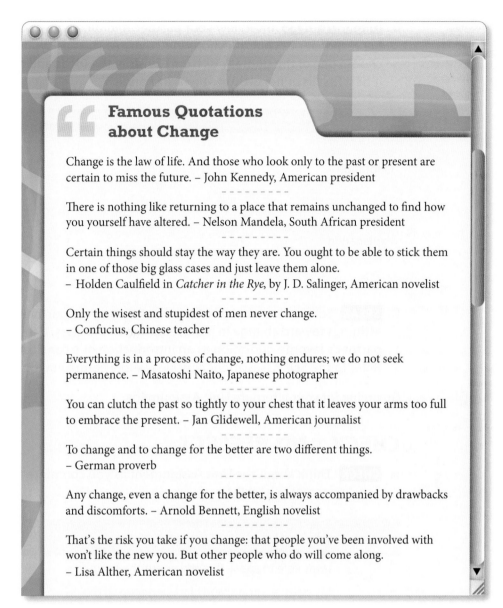

Famous Quotations about Change

Change is the law of life. And those who look only to the past or present are certain to miss the future. – John Kennedy, American president

- - - - - - - - -

There is nothing like returning to a place that remains unchanged to find how you yourself have altered. – Nelson Mandela, South African president

- - - - - - - - -

Certain things should stay the way they are. You ought to be able to stick them in one of those big glass cases and just leave them alone.
– Holden Caulfield in *Catcher in the Rye*, by J. D. Salinger, American novelist

- - - - - - - - -

Only the wisest and stupidest of men never change.
– Confucius, Chinese teacher

- - - - - - - - -

Everything is in a process of change, nothing endures; we do not seek permanence. – Masatoshi Naito, Japanese photographer

- - - - - - - - -

You can clutch the past so tightly to your chest that it leaves your arms too full to embrace the present. – Jan Glidewell, American journalist

- - - - - - - - -

To change and to change for the better are two different things.
– German proverb

- - - - - - - - -

Any change, even a change for the better, is always accompanied by drawbacks and discomforts. – Arnold Bennett, English novelist

- - - - - - - - -

That's the risk you take if you change: that people you've been involved with won't like the new you. But other people who do will come along.
– Lisa Alther, American novelist

PREPARE AND SPEAK

Critical Thinking (Tip)

In Activity A, you have to discuss the quotations and **defend** your ideas by giving explanations for your opinions. When you defend your opinions, you use your own personal values and beliefs.

A. **GATHER IDEAS** **Follow these steps to prepare for your interview.**

1. Work with a partner. Discuss the quotations above. Explain why you agree or disagree with them.

2. Write seven questions that will help you find out how your partner reacts to change. Your questions can cover different areas, including changes in family, school, careers, traditions, or reactions to the people in the recordings.

Tip for Success

In a conversation, it is important to have good eye contact so the speaker knows you are listening and interested in what he or she is saying.

B. ORGANIZE IDEAS Interview your partner, and take notes on his or her responses to your questions in Activity A. Then ask your partner to choose one of the quotations from Consider the Ideas and explain why it best fits his or her attitude toward change.

	Partner's responses
Quotation	
Explanation	

C. SPEAK Summarize what you found out about your partner's attitudes toward change in a presentation to the class. Use your partner's favorite quotation as an introduction or a conclusion. Refer to the Self-Assessment checklist below before you begin.

 Go online for your alternate Unit Assignment.

CHECK AND REFLECT

A. CHECK Think about the Unit Assignment as you complete the Self-Assessment checklist.

		SELF-ASSESSMENT
Yes	No	
☐	☐	I was able to speak fluently about the topic.
☐	☐	My partner, group, and class understood me.
☐	☐	I used phrasal verbs correctly and in appropriate situations.
☐	☐	I used gerunds and infinitives correctly and in a variety of sentence positions.
☐	☐	I pronounced consonants correctly.
☐	☐	I paraphrased to emphasize and to clarify understanding.

 B. REFLECT Go to the Online Discussion Board to discuss these questions.

1. What is something new you learned in this unit?

2. Look back at the Unit Question—How do people react to change? Is your answer different now than when you started this unit? If yes, how is it different? Why?

TRACK YOUR SUCCESS

Circle the words and phrases you have learned in this unit.

Nouns
attention span
breakthrough
elder
irony
nomad
obligation
payoff
psyche
roots 🗝
stability AWL
subsidy AWL

Verbs
accomplish
contemplate

cope 🗝
embrace
settle 🗝
sustain AWL

Phrasal Verbs
give away 🗝
give back
give up 🗝
keep at
keep away
keep up with
pick out
pick up 🗝

pick up on
turn back
turn down
turn in

Adjectives
critical 🗝
elite
evolved AWL
intrepid
marginal AWL
mundane

Phrase
make a living

🗝 Oxford 3000™ words
AWL Academic Word List

Check (✓) the skills you learned. If you need more work on a skill, refer to the page(s) in parentheses.

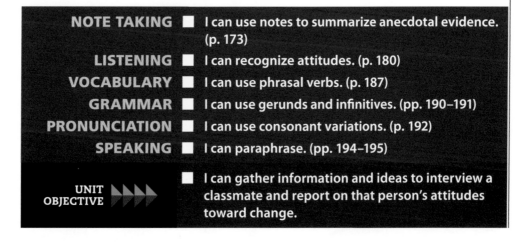

NOTE TAKING	☐ I can use notes to summarize anecdotal evidence. (p. 173)
LISTENING	☐ I can recognize attitudes. (p. 180)
VOCABULARY	☐ I can use phrasal verbs. (p. 187)
GRAMMAR	☐ I can use gerunds and infinitives. (pp. 190–191)
PRONUNCIATION	☐ I can use consonant variations. (p. 192)
SPEAKING	☐ I can paraphrase. (pp. 194–195)
UNIT OBJECTIVE ▶▶▶▶	☐ I can gather information and ideas to interview a classmate and report on that person's attitudes toward change.

UNIT **8**

Environmental Studies

NOTE TAKING	▶	organizing notes to prepare for a debate
LISTENING	▶	listening for cause and effect
VOCABULARY	▶	Greek and Latin word roots
GRAMMAR	▶	adverb clauses
PRONUNCIATION	▶	sentence rhythm
SPEAKING	▶	debating opinions

UNIT QUESTION

Where should the world's energy come from?

A Discuss these questions with your classmates.

1. Where does most of the energy in your community come from?

2. Why do environmentalists care whether energy is non-renewable (in limited supply) or renewable? What new energy sources can solve the world's energy needs?

3. Look at the photos. What types of energy do you see? Which ones do you think we should or should not use?

B Listen to *The Q Classroom* online. Match the ideas about energy in the box to the students in the chart. Then answer the questions.

a. We should use less energy and be more efficient.
b. The whole world is set up for fossil fuels.
c. We should use as much solar energy as possible.

Ideas about energy	
Sophy	
Felix	
Yuna	

1. Why does Marcus think that nuclear power is a good solution to the energy problem?

2. What answers does Felix have for where the world's energy should come from?

 **C** Go to the Online Discussion Board to discuss the Unit Question with your classmates.

D Work in a group. Do you know what these energy sources are? Label the pictures. Then discuss whether the sources are renewable or non-renewable.

1. _____ 2. _____ 3. _____

4. _____ 5. _____ 6. _____

E With your group, choose one energy type from Activity D. Complete the idea map. Then decide if you think this is an appropriate energy source for your community or not.

Energy type

Advantages/Benefits   Sources   Disadvantages/Risks

_____   _____   _____

_____   _____   _____

_____   _____   _____

A debate is a focused speaking activity in which people argue different sides of an issue. Each speaker presents evidence supporting his or her position while also making arguments against another speaker's position. It's common for arguments in debates to be framed in the following ways:

- pros and cons
- advantages and disadvantages
- strengths and weaknesses
- benefits and drawbacks
- positives and negatives

Learning about the issues involved in any one position or side of an argument requires research from written materials as well as interviews and news reports. Gathering the information necessary for a debate is often the easy part. Debates always have time limits, and many debates are team activities. Choosing the strongest points and deciding which material each participant will present are the more challenging parts of the debate-preparation process. When gathering evidence, it is important to zero in on the facts that will help you defend your position. In addition, while gathering information, it's also important to make note of the disadvantages of the other side so you can formulate questions and be prepared for arguments.

When taking notes and preparing your material for a debate, consider using these strategies:

- Make a note of what you need to do more research on or what parts of your argument need more explanation.

- Summarize your notes in a T-chart divided into pros and cons of your own position so you are prepared to defend it.

- List the pros and cons of the opposing position, too, so you are prepared to attack the weak points.

- Use different colored note cards for the pros of your side and the cons of your opponent.

- Annotate your notes with questions to ask your opponent and possible questions you think you may be asked.

- Highlight a few points that are the most crucial to your presentation in case you run out of time.

A. Listen to this excerpt from a debate on nuclear energy. Is Mr. Chen arguing for or against nuclear energy? Take notes on his main points.

> *Mr. Chen is arguing* _____ *nuclear energy.*
>
> *Main points:*

B. Compare your notes with a partner. Now imagine that you had to respond to Mr. Chen and argue the other side of the issue. Share your ideas and prepare notes.

C. Listen to a continuation of the debate. How does Ms. Regan respond to Mr. Chen's argument? Take notes on her main points. How do her ideas compare with yours?

_____

_____

_____

_____

_____

_____

_____

iQ ONLINE **D.** Go online for more practice organizing notes to prepare for a debate.

You are going to watch a video from BBC News about the debate over energy options. BBC's science editor David Shukman travels around England visiting energy facilities and asking residents about their attitudes toward different energy solutions. As you watch the video, gather information and ideas about where the world's energy should come from.

PREVIEW THE LISTENING

Drax power station in South Yorkshire

A. **PREVIEW** Shukman interviews both people who work in the energy industry and people he calls "NIMBYs" (Not in My Back Yard) who are against bringing certain types of energy to their communities. What do you know about different types of energy? Write a few adjectives to describe each option.

fossil fuels: _____

nuclear energy: _____

solar energy: _____

wind energy: _____

B. **VOCABULARY** Read aloud these words from Listening 1. Check (✓) the ones you know. Use a dictionary to define any new or unknown words. Then discuss with a partner how the words will relate to the unit.

catastrophic *(adj.)*	fracking *(n.)*
conflicted *(adj.)*	intermittent *(adj.)*
convert *(n.)*	potentially *(adv.)* 🔑
efficient *(adj.)* 🔑	priority *(n.)* 🔑
emission *(n.)*	retrofit *(v.)*

🔑 Oxford 3000™ words

 C. Go online to listen and practice your pronunciation.

WORK WITH THE LISTENING

A. **LISTEN AND TAKE NOTES** Go online to watch the video for Listening 1. Use the graphic organizer to take notes. Add the types of energy and the positive and negative points of each. Put a star next to the energy option you would choose to defend in a class debate. Put an *X* next to the one you would be least able to support.

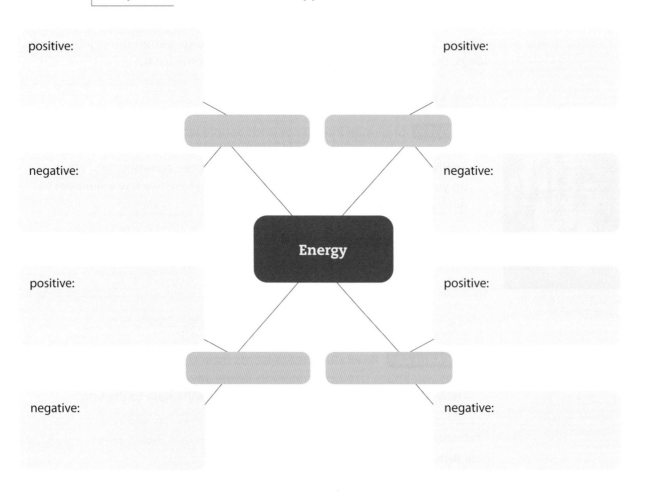

positive:

negative:

positive:

negative:

Energy

positive:

negative:

positive:

negative:

B. Compare notes with a partner. Fill in any missing information. Annotate your notes by writing questions you might ask someone defending the different options. Make notes where you feel you would need more details. Save these notes for your debate.

C. Watch or listen again. Circle the correct answers.

1. Which represents the correct order of energy production in England from high to low?

   a. nuclear, coal, gas   b. coal, gas, nuclear   c. gas, nuclear, coal

2. Which two types of power are available in Yorkshire?

   a. wind and coal   b. coal and solar   c. nuclear and wind

3. Who is an environmentalist?

    a. Smith   b. Garner   c. Linus

4. Which of the energy power stations produces the most carbon dioxide?

    a. coal   b. wind turbines   c. fracturing

5. Which of the following combinations is correct?

    a. nuclear – expensive   b. wind turbines – reliable c. gas – imported

D. Answer these questions.

1. What scientific theory do Smith and Garner argue against?

2. What point do the energy workers make about the problem with renewable energy such as solar and wind?

3. What form of energy does the woman on the street prefer and why?

4. What energy comes from fracking, and what is the risk one farmer worried about?

5. In the end, what conclusion does Shukman reach about the type of energy we choose?

E. Use your notes to write a short explanation of which side you would like to take in the debate and why. Make references to useful information from the video to support your position.

F. **VOCABULARY** **Here are some words from Listening 1. Read the sentences. Circle the answer that best matches the meaning of each bold word.**

Vocabulary
Skill Review

In Unit 7, you learned about phrasal verbs. Find one verb in these sentences that has three different meanings depending on the preposition or adverb that follows it. Write the three phrasal verbs and their meanings.

1. The debate over the pros and cons of nuclear energy leave the public **conflicted** about its safety.

    a. enthusiastically convinced

    b. emotionally confused

    c. clearly informed

2. The technicians needed to **retrofit** the old computers with new chips.

    a. put a new piece of equipment into a machine that did not have it when it was built

    b. replace new equipment with old equipment

    c. put old parts into a new machine

3. Nuclear waste materials have proven to have a **catastrophic** effect on life near the power plants.

    a. disastrous   b. fortunate   c. common

4. One concern with using gas, coal, and oil as fuels is the **emissions** they produce, which can cause illnesses in people and animals that breathe them.
   a. sticky, greasy substances
   b. liquid leaked into the environment
   c. gases sent out into the air

5. We look forward to the day when the reduction of greenhouse gases is a top **priority**.
   a. advantage   b. emphasis   c. pre-condition

6. The rain was only **intermittent** yesterday, so we could still go out for a walk.
   a. light
   b. pounding
   c. stopping and starting

7. The researcher's ideas were **potentially** dangerous because they were based more on theory than scientific evidence.
   a. strongly   b. incorrectly   c. possibly

8. The British invest more money in wave energy research than other countries, but do they really believe it could be an **efficient** way to produce energy?
   a. economical and useful
   b. new and unusual
   c. wasteful and powerful

9. That solar power company is full of a bunch of **converts** who used to be in favor of coal power.
   a. experienced engineers
   b. new believers
   c. unsure workers

10. Some energy campaigners believe we should look for other sources of energy besides **fracking** because it might cause pollution.
    a. installing wind turbines
    b. extracting gas from rock
    c. depending on solar power

 G. Go online for more practice with the vocabulary.

SAY WHAT YOU THINK

Discuss these questions in a group.

1. Do you agree with the views of the pro-nuclear or the pro-coal speaker regarding the best sources for future energy? Explain your reasons.

2. Which of the different energy sources discussed by the speakers do you think are the most efficient? Which are the least risky?

3. The speakers warn of three concerns when considering solutions to energy problems: climate change, nuclear waste, and an energy shortage. Which do you think should be our greatest concern?

Listening Skill | **Listening for cause and effect**

Many discussions are based on a presentation of causes and effects. Certain **organizational cues** or **signal words**, as well as some verbs, can indicate a cause and effect relationship.

Signal words/phrases for cause	since, because, because of, when, due to, on account of, if
Signal words/phrases for effect	so, as a result, consequently, for this reason, then, therefore, in order to
Signal verbs for cause	cause, bring about, give rise to, contribute to, initiate, trigger, affect, make happen, produce, set off, have an effect on, have an impact on, result in

Usually you will hear the cause in the first clause, followed by the effect. Sometimes, however, the speaker will give the effect in the first clause.

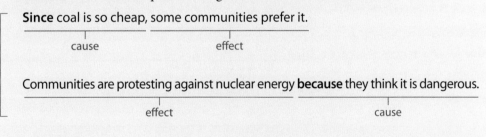

Since coal is so cheap, some communities prefer it.

   cause   effect

Communities are protesting against nuclear energy **because** they think it is dangerous.

     effect   cause

Sometimes the cause is the subject of a verb that shows the relationship to the effect.

Threats to the environment **have triggered** many concerns.

    cause   effect

A. Complete the chart with possible causes or effects.

Cause	Effect
1.	We're forced to import energy from other countries.
2. Emissions from fossil fuels escape into the air.	
3.	Wind and solar power can't provide enough energy.

B. Listen to the excerpts from news stories about energy. Write down the cause and effect relationships expressed by the speakers. Use the key words provided. Compare answers with a partner.

1. ethanol, fuel, fertilizer

   Cause: _____

   Effect: _____

2. electrons, generator, hydrogen

   a. Cause: _____

   Effect: _____

   b. Cause: _____

   Effect: _____

3. chemical reactions, leftovers, tank

   a. Cause: _____

   Effect: _____

   b. Cause: _____

   Effect: _____

   c. Cause: _____

   Effect: _____

   d. Cause: _____

   Effect: _____

 C. Go online for more practice listening for cause and effect.

LISTENING 2 | Tapping the Energy of the Tides

UNIT
OBJECTIVE
You are going to listen to a news report from New Hampshire Public Radio (NHPR). Reporter Amy Quinton investigates the possibility of using tidal energy (energy from the rise and fall of sea levels) to provide energy to residents in the state of New Hampshire. As you listen to the report, gather information and ideas about where the world's energy should come from.

PREVIEW THE LISTENING

an underwater turbine

A. **PREVIEW** What do you think might be some advantages and disadvantages of using tidal energy?

Advantages: _____

Disadvantages: _____

B. **VOCABULARY** Read aloud these words from Listening 2. Check (✓) the ones you know. Use a dictionary to define any new or unknown words. Then discuss with a partner how the words will relate to the unit.

bill (n.) 🔑	harness (v.)
center (n.) 🔑	present (adj.) 🔑
commission (n.) 🔑	power (n.) 🔑
current (n.) 🔑	state (n.) 🔑
free (adj.) 🔑	stretch (n.) 🔑
generation (n.) 🔑	tap (v.) 🔑

🔑 Oxford 3000™ words

 C. Go online to listen and practice your pronunciation.

WORK WITH THE LISTENING

⊛ **A.** **LISTEN AND TAKE NOTES** Take notes as you listen to Amy Quinton's report on tidal energy. Take notes on both the pros (positives) and cons (negatives) of this source of power.

B. Use your notes to answer these questions. Then compare your answers with a partner.

1. According to the speakers, what are some of the advantages of tidal power? Write at least two benefits.

   _____

   _____

2. Jack Pare states his support of tidal power by saying, "There's no single magic bullet … this is one pellet of that shotgun effect to be able to take the top off the global warming." What does he mean by this metaphor?

   _____

   _____

3. According to Vauthier, what effect will tidal power have on the energy available to New Hampshire residents?

   _____

   _____

4. According to the speakers, what are some of the problems that might be caused by trying to develop tidal power in New Hampshire? Write at least two problems.

   _____

   _____

C. Read the sentences. Then listen again. Circle the word or phrase that best completes each statement.

1. Tidal power is a (renewable / non-renewable) source of energy.

2. The first speaker says that energy from the tides, currents, and waves could produce (12 / 20) percent of American electricity.

3. New Hampshire state representatives appear to be (supporters / opponents) of pursuing tidal power.

4. According to Representative Tom Fargo, (wind / tidal) power is more reliable.

5. The underwater turbines in the East River resemble (windmills / vehicles).

6. The water in New Hampshire's Piscataqua River presents (more / fewer) problems for tidal technology than the water in New York's East River.

7. (Two / Four) companies hold federal permits to research tidal power in the Piscataqua River.

8. Small fish will (be turned away from / safely pass through) the screens in the turbine engines of the Underwater Electric Kite Company of Maryland.

9. The companies (agree / disagree) on how much power they will be able to produce from the tides.

10. Charles Cooper, one of the technical engineers, says that since the plant will generate 100 megawatts of power at most, it (can / cannot) produce enough energy for the region.

D. Match the causes with their corresponding effects.

Causes	Effects
____ 1. Concerns over global warming are increasing.	a. Not all equipment is appropriate everywhere.
____ 2. Engineers can capture free-flowing river energy.	b. Scientists are looking for alternative sources of energy.
____ 3. Advocates believe in tidal power.	c. Protective screens need to be added to turbines.
____ 4. Water is more than 800 times denser than air.	d. A commission has been established to study tidal power.
____ 5. Harnessing tidal power is expensive.	e. Tidal power might be a good source of renewable energy.
____ 6. There is marine life in the harbor.	f. Energy from the tides will not be able to supply a large region.
____ 7. Tidal power might only generate 100 megawatts.	g. Few companies are interested in investing in tidal power in the US.
____ 8. Rivers and harbors differ in many ways.	h. Water is very powerful.

E. Write a short letter to Representative Tom Fargo expressing your support for or concerns about investing state money in tidal power research.

F. **VOCABULARY** Here are some words from Listening 2. Read the sentences. Circle the answer that best matches the meaning of each bold word.

1. Engineers want to **harness** the energy from the ocean.
   a. attach a horse to a carriage with a device made of leather
   b. control and use the force of something to produce power
   c. use straps to hold something in place

2. The strong **current** from the ocean brings warm water from other areas.
   a. flow of electricity
   b. of the present time
   c. continuous flow of air or water

3. We need to **tap** the power of the wind by using windmills.
   a. make use of
   b. touch lightly
   c. listen to phone conversations

4. When there is a **free** flow of fast-moving water, the energy from a river could provide electricity for many homes.
   a. not paid for
   b. not controlled
   c. not being used

5. The secretary of the environment has the **power** to limit the use of fossil fuels.
   a. strength or energy
   b. right or authority of a person or group to do something
   c. public supply of electricity

6. New Hampshire residents hope that wind energy will provide energy for at least 20 percent of the homes in their **state**.
   a. mental, emotional, or physical condition that a person or thing is in
   b. to formally write or say something, especially in a careful or clear way
   c. a part of the country with its own governmental/political organization

7. Legislators passed a **bill** that provided funds for research into renewable energy.
   a. a plan for a new law
   b. a statement of how much money is owed
   c. the hard part of a bird's mouth

8. The local **commission** on energy conservation found the number of residents using green energy in their homes is on the rise.
   a. an official group of people with the responsibility to control or find out about something
   b. an amount of money paid to someone for selling goods or services, which increases with the amount sold
   c. a piece of work that someone has been asked to do

9. Some critics of tidal and wind energy argue that the power **generation** is intermittent and unreliable.
   a. the next stage of development
   b. the production of something
   c. all the people born around the same time

10. Marine animals such as stripers and lobster are **present** in the cold waters of the New Hampshire seacoast.
    a. a gift
    b. to introduce formally
    c. in a particular place

11. The factories along that **stretch** of the river use coal.
    a. to pull to become longer
    b. an area of land or water
    c. to extend one's arms and legs

12. The engine will have an open **center** that will allow animals to swim through.
    a. building or place used for a particular purpose or activity
    b. middle area of an object
    c. moderate political position between two extremes

 G. Go online for more practice with the vocabulary.

H. Go online to listen to *Energy Alternatives* and check your comprehension.

SAY WHAT YOU THINK

A. Discuss these questions in a group.

1. Are you convinced that tidal power is an idea worth pursuing as a solution to our energy problems? Why or why not?

2. What obstacles does tidal power have to overcome in order to compete with oil, gas, and nuclear power?

Critical Thinking **Tip**

These questions ask you to **interpret** someone else's ideas to decide what he or she might do or think. When you interpret, you are using your own knowledge and opinions to better understand and evaluate ideas.

B. Before you watch the video, discuss these questions in a group.

1. Considering the conditions needed for turbine technology to work well, in what countries would tidal power be a good energy source?

2. Would the supporters of nuclear energy agree or disagree about the potential of water as an energy source? What might they say to one another about this issue in a debate?

C. Go online to watch the video about tidal turbines and check your comprehension.

> **churn** (v.) move (something) around violently
>
> **durable** (adj.) strong, long-lasting
>
> **grid** (n.) a system of electric wires for sending power over a large area
>
> **retool** (v.) replace or change equipment to improve it
>
> **underestimate** (v.) guess an amount is smaller than it is

D. Think about the unit video, Listening 1, and Listening 2 as you discuss these questions.

1. What are some ways in which the human need for energy and personal interests are in conflict with environmental protection? Who should decide which is more important?

2. What are some ways that governments can encourage people to consume less energy and develop cleaner energy sources? Should these measures be voluntary or required?

A **root** is the part of a word that has the main meaning. We often add prefixes before a root and suffixes at the end to create different words.

Many English words can be traced back to Greek and Latin. Learning Greek and Latin word roots can help you build your vocabulary and figure out unfamiliar words. It can also help you recognize words that are part of the same word family.

Word Root	Meaning	Examples
aero	air	aerospace, aerodynamics
bene	good	benefit, benign
bi	two	bicycle, biped
bio	life	biology, biomedical
chron	time	chronological, chronicle
dict	say, speak	dictation, dictionary
geo	earth	geography, geodesic
hydro	water	hydrant, hydroelectric
phon	sound	telephone, phonetics
port	carry	portable, support
proto	first	prototype, protocol

A. Think about the meaning of the example words. Use your knowledge of these words to figure out the meaning of the underlined word root. Circle the correct answer.

1. de<u>flect</u>, re<u>flect</u>ion, <u>flex</u>ible

   flect =   (a.) bend   b. break

2. <u>di</u>ameter, <u>di</u>oxide, <u>di</u>alog

   di =   a. one   b. two

3. tele<u>vis</u>ion, <u>vis</u>ual, <u>vid</u>eo

   vid/vis =   a. see   b. hear

4. <u>tele</u>phone, <u>tele</u>vision, <u>tele</u>scope

   tele =   a. far   b. near

5. <u>sub</u>way, <u>sub</u>marine, <u>sub</u>terranean

   sub = _____   a. over   b. under

6. <u>scrib</u>ble, in<u>scrip</u>tion, de<u>scrib</u>e

   scrib = _____   a. write   b. destroy; undo

7. <u>therm</u>al, <u>therm</u>ometer, geo<u>therm</u>al

   therm = _____   a. heat   b. weather

B. Work with a partner. Look at the word root, its meaning, and the example. Without using a dictionary, write more words you know that come from that root. Then compare your lists with another pair.

Word Root	Meaning	Examples
1. *auto*	self	automobile,
2. *graph*	write	biography,
3. *meter/metr*	measure	metric,
4. *phys*	body/nature	physician,
5. *sol*	alone	solo,

C. Write two sentences with words from Activity B. Make sure that the meanings of the words are clear in the sentences. Read your sentences aloud to a new partner and ask him/her to identify and define the words that have Greek or Latin roots.

Top athletes work hard to have a perfect physique.

_____

_____

_____

_____

 D. Go online for more practice with Greek and Latin word roots.

At the end of this unit, you are going to participate in a class debate about the future of energy. In order to have an effective debate, you will need to be able to express your ideas and defend your opinions.

Grammar Adverb clauses

Adverb clauses are dependent clauses that modify independent clauses (or main clauses). They can start a sentence or come after the independent clause. Adverb clauses begin with a subordinator, and although they have a subject and verb, they cannot stand alone.

There are several types of adverb clauses; two of them are used to express reasons and concession.

Adverb clauses that express reasons tell *why* the action in the main clause happens. They start with the subordinators *since, because, as,* or *due to the fact that.*

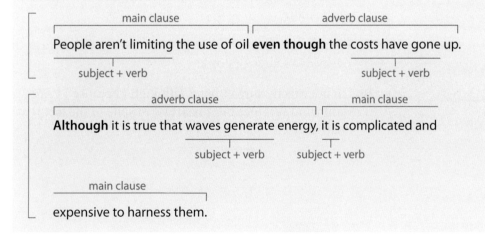

Adverb clauses that show concession acknowledge an idea and show that it is less important than the idea in the main clause. Subordinators for concession include *even though, although, though, while, despite the fact that,* and *in spite of the fact that.*

Be careful with the subordinators *despite the fact that* and *in spite of the fact that*. They can be confused with *despite* and *in spite of*, which introduce words or phrases, not clauses.

> ✓ Some people heat their homes with electricity **despite the fact that/ in spite of the fact that** it is so expensive.
> ✓ Some people heat their homes with electricity **despite/in spite of** the expense.
> ✗ Some people heat their homes with electricity **despite/in spite of** it is so expensive.

A. Listen to the sentences. What relationship do you hear between the two clauses? Circle *reason* or *concession*.

1. a. reason   b. concession   4. a. reason   b. concession

2. a. reason   b. concession   5. a. reason   b. concession

3. a. reason   b. concession   6. a. reason   b. concession

Tip for Success

When adverbial and other dependent clauses start a sentence, it is important to use a low- to mid-rise in pitch and add a slight pause before the main clause to show the sentence is not finished.

B. Work with a partner. Circle the correct expressions. Then practice the conversations.

1. **A:** (Even though / Because) we need to start consuming less energy, it's difficult for people to change their daily habits.

   B: I agree. We're not making as much progress as we could be (in spite of the fact that / due to the fact that) people stick to their old habits.

2. **A:** (Even though / Because) hybrid and electric cars are expensive, governments should provide subsidies so people can afford them.

   B: You've got a point, but is that really necessary? In my city, many people are already buying hybrids (in spite of the fact that / since) they cost a little more.

3. **A:** I'm not sure why wind energy isn't more popular, (as / though) it's a clean, renewable source of power.

   B: I'm not exactly sure either, (although / because) I know some people don't want wind turbines built nearby (in spite of the fact that / because) they're unattractive.

C. With a partner, create two conversations like those in Activity B. Take turns using the expressions in the skill box on pages 219–220 to add an adverb clause before or after one of the main clauses below.

1. . . . investing in solar energy seems unprofitable . . .

2. . . . many people around the world still rely mostly on coal . . .

3. . . . some people object to having wind turbines near their homes . . .

D. Go online for more practice with adverb clauses.

E. Go online for the grammar expansion.

Pronunciation	Sentence rhythm

Rhythm in language has contrasts between long and short, high and low, and soft and loud notes. In English, rhythm is produced by a combination of elements you've already learned: stress, linking, intonation, reduced forms, thought groups, and alternation of long and short syllables.

Listen to the difference in rhythm between these two sentences.

> BUY GAS NOW.
> It's too exPENsive to buy the GAS at this STAtion toDAY.

The first sentence has all short stressed words. The second has more rhythm, with multi-syllable words and stressed and unstressed syllables.

To have a natural-sounding rhythm in English, you need to:

- slow down and lengthen the vowels in stressed syllables of **content words** (verbs, nouns, adjectives, and adverbs) and vary your pitch. Listen to this example and repeat.

> If we WANT to prevent GLObal WARming, we have to CHANGE our
> conSUMPtion of FOssil FUELS.

- reduce and shorten function words (articles, prepositions, pronouns, conjunctions, and auxiliary verbs). Listen to this example and repeat.

> The BIKE-to-WORK PROgram was deSIGNED to help us SAVE Energy and
> SHOW that we can all aFFECT the PACE of CLImate CHANGE.

A. Listen to the sentences. Then take turns reading each set of sentences to a partner. Put the most stress on the capitalized syllables.

1. CARS CAUSE SMOG.
   The CARS in Los ANgeles cause SMOG.
   The OLD cars on the FREEways in Los ANgeles cause TOO much SMOG.

2. WE can TRY.
   We can TRY to SOLVE it.
   We can TRY to SOLVE the PROblem.
   We can TRY to SOLVE the ENergy problem with TIdal POwer.

B. Work with a partner. Circle the stressed syllables. Then listen to the conversation and check your answers. Make any necessary changes. Then practice the conversation with your partner.

A: Did you see the energy debate on TV last night?

B: No, I should have watched it, but I had to study for a math test. Give me the highlights.

A: Well, it was the big oil companies versus the environmentalists.

B: Which side had the best arguments?

A: Both sides presented good cases. The oil companies had more research, but the environmentalists made more compelling arguments. They convinced me that some of the oil companies' efforts are really misguided and that our reliance on fossil fuels has to end.

B: Was it possible to tell who won the debate?

A: Not really. Because the issues are so controversial, I think it's hard to come to any real resolution. I recorded it, so I'm going to watch it again.

B: There aren't any easy answers; that's for sure. Well, I'd like to watch that recording of the debate with you. It sounds thought-provoking.

A: Sure. And I think it'll be useful for our class discussion next week.

 **C.** Go online for more practice with sentence rhythm.

Tip for Success

In a conversation, stress often shifts to new information being provided or requested: Speaker A: *I just bought a CAR.* Speaker B: *Is it a NEW car or a USED one?*

Feeling comfortable **expressing ideas** and **defending opinions** is important in any conversation, and it's even more important in a debate. To keep a conversation going, when the other speaker gives a point, you can show your agreement and then add your own reason or a similar point; or you can disagree and explain why. Even close friends need to be careful about being too negative when presenting their own views, and direct disagreements should always be stated in a polite tone of voice.

Expressions to . . .	
Show agreement and add a further reason	**Concede a point and then disagree**
That's just it. I strongly believe that . . . *Exactly. The way I see it, . . .* *I couldn't agree more. The fact of the matter is . . .* *I think so, too. As far as I'm concerned . . .* *That's very true. Furthermore, another thing we need to consider is . . .*	*While that is true, it's clear that . . .* *You have some good points, but . . .* *You raise an important question; however, . . .* *Although I agree that . . ., I have to point out that . . .* *You might be right, but . . .* *I see what you're saying; on the other hand, . . .*

A. Listen to this excerpt from a debate on building a nuclear power plant in a community. Notice how both speakers present their ideas and concede some points while defending a point of view. Complete the sentences with the phrases you hear.

Moderator: Thank you. I'm sure we'll get back to some of those points later in the discussion. So, on the other side, now, Jack Chen, would you please present the case against nuclear energy?

Chen: I'd be happy to. _____ with

1

Emily that we need to reduce our consumption of fossil fuels,

_____ that nuclear energy is the

2

answer. Emily, you mentioned that nuclear energy is cleaner.

_____ if we're only talking about the

3

consumption of energy, but we have to look at how the energy

is produced and how waste is dealt with.

a city council debate

Regan: _____, but many scientists disagree
 4

with the notion that nuclear energy is somehow dangerous.

_____ that not one single person in North
 5

America has been injured at a nuclear power plant or died because of a

radiation-related accident. My research confirmed that this is a very

well-regulated industry. Right now, nuclear power plants supply 70 percent

of the emission-free electricity in the United States. It has a proven

safety record.

Chen: _____ that at the moment, nuclear
 6

energy is providing more power than other non-fossil fuel sources,

_____ that we need to develop our renewable
 7

options, energy that can be replaced naturally. Hydroelectric energy, or the

energy provided by moving water, provides 25 percent of non-fossil fuel

energy at the moment. _____ that we should also
 8

continue to invest in wind and solar energy. These sources are much safer

and cleaner than nuclear energy.

Moderator: Emily, what did you find out about the benefits of these

other sources?

Regan: _____, and scientists and
 9

environmentalists confirm, that renewable sources are safe and clean.

_____ that we're working
 10

at capacity in terms of hydroelectric power. More importantly, according

to Dr. David Scott, a professor at the University of Victoria, quote, "We've

gotta be very careful about what renewables can provide."

B. Work with a partner. Complete each conversation with one of the expressions from the Speaking Skill box on page 223. Are the speakers agreeing or disagreeing? Then read the conversations with your partner.

1. **A:** I really don't think we are going to run out of energy any time soon.

   B: _____ we are already using more energy than we can produce, especially during hot summers.

2. **A:** Students seem to be making an effort to save energy, like turning off their computers when they're not using them and biking to campus instead of driving.

   B: _____ even more people in our generation need to become aware of their energy consumption if we really want to fight global warming.

3. **A:** I'm shocked that people still support nuclear power, and scientists try to convince us it's not risky.

   B: _____; just think about how many people are exposed to radiation from aging nuclear power plants.

4. **A:** Politicians should support researchers working to harness the power of the tides and the wind.

   B: _____ we could never really get enough power from those sources to make it worth the investment.

5. **A:** Fossil fuels should be eliminated as an energy source as they put pollutants into the air and decrease the ozone layer.

   B: _____ banning fossil fuels completely is not a realistic solution.

6. **A:** I believe everyone should drive a hybrid or electric car to reduce harmful emissions.

   B: _____ these types of vehicles are currently too expensive for most people to buy.

C. Role-play the conversations in Activity B. Take turns giving your own reactions and opinions.

iQ ONLINE **D.** Go online for more practice debating opinions.

UNIT OBJECTIVE ▶▶▶▶

In this assignment, you are going to have a class debate on the future of energy. As you prepare for the debate, think about the Unit Question, "Where should the world's energy come from?" Use information from Listening 1, Listening 2, the unit video, and your work in this unit to support your debate. Refer to the Self-Assessment checklist on page 228.

CONSIDER THE IDEAS

A. Read these posts to an online discussion thread by an instructor and students in an environmental studies class.

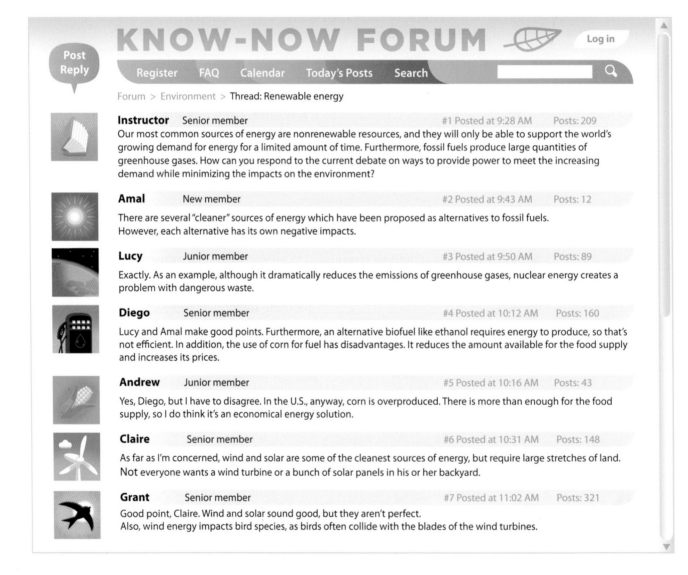

KNOW-NOW FORUM 🍃 Log in

Post Reply

Register   FAQ   Calendar   Today's Posts   Search

Forum > Environment > Thread: Renewable energy

Instructor   Senior member   #1 Posted at 9:28 AM   Posts: 209

Our most common sources of energy are nonrenewable resources, and they will only be able to support the world's growing demand for energy for a limited amount of time. Furthermore, fossil fuels produce large quantities of greenhouse gases. How can you respond to the current debate on ways to provide power to meet the increasing demand while minimizing the impacts on the environment?

Amal   New member   #2 Posted at 9:43 AM   Posts: 12

There are several "cleaner" sources of energy which have been proposed as alternatives to fossil fuels. However, each alternative has its own negative impacts.

Lucy   Junior member   #3 Posted at 9:50 AM   Posts: 89

Exactly. As an example, although it dramatically reduces the emissions of greenhouse gases, nuclear energy creates a problem with dangerous waste.

Diego   Senior member   #4 Posted at 10:12 AM   Posts: 160

Lucy and Amal make good points. Furthermore, an alternative biofuel like ethanol requires energy to produce, so that's not efficient. In addition, the use of corn for fuel has disadvantages. It reduces the amount available for the food supply and increases its prices.

Andrew   Junior member   #5 Posted at 10:16 AM   Posts: 43

Yes, Diego, but I have to disagree. In the U.S., anyway, corn is overproduced. There is more than enough for the food supply, so I do think it's an economical energy solution.

Claire   Senior member   #6 Posted at 10:31 AM   Posts: 148

As far as I'm concerned, wind and solar are some of the cleanest sources of energy, but require large stretches of land. Not everyone wants a wind turbine or a bunch of solar panels in his or her backyard.

Grant   Senior member   #7 Posted at 11:02 AM   Posts: 321

Good point, Claire. Wind and solar sound good, but they aren't perfect.
Also, wind energy impacts bird species, as birds often collide with the blades of the wind turbines.

B. Discuss the questions in a group.

1. What ideas would you have contributed to this discussion if you were a student in this environmental studies class?

2. Do the students mostly agree with each other or mostly disagree? Do you agree or disagree with any of the posts?

PREPARE AND SPEAK

A. GATHER IDEAS Work in groups of four. Prepare for a debate.

1. Divide into two teams of two students each.
   - Team 1 will represent energy producers by supporting at least two sources of energy and inform Team 2 of the choices.
   - Team 2 will represent environmentalists by presenting the environmental impacts of those two energy sources and offering alternatives.

2. Share your information. Review details from the unit with your teammate, and take notes on information that might help to support your argument.

3. Plan for arguments. How do you think the other team might respond to your opinions? Write down three arguments your opponents might make. Then decide how you might defend your opinion.

B. ORGANIZE IDEAS Study this format for a simple debate.

1. The first member of Team 1 and then Team 2 will give an overview of their opinion. (five minutes per team)

2. Team 2 will ask Team 1 questions to check understanding or get further information. Then Team 1 will ask Team 2 questions. (five minutes per team)

3. The second member of Team 1 and then Team 2 will respond to the other team's position and then give a conclusion. (six minutes per team)

C. SPEAK Conduct the debate. Refer to the Self-Assessment checklist on page 228 before you begin. After the debate, discuss the results.

 Go online for your alternate Unit Assignment.

CHECK AND REFLECT

A. **CHECK** Think about the Unit Assignment as you complete the Self-Assessment checklist.

SELF-ASSESSMENT		
Yes	No	
☐	☐	I was able to speak fluently about the topic.
☐	☐	My partner, group, and class understood me.
☐	☐	I used adverb clauses to express my ideas.
☐	☐	I used vocabulary from the unit to express my ideas.
☐	☐	I stressed the correct syllables and words in sentences.
☐	☐	I agreed and disagreed with opinions appropriately and politely.

B. **REFLECT** Go to the Online Discussion Board to discuss these questions.

1. What is something new you learned in this unit?

2. Look back at the Unit Question—Where should the world's energy come from? Is your answer different now than when you started this unit? If yes, how is it different? Why?

TRACK YOUR SUCCESS

Circle the words you have learned in this unit.

Nouns
bill 🔑
center 🔑
commission 🔑 AWL
convert AWL
current 🔑
emission
fracking
generation 🔑 AWL

power 🔑
priority 🔑 AWL
state 🔑
stretch 🔑

Verbs
harness
retrofit
tap 🔑

Adjectives
catastrophic
conflicted AWL
efficient 🔑
free 🔑
intermittent
present 🔑

Adverb
potentially 🔑 AWL

🔑 Oxford 3000™ words
AWL Academic Word List

Check (✓) the skills you learned. If you need more work on a skill, refer to the page(s) in parentheses.

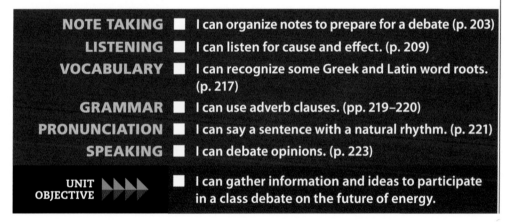

NOTE TAKING	☐ I can organize notes to prepare for a debate (p. 203)
LISTENING	☐ I can listen for cause and effect. (p. 209)
VOCABULARY	☐ I can recognize some Greek and Latin word roots. (p. 217)
GRAMMAR	☐ I can use adverb clauses. (pp. 219–220)
PRONUNCIATION	☐ I can say a sentence with a natural rhythm. (p. 221)
SPEAKING	☐ I can debate opinions. (p. 223)
UNIT OBJECTIVE ▶▶▶▶	☐ I can gather information and ideas to participate in a class debate on the future of energy.

Audio can be found in the *iQ Online* Media Center. Go to <u>iQOnlinePractice.com</u>. Click on the Media Center. Choose to stream or download the audio file you select. Not all audio files are available for download.

Page	Track Name: Q2e_05_LS_
2	U01_Q_Classroom.mp3
6	U01_Listening1_ActivityA.mp3
7	U01_Listening1_ActivityC.mp3
11	U01_ListeningSkill_ActivityA.mp3
12	U01_NoteTakingSkill_ActivityA.mp3
12	U01_NoteTakingSkill_ActivityB.mp3
14	U01_Listening2_ActivityA.mp3
15	U01_Listening2_ActivityC.mp3
23	U01_Pronunciation_Example1.mp3
23	U01_Pronunciation_Example2.mp3
23	U01_Pronunciation_ActivityA.mp3
30	U02_Q_Classroom.mp3
34	U02_Listening1_ActivityA.mp3
35	U02_Listening1_ActivityC.mp3
38	U02_ListeningSkill_Examples.mp3
38	U02_ListeningSkill_ActivityA.mp3
40	U02_NoteTakingSkill_ActivityB.mp3
41	U02_Listening2_ActivityA.mp3
42	U02_Listening2_ActivityC.mp3
50	U02_Pronunciation_Example1.mp3
50	U02_Pronunciation_Example2.mp3
50	U02_Pronunciation_Example3.mp3
50	U02_Pronunciation_Example4.mp3
51	U02_Pronunciation_ActivityA.mp3
59	U03_Q_Classroom.mp3
61	U03_NoteTakingSkill_ActivityC.mp3
63	U03_Listening1_ActivityA.mp3
64	U03_Listening1_ActivityC.mp3
66	U03_ListeningSkill_Examples.mp3
67	U03_ListeningSkill_ActivityA.mp3
68	U03_Listening2_ActivityA.mp3
70	U03_Listening2_ActivityC.mp3
77	U03_Grammar_ActivityA.mp3
79	U03_Pronunciation_Examples.mp3
79	U03_Pronunciation_ActivityA.mp3
86	U04_Q_Classroom.mp3
89	U04_NoteTakingSkill_Examples.mp3
90	U04_NoteTakingSkill_ActivityB.mp3
92	U04_Listening1_ActivityA.mp3
93	U04_Listening1_ActivityD.mp3
96	U04_ListeningSkill_ActivityA.mp3
97	U04_Listening2_ActivityA.mp3
99	U04_Listening2_ActivityD.mp3
106	U04_Pronunciation_ Examples.mp3
107	U04_Pronunciation_ ActivityA.mp3
115	U05_Q_Classroom.mp3
118	U05_NoteTakingSkill_ActivityA.mp3
120	U05_Listening1_ActivityA.mp3
121	U05_Listening1_ActivityC.mp3
126	U05_ListeningSkill_ ActivityA.mp3

Page	Track Name: Q2e_05_LS_
126	U05_ListeningSkill_ ActivityB.mp3
127	U05_Listening2_ActivityA.mp3
128	U05_Listening2_ActivityC.mp3
136	U05_Pronunciation_Examples.mp3
136	U05_Pronunciation_ActivityA.mp3
139	U05_UnitAssignment.mp3
142	U06_Q_Classroom.mp3
146	U06_Listening1_ActivityA.mp3
147	U06_Listening1_ActivityC.mp3
150	U06_ListeningSkill_Examples.mp3
151	U06_ListeningSkill_ActivityA.mp3
151	U06_ListeningSkill_ActivityB.mp3
153	U06_NoteTakingSkill_ActivityA.mp3
153	U06_NoteTakingSkill_ActivityB.mp3
154	U06_Listening2_ActivityA.mp3
156	U06_Listening2_ActivityC.mp3
160	U06_VocabularySkill_ActivityB.mp3
164	U06_Pronunciation_Examples.mp3
164	U06_Pronunciation_ActivityA.mp3
164	U06_Pronunciation_ActivityB.mp3
166	U06_UnitAssignment_ActivityA.mp3
171	U07_Q_Classroom.mp3
176	U07_Listening1_ActivityA.mp3
176	U07_Listening1_ActivityC.mp3
180	U07_ListeningSkill_Examples.mp3
181	U07_ListeningSkill_ActivityA.mp3
181	U07_ListeningSkill_ActivityB.mp3
183	U07_Listening2_ActivityA.mp3
183	U07_Listening2_ActivityC.mp3
192	U07_Pronunciation_Examples.mp3
193	U07_Pronunciation_ActivityA.mp3
193	U07_Pronunciation_ActivityB.mp3
194	U07_Pronunciation_ActivityC.mp3
194	U07_SpeakingSkill_Example.mp3
201	U08_Q_Classroom.mp3
204	U08_NoteTakingSkill_ActivityA.mp3
204	U08_NoteTakingSkill_ActivityC.mp3
206	U08_Listening1_ActivityC.mp3
210	U08_ListeningSkill_ActivityB.mp3
211	U08_Listening2_ActivityA.mp3
212	U08_Listening2_ActivityC.mp3
220	U08_Grammar_ActivityA.mp3
221	U08_Pronunciation_Example1.mp3
221	U08_Pronunciation_Example2.mp3
221	U08_Pronunciation_Example3.mp3
222	U08_Pronunciation_ActivityA.mp3
222	U08_Pronunciation_ActivityB.mp3
223	U08_SpeakingSkill_ActivityA.mp3

Author

Susan Earle-Carlin earned a Ph.D. in Reading, Language, and Cognition from Hofstra University. She has taught at SUNY Old Westbury and Rutgers University and is now the coordinator of the Test of Oral Proficiency at the University of California, Irvine. Her interests include addressing the needs of generation 1.5 students at the university and improving the communication skills of international teaching assistants. *Q* is her third ESL textbook.

Series Consultants

ONLINE INTEGRATION

Chantal Hemmi holds an Ed.D. TEFL and is a Japan-based teacher trainer and curriculum designer. Since leaving her position as Academic Director of the British Council in Tokyo, she has been teaching at the Center for Language Education and Research at Sophia University on an EAP/CLIL program offered for undergraduates. She delivers lectures and teacher trainings throughout Japan, Indonesia, and Malaysia.

COMMUNICATIVE GRAMMAR

Nancy Schoenfeld holds an M.A. in TESOL from Biola University in La Mirada, California, and has been an English language instructor since 2000. She has taught ESL in California and Hawaii, and EFL in Thailand and Kuwait. She has also trained teachers in the United States and Indonesia. Her interests include teaching vocabulary, extensive reading, and student motivation. She is currently an English Language Instructor at Kuwait University.

WRITING

Marguerite Ann Snow holds a Ph.D. in Applied Linguistics from UCLA. She teaches in the TESOL M.A. program in the Charter College of Education at California State University, Los Angeles. She was a Fulbright scholar in Hong Kong and Cyprus. In 2006, she received the President's Distinguished Professor award at Cal State, LA. She has trained EFL teachers in Algeria, Argentina, Brazil, Egypt, Libya, Morocco, Pakistan, Peru, Spain, and Turkey. She is the author/editor of publications in the areas of integrated content, English for academic purposes, and standards for English teaching and learning. She recently served as a co-editor of *Teaching English as a Second or Foreign Language* (4th ed.).

VOCABULARY

Cheryl Boyd Zimmerman is a Professor at California State University, Fullerton. She specializes in second-language vocabulary acquisition, an area in which she is widely published. She teaches graduate courses on second-language acquisition, culture, vocabulary, and the fundamentals of TESOL and is a frequent invited speaker on topics related to vocabulary teaching and learning. She is the author of *Word Knowledge: A Vocabulary Teacher's Handbook* and Series Director of *Inside Reading, Inside Writing,* and *Inside Listening and Speaking,* all published by Oxford University Press.

ASSESSMENT

Lawrence J. Zwier holds an M.A. in TESL from the University of Minnesota. He is currently the Associate Director for Curriculum Development at the English Language Center at Michigan State University in East Lansing. He has taught ESL/EFL in the United States, Saudi Arabia, Malaysia, Japan, and Singapore.

iQ ONLINE extends your learning beyond the classroom. This online content is specifically designed for you! *iQ Online* gives you flexible access to essential content.

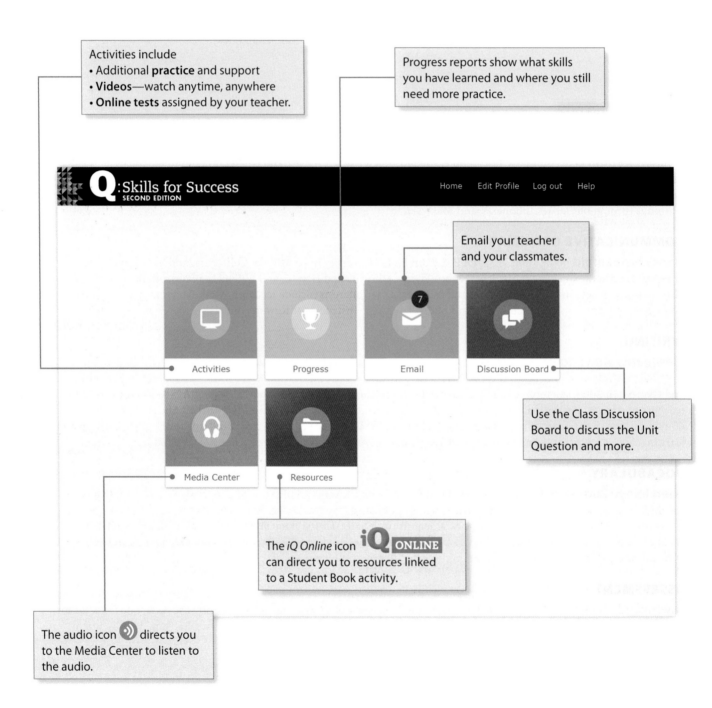

Activities include
• Additional **practice** and support
• **Videos**—watch anytime, anywhere
• **Online tests** assigned by your teacher.

Progress reports show what skills you have learned and where you still need more practice.

Email your teacher and your classmates.

Use the Class Discussion Board to discuss the Unit Question and more.

The *iQ Online* icon can direct you to resources linked to a Student Book activity.

The audio icon directs you to the Media Center to listen to the audio.

Q:Skills for Success
SECOND EDITION

Home   Edit Profile   Log out   Help

Activities   Progress   Email   Discussion Board

Media Center   Resources

SEE THE INSIDE FRONT COVER FOR HOW TO REGISTER FOR *iQ ONLINE* FOR THE FIRST TIME.

Take Control of Your Learning

You have the choice of where and how you complete the activities. Access your activities and view your progress at any time.

Your teacher may

- assign *iQ Online* as homework,
- do the activities with you in class, or
- let you complete the activities at a pace that is right for you.

iQ Online makes it easy to access everything you need.

Set Clear Goals

STEP 1 If it is your first time, look through the site. See what learning opportunities are available.

STEP 2 The Student Book provides the framework and purpose for each online activity. Before going online, notice the goal of the exercises you are going to do.

STEP 3 Stay on top of your work, following the teacher's instructions.

STEP 4 Use *iQ Online* for review. You can use the materials any time. It is easy for you to do follow-up activities when you have missed a class or want to review.

Manage Your Progress

The activities in *iQ Online* are designed for you to work independently. You can become a confident learner by monitoring your progress and reviewing the activities at your own pace. You may already be used to working online, but if you are not, go to your teacher for guidance.

Check 'View Reports' to monitor your progress. The reports let you track your own progress at a glance. Think about your own performance and set new goals that are right for you, following the teacher's instructions.

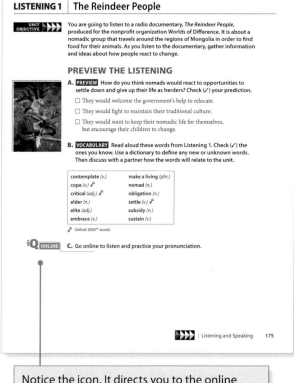

Notice the icon. It directs you to the online materials linked to the Student Book activities.

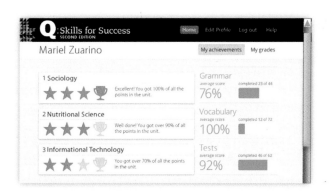

iQ Online is a research-based solution specifically designed for English language learners that extends learning beyond the classroom. I hope these steps help you make the most of this essential content.

C. N. Hemmi

Chantal Hemmi, EdD TEFL
Center for Language Education and Research
Sophia University, Japan

🔑 The keywords of the **Oxford 3000**™ have been carefully selected by a group of language experts and experienced teachers as the words which should receive priority in vocabulary study because of their importance and usefulness.

AWL **The Academic Word List** is the most principled and widely accepted list of academic words. Averil Coxhead gathered information from academic materials across the academic disciplines to create this word list.

The Common European Framework of Reference for Languages (CEFR) provides a basic description of what language learners have to do to use language effectively. The system contains 6 reference levels: **A1, A2, B1, B2, C1, C2**. CEFR leveling provided by the Word Family Framework, created by Richard West and published by the British Council. http://www.learnenglish.org.uk/wff/

UNIT 1

adequate *(adj.)* 🔑 AWL, B1
external *(adj.)* AWL, B1
function *(n.)* 🔑 AWL, A1
incident *(n.)* 🔑 AWL, A2
insight *(n.)* AWL, B1
intense *(adj.)* 🔑 AWL, B1
invariably *(adv.)* AWL, B2
overall *(adj.)* 🔑 AWL, A2
perception *(n.)* AWL, B1
persist *(v.)* AWL, B2
recovery *(n.)* 🔑 AWL, B1
reveal *(v.)* 🔑 AWL, A1
structure *(n.)* 🔑 AWL, C2

UNIT 2

atmosphere *(n.)* 🔑, B1
coordinator *(n.)* AWL, C1
diverse *(adj.)* AWL, B2
exhibit *(n.)* 🔑 AWL, B2
impact *(n.)* 🔑 AWL, B1
interactive *(adj.)* AWL, C1
prompt *(v.)* 🔑, B2
range *(n.)* 🔑 AWL, B1
resource *(n.)* 🔑 AWL, A1
restore *(v.)* 🔑 AWL, C2
site *(n.)* 🔑 AWL, A1
validate *(v.)* AWL, C2

UNIT 3

accurate *(adj.)* 🔑 AWL, B1
adapt *(v.)* 🔑 AWL, B1
capability *(n.)* AWL, B1
enhance *(v.)* AWL, B1
infinite *(adj.)* AWL, B1
manipulate *(v.)* AWL, B2
mature *(v.)* AWL, C2
objective *(n.)* 🔑 AWL, B1
obvious *(adj.)* 🔑 AWL, A2
operation *(n.)* 🔑, B2
revolution *(n.)* 🔑 AWL, B2
survival *(n.)* AWL, B1
utilize *(v.)* AWL, B2
virtually *(adv.)* 🔑 AWL, A2

UNIT 4

activist *(n.)* 🔑, C1
afford *(v.)* 🔑, A2
commodity *(n.)* AWL, B2
exploit *(v.)* AWL, B2
guarantee *(v.)* 🔑 AWL, B1
massive *(adj.)* 🔑, A2
roughly *(adv.)* 🔑, B1
transform *(v.)* 🔑 AWL, B1

UNIT 5

adjacent *(adj.)* AWL, B2
clarify *(v.)* AWL, C1
crucial *(adj.)* 🔑 AWL, B1
domain *(n.)* AWL, B2
engage in *(phr. v.)* 🔑, C2
framework *(n.)* AWL, C2
gender *(n.)* AWL, B2
modify *(v.)* AWL, B2
profile *(n.)* 🔑, B1
propose *(v.)* 🔑, B1
remarkable *(adj.)* 🔑, B1

UNIT 6

compound *(n.)* AWL, B2
consistently *(adv.)* AWL, B2
container *(n.)* 🔑, B2
convert *(v.)* 🔑 AWL, B1
convince *(v.)* 🔑 AWL, B1
deny *(v.)* 🔑 AWL, B2
grant *(n.)* 🔑 AWL, B1
implement *(v.)* AWL, B1
incentive *(n.)* AWL, C1
infrastructure *(n.)* AWL, C1
periodically *(adv.)* AWL, C2
protocol *(n.)* AWL, C1
reluctant *(adj.)* AWL, B2
submit *(v.)* AWL, B2
substantial *(adj.)* 🔑, A2

UNIT 7

cope *(v.)* 🔑, B1
critical *(adj.)* 🔑, B2
evolved *(adj.)* AWL, B1
marginal *(adj.)* AWL, C2
roots *(n.)* 🔑, B2
settle *(v.)* 🔑, B2
stability *(n.)* AWL, B2
subsidy *(n.)* AWL, B2
sustain *(v.)* AWL, B1

UNIT 8

bill *(n.)* 🔑, B1
center *(n.)* 🔑, A1
commission *(n.)* 🔑 AWL, A2
conflicted *(adj.)* AWL, C1
convert *(n.)* AWL, C2
current *(n.)* 🔑, B1
efficient *(adj.)* 🔑, B1
free *(adj.)* 🔑, A2
generation *(n.)* 🔑 AWL, C1
potentially *(adv.)* 🔑 AWL, B1
power *(n.)* 🔑, A2
present *(adj.)* 🔑, A1
priority *(n.)* 🔑 AWL, A2
state *(n.)* 🔑, B1
stretch *(n.)* 🔑, B2
tap *(v.)* 🔑, B1